Naqshbandi Awrad of Mawlana Shaykh Muhammad Nazim Adil al-Haqqani

Second Edition

Compiled by
Shaykh Muhammad Hisham Kabbani

INSTITUTE FOR SPIRITUAL & CULTURAL ADVANCEMENT

ISBN: 978-1-938058-56-1

Original Library of Congress Cataloging-in-Publication Data

Naqshbandi, Muhammad Nazim Adil al-Haqqani, 1922-
Naqshbandi awrad of Mawlana Shaykh Muhammad Nazim Adil al-Haqqani / compiled by Shaykh Muhammad Hisham Kabbani.
p. cm.
Includes bibliographical references.
ISBN 1-930409-25-7
1. Naqshabandeiyah--Prayer-books and devotions. 2. Sufism--Prayer-books and devotions. 3. Sufi chants. I. Kabbani, Shaykh Muhammad Hisham. II. Title.
BP189.7.N35N35 2004
297.4'8--dc22
2004019197

Published and Distributed by:
Institute for Spiritual & Cultural Advancement
17195 Silver Parkway, #401
Fenton, MI 48430 USA
Tel: (888) 278-6624 Fax: (810) 815-0518
Email: staff@sunnah.org
Web: http://www.isn1.net

بسم الله الرحمن الرحيم

وَاتَّقُوا اللَّهَ وَيُعَلِّمُكُمُ اللَّهُ

Observe your duty to God and God will teach you. (2:283)

يَا أَيُّهَا الَّذِينَ آمَنُوا اتَّقُوا اللَّهَ وَكُونُوا مَعَ الصَّادِقِينَ

O ye who believe! Fear God and be with those who are true (in word and deed). (9:119)

وَاذْكُر رَّبَّكَ فِي نَفْسِكَ تَضَرُّعاً وَخِيفَةً وَدُونَ الْجَهْرِ مِنَ الْقَوْلِ بِالْغُدُوِّ وَالآصَالِ وَلاَ تَكُن مِّنَ الْغَافِلِينَ

And (O Muhammad!) bring thy Lord to remembrance in thy (very) soul, with humility and in reverence, without loudness in words, in the mornings and evenings; and be not thou of those who are unheedful. (7:205)

إِنَّ اللَّهَ وَمَلاَئِكَتَهُ يُصَلُّونَ عَلَى النَّبِيِّ يَا أَيُّهَا الَّذِينَ آمَنُوا صَلُّوا عَلَيْهِ وَسَلِّمُوا تَسْلِيماً

Lo! Allah and His angels shower blessings on the Prophet. O ye who believe! Ask blessings on him and salute him with a worthy salutation. (33:56)

The late Shaykh Muhammad Nazim Adil al-Haqqani with his son-in-law, Shaykh Muhammad Hisham Kabbani (right), and his brother, the late Shaykh Muhammad Adnan Kabbani (left).

CONTENTS

Foreword 11

Publisher's Notes 13

Author's Note 16

The Naqshbandi Way of Dhikr: the Spiritual Practices 17

- Daily Spiritual Practices for Initiates 17
- Spiritual Practices for the Prepared 21
- Spiritual Practices for People of Determination 22

Notes to the Spiritual Practices 23

- The Verse "The Messenger believeth..." (2:285-286) 23
- Chief of prayers on the Prophet 25
- Dedication 28

Dhikr in Congregation: Khatmu-l-Khwajagan .. 31

- The Long Khatm 31
- Short Khatm (Aloud) 49

Invoking the Masters 51

Invocation of Imam al-Mahdi and His Deputies 56

Salatu-l-Maghrib 58

- Salatu-l-Janazah 70
- Salatu-l-Awwabin 76

Salatu-l-Isha 81

Salatu-l-Fajr 85

- Salatu munajiyyah 97
- 99 Beautiful Names of God 131

Salatu-z-Zuhr 140

Salatu-l-Asr 141
Practices During Rajab, Shaban, Ramadan and Muharram 143
Practice of the Month of Rajab 143
Daily Evening Practices in Rajab 160
Invocation of Rajab 163
Practices of the Blessed Laylat al-Raghaib (the Night of Desires) 167
Practices on the Night of Ascension 170
Practices of the 15th of Shaban (nisf Shaʿbān) 173
The Grand Transmitted Supplication 179
Greeting Ramadan 208
Ramadan Salatu-t-Tarawih 216
Practices on Ashura 219
Notes to the Guidebook 223
Voluntary Worship 223
Special Practices 224
Sunan Prayers 224
Salatu-l-Maghrib 226
Salatu-l-Janazah 226
Salatu-l-Awwabin 226
Salatu-l-Witr 227
Salatu-n-Najat 228
Salatu-t-Tasabih 235
Salatu-l-Fajr 237
Salatu-l-Ishraq 238
Salatu-d-Duha 238

Conduct of Pilgrimage - Hajj 239
Hajj Obligations as per the Four Schools 239
Restrictions of Ihram 241
Summarized Steps of Hajj 242
Summarized Steps of Umrah 246
Detailed Steps of Hajj and Umrah 247
Ihram 250
Tawaf al-Qudum 261
Sai 268
Standing at Arafah 270
Stoning the Jamarat 271
Stay at Mina 272
Zamzam 273
Holy Places of Visitation in Makkah 276
Visiting Madinat al-Munawwarah 281
Etiquette in the Rawdah 281
Greeting the Prophet ﷺ 288
Holy Places of Visitation in Madinah 302
Funeral Procedures 308
Approach of Death 308
Washing the Dead 309
The Funeral Prayer 314
Funeral Procession 319
The Grave 319
Burial 320
Coaching the Deceased 322
Finishing the Grave 324

Quranic Readings 325
Surat al-Fatihah: The Opening (1) 325
Surah Ya Sin (36) 327
Surat al-Mulk: Kingship (67) 353
Surat an-Naba: The Event (78) 364
Surat as-Sajdah: The Prostration (32) 372
Surat al-Ikhlas: Sincerity (112)................................. 385
Surat al-Falaq: The Daybreak (113) 386
Surat an-Nas: Mankind (114).................................... 387
Other titles from ISCA 389

Foreword

Praise be to God who has revealed to the purest of mankind, our master Muhammad the Messenger of God ﷺ, the wonderful signs of His Wisdom, bestowed on him the goodness of His knowledge and love, and honored him with the stewardship of this life and the next. He is the source from whom all saints draw their secret. He is the ocean of plenitude in which the Gnostics sail forth in search of the knowledge of God, of His Attributes and of the manifestations of His Glory.

Sainthood's azimuth was manifest distinctly in the Naqshbandi spiritual path. In particular this century has been blessed, for in this time of flagrant materialism and unlimited freedom for the rampant extremes of the ego, there yet lives a man who brings to bear a miracle in every encounter: Shaykh Muhammad Nazim Adil al-Haqqani, may God sanctify his secret.

The Naqshbandi devotions of Mawlana Shaykh Nazim are a source of light and energy, an oasis in a worldly desert and the secret behind the motion of every living cell. Through the manifestations of Divine Blessings bestowed on the practitioners of these magnificent rites, they will be granted the power of magnanimous healing, by which they seek to cure the hearts of mankind darkened by the gloom of spiritual poverty and materialism and scorched in the flames of iniquity and heedlessness.

We present this volume of select and spiritual devotions with the prayer that each person who picks it up with sincere intention to observe any of its efficacious practices receive the blessings and manifestations bestowed on the greatest saints of earlier times.

As with any method of approach to the Divine Presence, proper conduct must be observed in its performance. May God support and guide the seeker to the best conduct in observing these devotions; in every step, in every breath, and in every heartbeat.

Shaykh Muhammad Hisham Kabbani
Chairman, Islamic Supreme Council of
America

Publisher's Notes

References from the Quran and the *hadith* (holy traditions) are most commonly italicized and offset. References from the Quran are noted in parenthesis, i.e. (3:127), indicating the third chapter, verse 127. References from *hadith* are attributed to their transmitter, i.e. Bukhari, Muslim, Ahmed, etc. Quotes from other sources are offset without italics.

Dates of events are characterized as "AH/CE," which infers "after Hijrah (migration)" on which the Islamic calendar is based, and "Christian Era," respectively.

Muslims around the world typically offer praise upon speaking, hearing, or reading the name "Allah" and any of the Islamic names of God. Muslims also offer salutation and/or invoke blessing upon speaking, hearing or reading the names of Prophet Muhammad, other prophets, his family, his companions, and saints. We have applied the following international standards, using Arabic calligraphy and lettering:

- سبحانه وتعالى *subḥānahu wa taʿala* (Glorified and Exalted), after the proper name of God, "*Allah*" in Arabic.
- ﷺ *ṣall-Allāhu ʿalayhi wa sallam* (God's blessings and greetings of peace be upon him) following the names of the Prophet.
- عليه السلام *ʿalayhi 's-salām* (peace be upon him) following the names of other prophets, angels, and Khidr.
- عليها السلام *ʿalayhā 's-salām* (peace be upon her) following the name of Mary, Mother of Jesus.
- رضي الله عنه/رضي الله عنها *radī-Allahu ʿanhu/ʿanhā* (may God be pleased with him/her) following the name of a male or female companion of the Prophet.
- ق *qaddas-Allāhu sirrah* (may God sanctify his secret) following the name of a saint.

Transliteration

Transliteration is provided in the glossaries and in the section on the spiritual practices to facilitate correct pronunciation and is based on the following system:

Symbol	Transliteration	Symbol	Transliteration	Vowels:	
ء	ʼ	ط	ṭ	Long	
ب	b	ظ	ẓ	آ ى	ā
ت	t	ع	ʻ	و	ū
ث	th	غ	gh	ي	ī
ج	j	ف	f	Short	
ح	ḥ	ق	q	َ	a
خ	kh	ك	k	ُ	u
د	d	ل	l	ِ	i
ذ	dh	م	m		
ر	r	ن	n		
ز	z	ه	h		
س	s	و	w		
ش	sh	ي	y		
ص	ṣ	ة	ah; at		
ض	ḍ	ال	al-/'l-		

Author's Note

While the practices specified in this book were compiled by the shaykhs of the Naqshbandi Sufi Order, they are all derived from the Sunnah of the Prophet ﷺ and his Companions ؓ and for that reason anyone may feel free to use these spiritually efficacious practices, and there is permission to do so, including the conduct of pilgrimage and visiting the Holy Prophet in Madinah.

The Naqshbandi Way of *Dhikr*: the Spiritual Practices

The spiritual practices of seekers are of three kinds: for Initiates, for the Prepared, and for the People of Determination.

Daily Spiritual Practices for Initiates

ADAB		ادب	
Practice	Dhikr	Arabic	Re-peat
Bear witness - shahāda	ash-hadu an lā ilāha ill-Allāh wa ash-hadu anna Muḥammadan ʿabduhū wa rasūluh	أَشْهَدُ أنْ لا إلَهَ إلا الله وأَشْهَدُ أنَّ مُحَمَّدًا عَبْدُهُ ورَسُولُهُ	3
I testify that there is no god but God, and I testify that Muhammad is the Servant and Messenger of God.			
Seek forgiveness – istighfār	Astaghfirullāh	أستغفر الله	70

God forgive me.			
Seek blessings	Sūratu 'l-Fātiḥah (see page 325)	الفاتحة الشريفة	1
	Āman ar-rasūlu (Quran 2:285-6)	See Page 23	1
	Sūratu 'l-Ikhlāṣ (see page 385)	سُورةُ الإخْلاصِ	11
	Sūratu 'l-Inshirāḥ	سُورةُ الانْشراح	7
	Sūratu 'l-Falaq (see page 386).	سورة الفلق	1
	Sūratu 'n-Nās (see page 387)	سورة الناس	1
kalimah	Lā ilāha illa-Allāh	لا إله إلا اللهُ	9
There is no god but God.			
	Lā ilāha illa-Allāh Muḥammadun Rasūl Allāh	لا إله إلا اللهُ مُحَمَّدٌ رَسُولُ الله	1

There is no god but God, and Muhammad is the Servant and Messenger of God.			
Prayers on the Prophet - ṣalawāt	Allāhumma ṣalli ʿalā Muḥammadin wa ʿalā āli Muḥammadin wa sallim	اللَّهُمَّ صلِّ على مُحَمَّدٍ وعلى آل مُحَمَّدٍ وسلّم	10
O God send blessings and peace upon Muhammad and the family of Muhammad.			
Gift the reward - Ihdā	See page 28	إهداء	1
Recitation	Sūratu 'l-Fātiḥah (see page 325)	الفَاتِحَةُ الشَّرِيفَةُ	1
WIRD		ورد	
Practice	Dhikr	Arabic	Re-peat

Remember God-dhikr	Allāh, Allāh	ذِكرُ الجَلالة: اللهُ اللهُ حَقْ	1500
God, God.			
Prayers on the Prophet-ṣalawāt	Allāhumma ṣalli ʿalā Muḥammadin wa ʿalā āli Muḥammadin wa sallim	اللَّهُمَّ صلِّ على مُحَمَّدٍ وعلى آل مُحَمَّدٍ وسلِّم	100
O God send blessings and peace upon Muhammad and the family of Muhammad.			
Recitation of Qur'ān	One juz' (1/30) of the Qur'ān -or- Sūratu 'l-Ikhlāṣ (see page 385)	جُزْءٌ من القرآن او سورة الإخلاَصُ الشريفةِ	1 -or- 100

Prayers on the Prophet-Ṣalawāt	Dalā'il al-Khayrāt -or- Allāhumma ṣalli ʿalā Muḥammadin wa ʿalā āli Muḥammadin wa sallim	دلائلُ الخَيْراتِ او اللَّهُمَّ صلّ على مُحَمَّدٍ وعلى آل مُحَمَّدٍ وسلّم	1 chapter -or- 100
O God send blessings and peace upon Muhammad and the family of Muhammad			

Spiritual Practices for the Prepared

The *adab* and *wird* for the Prepared (*musta'id*) seeker is identical to that of the Initiate (*muḥib*), with the following additions:

- Increase the number of repetitions of God's name from 1,500 to 2,500 by tongue and add another 2,500 by heart, meditating upon it.
- Increase the number of *ṣalawāt* from 100 to 300 on all days except Monday, Thursday, and Friday when it is done 500 times.

Spiritual Practices for People of Determination

The *adab* and *wird* for the People of Determination are similar to that of the Prepared (*musta'id*), with the following additions:

- *Sayyid aṣ-ṣalawāt* (chief of the Prayers on the Prophet) is recited before the *Ihdā* (see page 28).
- After the *Sūratu 'l-Fātiḥah* of the *Ihdā*, the seeker repeats *Allāh Hū Allāh Hū Allāh Hū Ḥaqq* three times, imagining himself between the Hands of his Lord.
- Increase the number of repetitions of God's name from 2,500 to 5,000 each by tongue and by heart.
- Increase the number of *ṣalawāt* from 300 to 1,000 on all days except Monday, Thursday, and Friday, when it is done 2,000 times.

Notes to the Spiritual Practices

The Verse "The Messenger believeth..." (2:285-286)

ĀYAT ĀMAN AR-RASŪLU (2:285-286)		آمَنَ الرَّسُولُ
Āmana ar-rasūlu bimā unzila ilayhi min rabbihi wa 'l-mu'minūn. kullun āmana billāhi wa malā'ikatihi wa kutubihi wa rusulihi lā nufarriqu bayna āhadin min rusulihi wa qālū samʿinā wa aṭʿanā ghufrānaka rabbanā wa ilayka 'l-maṣīr. Lā yukallif-ullāhu nafsan illa wusʿahā. lahā mā kasabat wa ʿalayhā māktasabat. Rabbanā lā tū'ākhidhnā in nasīnā aw akhṭānā. Rabbanā wa lā taḥmil ʿalaynā iṣran kamā ḥamaltahu ʿalā alladhīnā min qablinā. Rabbanā wa lā tuḥamilnā mā lā ṭāqata lanā		آمَنَ الرَّسُولُ بِمَا أُنزِلَ إِلَيْهِ مِن رَّبِّهِ وَالْمُؤْمِنُونَ كُلٌّ آمَنَ بِاللّهِ وَمَلآئِكَتِهِ وَكُتُبِهِ وَرُسُلِهِ لاَ نُفَرِّقُ بَيْنَ أَحَدٍ مِّن رُّسُلِهِ وَقَالُواْ سَمِعْنَا وَأَطَعْنَا غُفْرَانَكَ رَبَّنَا وَإِلَيْكَ الْمَصِيرُ لاَ يُكَلِّفُ اللّهُ نَفْساً إِلاَّ وُسْعَهَا لَهَا مَا كَسَبَتْ وَعَلَيْهَا مَا اكْتَسَبَتْ رَبَّنَا لاَ تُؤَاخِذْنَا إِن نَّسِينَا أَوْ أَخْطَأْنَا رَبَّنَا وَلاَ تَحْمِلْ عَلَيْنَا إِصْراً

bihi w'afu 'anā waghfir lanā warḥamnā Anta mawlānā f'anṣurnā 'alā l-qawmi 'l-kāfirīn.		كَمَا حَمَلْتَهُ عَلَى الَّذِينَ مِن قَبْلِنَا رَبَّنَا وَلاَ تُحَمِّلْنَا مَا لاَ طَاقَةَ لَنَا بِهِ وَاعْفُ عَنَّا وَاغْفِرْ لَنَا وَارْحَمْنَا أَنتَ مَوْلاَنَا فَانصُرْنَا عَلَى الْقَوْمِ الْكَافِرِينَ

The Messenger believeth in what hath been revealed to him from his Lord, as do those who have faith. Each one (of them) believeth in God, His angels, His books, and His apostles. "We make no distinction (they say) between one and another of His apostles." And they say: "We hear, and we obey: (We seek) Thy forgiveness, our Lord, and to Thee is the end of all journeys." On no soul doth God place a burden greater than it can bear. It gets every good that it earns, and it suffers every ill that it earns. (Pray:) "Our Lord! Condemn us not if we forget or fall into error; our Lord! Lay not on us a burden like that which Thou didst lay on those before us; Our Lord! Lay not on us a burden greater than we have strength to bear. Blot out our sins, and grant us forgiveness. Have mercy on us. Thou art our Protector; Help us against those who stand against faith."

Chief of prayers on the Prophet

SAYYID AṢ-ṢALAWĀT		سَيِّدُ الصلَاةُ الشَّرِيفة المأثُورَة
'Alā ashrafi 'l-'ālamīna Sayyidinā Muḥammadini 'ṣ-ṣalawāt ṣall-Allāhū 'alayhi wa sallam. 'Alā afḍali 'l-'ālamīna Sayyidinā Muḥammadini 'ṣ-ṣalawāt ṣall-Allāhū 'alayhi wa sallam. 'Alā akmali 'l-'ālamīna Sayyidinā Muḥammadini 'ṣ-ṣalawāt ṣall-Allāhū 'alayhi wa sallam.		على أشْرَفِ العالَمِينَ سَيِّدِنا مُحَمَّدٍ الصَّلَوات. على أفْضَلِ العالَمِينَ سَيِّدِنا مُحَمَّدٍ الصَّلَوات. على أكْمَلِ العالَمِينَ سَيِّدِنا مُحَمَّد الصَّلَوات.

Upon the Noblest of all Creation, our Master Muhammad, blessings.

Upon the most Preferred of all Creation, our Master Muhammad, blessings.

Upon the most Perfect of all Creation, our Master Muhammad, blessings.

Ṣalawātullāhi taʿalā wa malā'ikatihi wa anbīyā'ihi wa rusulihi wa jamīʿi khalqihi ʿalā Muḥammadin wa ʿalā āli Muḥammad, ʿalayhi wa ʿalayhimu 's-salām wa raḥmatullāhi taʿalā wa barakātuhu, wa raḍī-Allāhū tabāraka wa taʿalā ʿan sādātinā aṣḥābi Rasūlillāhi ajmaʿīn, wa ʿani 't-tabiʿīna bihim bi iḥsān, wa ʿani 'l-a'immati 'l-mujtahidīni 'l-māḍīn, wa ʿani 'l-ʿulamā il-muttaqqīn, wa ʿani 'l-awlīyā 'iṣ-ṣāliḥīn, wa ʿam-mashayikhinā fi 'ṭ-ṭarīqati 'n-Naqshbandīyyati 'l-ʿalīyyah, qaddas-Allāhū taʿalā arwāḥahumu 'z-		صَلَواتُ الله تعالى ومَلائِكَتِهِ وأنبيائِهِ ورُسُلِهِ وجَمِيعِ خَلْقِهِ على مُحَمَّدٍ وعلى آلِ مُحَمَّدٍ، عليه وعَلَيْهِمُ السَّلامُ ورَحْمَةُ الله تَعالى وبَرَكاتُهُ ورَضِيَ الله تَبارَكَ وتَعالى عَنْ ساداتِنا أَصْحابِ رَسُولِ الله أَجْمَعين وعَنِ التَّابِعينَ بِهِم بِإِحْسان وعَنِ الأَئِمَّةِ المُجْتَهِدين الماضين وعَنِ العُلَماءِ المُتَّقين وعَنِ الأَوْلِياءِ الصَّالِحِين وعَن

zakīyya, wa nawwar Allāhū ta'alā aḍriḥatahumu 'l-mubāraka, wa a'ād-Allāhū ta'alā 'alaynā min barakātihim wa fuyūḍātihim dā'iman wa 'l-ḥamdulillāhi Rabb il-'ālamīn, al-Fātiḥā.		مَشايِخِنا في الطَّريقةِ النَّقْشَبَنْدِيّة العَلِيّة، قدَّسَ اللهُ تَعالى أرْواحَهُمُ الزَّكِيّة ونَوَّرَ اللهُ تَعالى أضْرِحَتَهُمُ المُبارَكة وأعادَ اللهُ تَعالى علَيْنا من بَرَكاتِهِم وفُيُوضاتِهِم دائِمًا والحَمدُ لله رَبِّ العالَمِين - الفاتِحة

Blessings of God (Exalted is He!), of His angels, of His prophets, of His Emissaries, and of all creation be upon Muhammad and the family of Muhammad; may the peace and mercy of God (Exalted is He!) and His blessings be upon him and upon them. May God, the Blessed and Most High, be pleased with every one of our Masters, the Companions of the Emissary of God, and with those who followed them in excellence, and with the early masters of juristic reasoning, and with the pious scholars, and the righteous saints and with our Shaykhs in the exalted Naqshbandi Order. May

God (Exalted is He!) sanctify their pure souls, and illuminate their blessed graves. May God (Exalted is He!) return to us of their blessings and overflowing bounty, always. Praise belongs to God, the Lord of the worlds, al-Fātiḥah (see page 325).

Dedication

IHDĀ		إِهدَاء
Allāhumma balligh thawāba mā qarā'nāhū wa nūra mā talawnāhū hadīyyatan wāṣilatan minnā ila rūḥi Nabīyyīnā Sayyidinā wa Mawlānā Muḥammadin ṣall-Allāhū ʿalayhi wa sallam. Wa ilā arwāḥi ikhwānihi min al-anbiyā'i wa 'l-mursalīn wa khudamā'i sharāʿihim wa ila arwāḥi 'l-a'immati 'l-arbaʿah wa ila arwāḥi mashāyikhinā fi 'ṭ-ṭarīqati 'n-naqshbandīyyati 'l-		اللَّهُمَّ بَلِّغْ ثَوابَ ما قَرأناهُ ونُورَ ما تَلَوْناهُ هَدِيّةً واصِلةً منّاإلى رُوحِ نَبِيِّنا مُحَمَّدٍ (صلّى الله عليه وسلّم) وإلى أرواحِ إخْوانِهِ من الأنبِياءِ والمُرسَلينَ وخُدَماءِ شَرائِعهِم وإلى أرواحِ الأئِمّةِ الأرْبَعَة وإلى أرْواحِ مَشايِخِنا في الطَّريقةِ

ʿaliyyah khāṣṣatan ila rūḥi Imāmi 'ṭ-ṭarīqati wa ghawthi 'l-khalīqati Khwājā Bahā'uddīn an-Naqshband Muḥammad al-Uwaisī 'l-Bukhārī wa ḥaḍarati Mawlanā Sulṭānu 'l-awlīyā ash-Shaykh ʿAbd Allāh al-Fā'iz ad-Dāghestanī wa sayyidunā ash-Shaykh Muḥammad Nāẓim al-Ḥaqqānī Mu'ayyad ad-dīn wa sa'iri sādātinā waṣ-ṣiddiqīna al-Fātiḥā.	النَّقْشْبَنْدِيَّةِ العَلِيَّة، خاصة إلى روحِ إمامِ الطَّرِيقة وغَوْثِ الخَلِيقةِ خَواجه بَهاءُ الدِّينِ النَّقْشْبند مُحَمَّد الأُوَيْسي البُخاري وإلى حضْرة مَوْلانا سُلْطانُ الأَوْلياءِ الشَّيْخ عَبْدُ الله الفائِز الدّاغَسْتاني وإلى مولانا سيِّدِنا الشَّيْخ محمَّدُ ناظِمُ الحقّاني مؤيِّد الدِّين وإلى سائِرِ ساداتِنا والصِّدِّيقِين الفاتحة

O God! Grant that the merit of what we have read, and the light of what we have recited, are (considered) an offering and gift from us to the soul of our Prophet Muhammad, and to the souls of the prophets, and the saints; in particular the soul of the Imām of the ṭarīqat and arch-Intercessor of the created world, Khwājā Bahā'uddīn an-Naqshband Muḥammad al-Uwaisī 'l-Bukhārī, and our venerable teacher and master, the Sultan of Saints, our Shaykh 'Abd Allāh al-Fā'iz ad-Dāghestanī, and our master Shaykh Muḥammad Nāẓim al-Ḥaqqānī Mu'ayyad ad-dīn, and to all our masters and to the righteous, al-Fātiḥah (see page 325).

This presents the reward of the preceding recitations to the Prophet ﷺ and to the shaykhs of the Naqshbandi Order.

Dhikr in Congregation: Khatmu-l-Khwajagan

In the Naqshbandi Order, the daily spiritual exercises and the weekly congregational *dhikr,* known as *Khatmu 'l-Khwājagān,* are important practices which the disciple must not leave. The *Khatmu 'l-Khwājagān* is done sitting with the shaykh in congregation. This is held once a week, preferably on Thursday night or Friday, two hours before sunset. The *Khatmu 'l-Khwājagān* is of two categories: the long *khatm* and the short *khatm.*

The Long Khatm		خَتْمُ الخَواجَكانِ الكبير
1. 108 stones, consisting of 100 pebbles, 7 somewhat larger ones and one large stone, are used for counting repetitions of Dhikr. *Distribute 79 of the smaller pebbles among the attendees and the shaykh, dividing them as evenly as possible based on the number of those present. The Imam retains 21 of the pebbles, along with the 7 larger ones and the one large stone.*		

2. *The shaykh begins the Khatm, which is performed silently:*	
Intention: Niyyatu ādā' al-khatm ibtighā' riḍwān Allāhi ta'la	نِيَّةَ أَدَاءِ الخَتْمِ إِبْتِغَاءَ رِضْوانُ الله تعالى
Intention to perform the Khatm seeking the pleasure of God the most High.	
Shahāda (3 times): Ash-hadu an lā ilāha ill-Allāh wa ash-hadu anna Muḥammadan 'abduhu wa rasūluh I testify that there is no god but God, and I testify that Muhammad is the Servant and Messenger of God.	كَلِمَةُ الشَّهادتين (٣ مرات) أَشْهَدُ أَنْ لا إله إلا الله وأَشْهَدُ أَنَّ مُحَمَّدًا عَبْدُهُ وَرَسُولُهُ
Istighfār (70 times): Astaghfirullāh God forgive me.	إستغفار: ٧٠ مرة أَسْتَغْفِرُ الله

Astaghfirullāhi 'l-'Aẓīm alladhī lā ilāha illa Hū al-Ḥayyu 'l-Qayyūm wa atūbu ilayh innahu hūwa 't-tawābu 'r-raḥīm min kulli dhanbin wa ma'ṣīyatin wa min kulli mā yukhālifu dīn al-Islām, yā Arḥam ar-Rāḥimīn, min kulli mā yukhālifu 'sh-sharī'at, min kulli mā yukhālifu 'ṭ-ṭarīqata, min kulli mā yukhālifu 'l-ma'rifata, min-kulli mā yukhālifu 'l-ḥaqīqata, min kulli mā yukhālifu 'l-'azīmata, yā Arḥam ar-rāḥīmin.	يتلو الإمام: أَسْتَغْفِرُ اللهَ العَظِيمَ الذي لا إله إلا هُوَ الحَيُّ القَيُّوم وأَتُوبُ إليْه إنَّهُ هو التَّوّابُ الرَّحيم. من كُلِّ ذَنْبٍ ومَّعْصيَّةٍ ومن كُلِّ ما يُخالِفُ دينَ الإِسْلام ومن كُلِّ ما يُخالِفُ الشَّريعة ومن كُلِّ ما يُخالِفُ الطَّريقةَ ومن كُلِّ ما يُخالِفُ المَعْرِفةَ ومن كُلِّ ما يُخالِفُ الحَقيقةَ ومن كُلِّ ما يُخالِفُ العَزيمةَ يا أَرْحَمَ الرّاحِمين

I ask forgiveness from God Almighty, there is no god but He, the Living, the Self-Subsisting, and I turn in repentance to Him, verily He is the Forgiver, the Merciful, from every sin and disobedience and from all that opposes the religion of Islam, from all that opposes the Divine Law, from all that opposes the Path, from all that opposes Spiritual Realization, from all that opposes Reality, from all that opposes firm Intention, O most Merciful of the Merciful.

The shaykh recites the following supplication: Allāhumma yā Musabbib al-asbāb, yā Mufattiḥ al-abwāb, yā Muqallib al-qulūbi wa 'l-abṣār, yā Dalīl al-mutaḥayyirīn, yā Ghiyāth al-mustaghīthīn, yā Ḥayyu, yā Qayyūm, yā Dhā 'l-Jalāli wa 'l-Ikrām! Wa ufawwiḍu amrī ilā-Allāh, inna-Allāha baṣīrun bil-ʿibād.		يَتْلُو الإمامُ: اللَّهُمَّ يا مُسَبِّبَ الأَسْباب ويا مُفَتِّحَ الأَبْوابِ. يا مُقَلِّبَ القُلُوبِ والأبصار. يا دَليلَ المُتَحَيِّرِين يا غِياثَ المُسْتَغِيثِين يا حيُّ يا قَيُّوم. يا ذا الجَلالِ والإكْرام. وأُفَوِّضُ أمْري إلى الله. إنَّ اللهَ بَصيرٌ بالعِبادِ

O Bestower! O Bestower! O Bestower! O Originator of causes! O Opener of doors! O Turner of hearts and

eyes! O Guide of the perplexed! O Succor for those who seek Your aid! O Living! O Self-Subsisting One! O (You who are) possessed of Majesty and Bounty! I entrust my affair unto God. Truly, God is aware of His servants.		
Rābiṭatu 'sh-sharīfā.		الرّابِطةُ الشَّريفة
Connect your heart to the heart of the shaykh, from him to the heart of the Prophet, from the Prophet to the Divine Presence; *3. The shaykh then distributes 7 of the larger stones, keeping 1 for himself and passing the other 6 among the attendees to his right. Those who receive a large stone recite the Fātiḥā. The larger stones are then returned to the shaykh.*		
Sūratu 'l-Fātiḥah (7 times) (see page 325)		سورة الفاتحة (٧ مَرات)
4. The shaykh then asks the group to recite As-Ṣalawātu 'sh-Sharīfah. Each person recites it one time for each pebble that he holds in his hand. The Imam completes the recitation by counting on the 21 pebbles he reserved.		
Ṣalawāt (100 times):		صلوات: ١٠٠ مرة

Allāhumma ṣalli ʿalā Muḥammadin wa ʿalā āli Muḥammadin wa sallim.		اللَّهُمَّ صلّ على مُحَمَّدٍ وعلى آل مُحَمَّدٍ وسلّم

5. The shaykh then asks the group to recite Sūratu 'l-Inshirāḥ, following the same methodology.

Sūratu 'l-Inshirāḥ (79 times)		سُورَةُ الانْشراح (٧٩ مَرة)

6. The shaykh then distributes the remaining 21 pebbles among the attendees as evenly as possible.

7. Then the shaykh asks the group to recite Sūratu 'l-Ikhlāṣ, with the Basmalah. Each one recites according to the number of pebbles in his hand. This is repeated 10 times.

After completing the tenth round of recitation, the shaykh takes the big stone and reads Ikhlāṣ on it, making for 1,001 recitations of this surah.

Sūratu 'l-Ikhlāṣ (1,001 times) (see page 385)		سُورَةُ الإِخْلاصِ (١٠٠١ مَرّة)

8. The shaykh again distributes 7 of the larger stones, keeping one for himself and passing the other 6 to the attendees to his left. Once again, those who receive a large

stone recite the Fātiḥā and the stones are then returned to the shaykh.		
Sūratu 'l-Fātiḥā (7 times)		سُورةُ الفَاتحة (٧ مَرّات)
9. The shaykh again asks the group to recite aṣ-Ṣalawātu 'sh-Sharīfah, each according to the number of pebbles in his hand.		
Ṣalawāt (100 times): Allāhumma ṣalli ʿalā Muḥammadin wa ʿalā āli Muḥammadin wa sallim.		صَلَوات ١٠٠ مرة اللَّهُمَّ صلّ على مُحَمَّدٍ وعلى آل مُحَمَّدٍ وسلّم
O God send blessings and peace upon Muhammad and the family of Muhammad.		
10. The shaykh, or a person designated by him, then recites Chapter 12, Verse 101 (12:101) of the Holy Quran.		
Aʿūdhu billāhi min ash-shayṭāni 'r-rajīm Bismillāhi 'r-Raḥmāni 'r-Raḥīm. Rabbi qad ātaytanī min al-mulki wa ʿallamtanī min		يتْلُو الإمامُ: أعُوذُ بِالله من الشَّيْطانِ الرَّجيم. بِسْمِ الله الرَّحْمنِ الرَّحيمِ. رَبِّ

ta'wīli 'l-aḥādīth fāṭira 's-samāwāti wa-'l-arḍi anta walīyyī fī d-dunyā wa 'l-ākhirati tawaffanī musliman wa alḥiqnī bi ṣ-ṣāliḥīn; Āmantu billāhi sadaq-Allāhu 'l-'Aẓīm. Subḥāna rabbika rabbi 'l-'izzati 'amā yaṣifūn wa salāmun 'alā 'l-mursalīn wa 'lḥamdulillāhi rabbi 'l-'alamīn.	قَدْ آتَيْتَنِي مِنَ الْمُلْكِ وَعَلَّمْتَنِي مِن تَأْوِيلِ الأَحَادِيثِ فَاطِرَ السَّمَاوَاتِ وَالأَرْضِ أَنتَ وَلِيِّي فِي الدُّنُيَا وَالآخِرَةِ تَوَفَّنِي مُسْلِماً وَأَلْحِقْنِي بِالصَّالِحِينَ. آمَنْتُ بِاللهِ صَدَقَ اللهُ العَظِيم. سُبْحَانَ رَبِّكَ رَبِّ العِزَّةِ عَمَّا يَصِفُونَ وسَلامٌ على الْمُرْسَلِينَ والحَمْدُ لله رَبِّ العالَمِينَ

I seek refuge in God from the accursed Satan. In the name of God, the Merciful, the Beneficent. O my Lord! You have indeed bestowed on me some power, and taught me something of the interpretation of dreams and events. Creator of the Heavens and the Earth! You

are my Protector in this world and in the Hereafter. Take my soul (at death) as one submitting to Your Will (as a Muslim), and unite me with the righteous.		
11. The shaykh reads the dedication.		
Ihdā: (see page 28)		إِهدَاء
12. The shaykh then proceeds with the loud portion of the dhikr.		
Loud Part		
F'alam annahū: Lā ilāhā ill-Allāh (100 times) There is no god but God.		فَاعْلَمْ أَنَّهُ: لا إله إلا الله (١٠٠ مَرّة)
The shaykh then recites the Ihdā (see page 28) presenting the reward of the preceding recitations to the Prophet ﷺ and to the shaykhs of the Naqshbandi Order:		إِهدَاء
Ila sharafi 'n-Nabī ṣall-Allāhū 'alayhi wa sallam wa ālihi wa ṣaḥbih, wa ila		إلى شَرَفِ النَّبِي صلى اللهُ عليهِ وسلّم وإلى آلِهِ

<table>
<tr><td>arwāḥi sā'iri sādātinā wa 'ṣ-ṣīddiqīn, al-Fātiḥah. (see page 325)</td><td></td><td>وصَحْبِهِ وإلى أرْواحِ مشائِخِنا وسائِرِ ساداتِنا والصِّدّيقين الفاتِحة</td></tr>
<tr><td colspan="3">For the honor of the Prophet ﷺ and his family and companions, and to the souls of the preceding masters and the veracious ones ... al-Fātiḥah (see page 325).</td></tr>
<tr><td>Dhikr al-Jālāla:
Allāh, Allāh (100 times)
God, God</td><td></td><td>ذِكرُ الجَلالةِ
الله الله الله (حَوالي ١٠٠ مَرّة)</td></tr>
<tr><td>Ḥasbun-Allāh wa ni‘m al-wakīl, ni‘m al-Mawlā wa ni‘m an-Naṣīr, lā ḥawla wa lā quwwata illa billāhi 'l-‘Alīyyi 'l-‘Aẓīm.</td><td></td><td>الإمام: حَسْبُنا الله ونِعْمَ الوَكيل نِعْمَ المولى ونِعْمَ النَّصيرُ لا حَوْلَ ولا قُوَّةَ إلا بِالله العَلِيِّ العَظيم</td></tr>
<tr><td colspan="3">God is sufficient for us and the Best of Protectors, the Best Patron, and the Best of Helpers; there is no power</td></tr>
</table>

and no strength save in God, the Most High, the Great.		
Hū, Hū (33 times) He, the Absolute Unknown One.		هُو. هُو. هُو.(حَوالي ٣٣ مَرّة)
Ḥasbun-Allāh wa niʿm al-wakīl, niʿm al-Mawlā wa niʿm an-Naṣīr, lā ḥawla wa lā quwwata illa billāhi 'l-ʿAlīyyi 'l-ʿAẓīm.		الإمام: حَسْبُنا الله ونِعْمَ الوكيل نِعْمَ المولى ونِعْمَ النَّصِيرُ لا حَوْلَ ولا قُوَّةَ إلا بِالله العَلِيِّ العَظيم
God is sufficient for us and the Best of Protectors, the Best Patron, and the Best of Helpers; there is no power and no strength save in God, the Most High, the Great.		
Ḥaqq, Ḥaqq (33 times) The Ultimate Reality.		حَق. حَق. حَق.(حَوالي ٣٣ مَرّة)
Ḥasbun-Allāh wa niʿm al-wakīl, niʿm al-Mawlā wa niʿm an-Naṣīr, lā ḥawla wa		الإمام: حَسْبُنا الله ونِعْمَ الوكيل نِعْمَ المولى ونِعْمَ

Lā quwwata illa billāhi 'l-ʿAlīyyi 'l-ʿAẓīm.	المصيرُ ولا حَوْلَ ولا قُوَّةَ إلا بِاللهِ العَلِيِّ العَظيم

God is sufficient for us and the Best of Protectors, the Best Patron, and the Best of Helpers; there is no power and no strength save in God, the Most High, the Great.

Ḥayy, Ḥayy (33 times) Ever-living One.	حَيّ. حَيّ. حَيّ.(حَوالي ٣٣ مَرَّة)
Ḥasbun-Allāh wa niʿm al-wakīl, niʿm al-Mawlā wa niʿm an-Naṣīr, lā ḥawla wa lā quwwata illa billāhi 'l-ʿAlīyyi 'l-ʿAẓīm.	الإمام: حَسْبُنا الله ونِعْمَ الوكيل ولا حَوْلَ نعم المولى ونعم المصير لا قُوَّةَ إلا بِاللهِ العَلِيِّ العَظيم

God is sufficient for us and the Best of Protectors, the Best Patron, and the Best of Helpers; there is no power and no strength save in God, the Most High, the Great.

Allāh Hū, Allāh Ḥaqq (10-12 times) God is He the Absolute Unknown One, God is the Ultimate Reality.		الله هُو الله حَقّ الله هُو الله حَقّ (١٠ أو ١٢ مَرّة)
Allāh Hū, Allāh Ḥayy (10-12 times) God is He the Absolute Unknown One, God is Ever-living		الله هُو الله حَيّ . الله هُو الله حَيّ (١٠ أو ١٢ مَرّة)
Allāh Ḥayy Yā Qayyūm (10-12 times) God Ever-living, O Self-sufficient One		الله حَيّ يا قَيُّوم الله حَيّ يا قَيُّوم (١٠ أو ١٢ مَرّة)
Ḥasbun-Allāh wa niʿm al-wakīl, niʿm al-Mawlā wa niʿm an-Naṣīr, lā ḥawla wa lā quwwata illa billāhi 'l-ʿAlīyyi 'l-ʿAẓīm.		الإمام: حَسْبُنا الله ونِعْمَ الوكيل ولا حَوْلَ لا قُوَّةَ إلا بالله العَلِيّ العَظيم
God is sufficient for us and the Best of Protectors, the Best Patron, and the Best of Helpers; there is no power		

and no strength save in God, the Most High, the Great.		
Yā Hū, Yā Hū, Yā Dā'im (3 times); Allāh Yā Hū, Yā Dā'im (1 time) O Absolute Unknown One, O Eternal One, God is He the Absolute Unknown One, O Eternal One.		الإمام: يا هُو يا هُو يا دائِم (٣ مَرّة) الله يا هو يا دائِم
Yā Dā'im x3, Yā Allāh (2 times) O Eternal One x3, O God		يا دائِمْ. يا دائِمْ. يا دائِمْ يا الله (مَرّتانِ)
Yā Ḥalīm x3, Yā Allāh (2 times) O Clement One, x3, O God		يا حَليمْ. يا حَليمْ. يا حَليمْ يا الله (مَرّتانِ)
Yā Ḥafīẓ x3 Yā Allāh (2 times) O Preserver x3, O God		يا حَفيظْ. يا حَفيظْ. يا حَفيظْ يا الله (مَرّتانِ)

Yā Laṭīf x3, Yā Allāh (2 times) O Subtle One x3, O God	يا لَطيفْ. يا لَطيفْ. يا لَطيفْ يا الله (مَرَّتانِ)
Yā Ghaffār x3, Yā Allāh (2 times) O Forgiver x3, O God	يا غَفّارْ. يا غَفّارْ. يا غَفّارْ يا الله (مَرَّتانِ)
Yā Sattār x3 Yā Allāh (2 times) O Concealer x3, O God	يا سَتّارْ. يا سَتّارْ. يا سَتّارْ يا الله (مَرَّتانِ)
Yā Fattāḥ x3, Yā Allāh (2 times) O Opener x3, O God	يا فَتّاحْ. يا فَتّاحْ. يا فَتّاحْ يا الله (مَرَّتانِ)
Yā Mujīb x3, Yā Allāh (2 times) O Answerer of Prayers x3, O God	يا مُجيبْ. يا مُجيبْ. يا مُجيبْ يا الله (مَرَّتانِ)
Yā Muʿiz x3, Yā Allāh (2 times) O Honorer x 3, O God	يا مُعِزْ. يا مُعِزْ. يا مُعِزْ يا الله (مَرَّتانِ)

Yā Mu'īn x3, Yā Allāh (2 times) O Giver of Aid, x 3, O God		يا مُعِينْ . يا مُعِينْ . يا مُعِينُ يا الله (مَرّتانِ)
Yā Wadūd x3, Yā Allāh (2 times) O Most Loving x3, O God		يا وَدودْ. يا وَدودْ. يا وَدودْ يا الله (مَرّتانِ)
Yā Raḥmān x3, Yā Allāh (2 times) O Most Compassionate x3, O God		يا رَحْمنْ. يا رَحْمنْ. يا رَحْمنْ يا الله (مَرّتانِ)
Yā Raḥīm x3, Yā Allāh (2 times) O Most Merciful x3, O God		يا رَحْيمْ. يا رَحْيمْ. يا رَحْيمْ يا الله (مَرّتانِ)
Yā Ḥannān x3, Yā Allāh (2 times) O Most Caring x3, O God		يا حَنّانْ. يا حنّانْ. يا حَنّانْ. يا الله (مَرّتانِ)
Yā Mannān x3, Yā Allāh (2 times) O Beneficent x3, O God		يا مّنّانْ. يا مّنّانْ. يا مّنّانْ. يا الله (مَرّتان)

Yā Dayyān x3, Yā Allāh (2 times) O Most Just x3, O God		يا دَيّانْ. يا دَيّانْ. يا دَيّانْ. يا الله (مَرّتانِ)
Yā Subḥān x3 , Yā Allāh (2 times) O Most Glorious One x3, O God		يا سُبْحانْ. يا سُبْحانْ. يا سُبْحانْ. يا الله (مَرّتانِ)
Yā Sulṭān x3, Yā Allāh (2 times) O Supreme Ruler x3, O God		يا سُلْطانْ. يا سُلْطانْ. يا سُلْطانْ. يا الله (مَرّتان)
Yā Amān x3, Yā Allāh (2 times) O Giver of Safety x3, O God		يا أمانْ. يا أمانْ. يا أمانْ. يا الله (مَرّتانِ)
Yā Allāh x3, Yā Allāh (2 times) O God x 4		يا الله. يا الله. يا الله. يا الله....(مَرّتان)
The Shaykh may add more of God's Beautiful Names as he is inspired.		
Ḥasbun-Allāh wa ni'm al-wakīl, ni'm al-Mawlā wa ni'm an-Naṣīr, lā ḥawla wa		الإمام: حَسْبُنا الله ونِعْمَ الوكيل نعم المولى ونعم

lā quwwata illa billāhi 'l-'Alīyyi 'l-'Aẓīm.		المصير لا حَوْلَ ولا قُوَّةَ إلا بالله العَليّ العَظيم
God is sufficient for us and the Best of Protectors, the Best Patron, and the Best of Helpers; there is no power and no strength save in God, the Most High, the Great.		
Inna-Allāha wa malā'ikatahū yuṣallūna 'alā an-Nabī, yā ayyuh-alladhīnā āmanū, ṣallū 'alayhi wa sallimū taslīmā. (Ṣadaq-Allāhu 'l-'Aẓīm)		إِنَّ اللهَ وَمَلَائِكَتَهُ يُصَلُّونَ عَلَى النَّبِيِّ يَا أَيُّهَا الَّذِينَ آمَنُوا صَلُّوا عَلَيْهِ وَسَلِّمُوا تَسْلِيماً
God and His angels send blessings on the Prophet: O you who believe! Send blessings on him and greet him with all respect. (God speaks the Truth).		
Ṣalawāt (10 times): Allāhumma ṣalli 'alā Muḥammadin wa 'alā āli Muḥammadin wa sallim		صلوات: ١٠ مرات – اللَّهُمَّ صلّ على مُحَمَّدٍ وعلى آل مُحَمّدٍ وسلّم

O God send blessings and peace upon Muhammad and the family of Muhammad.		
The Shaykh then makes invocation as he is inspired.		
The Shaykh then recites the Chief of Prayers (see page 25)		الصلَاةُ الشَّرِيفَةِ المأثُورة
The Shaykh then recites the Ihdā (see page 28).		إهدَاء
Short Khatm (Aloud)		خَتْمُ الخَواجَكانِ الصغير - جَهْر
The Short Khatm is identical to the Long Khatm except that it is recited aloud in its entirety, and has the following differences in number of repetitions in the Adab.		
Sūratu 'l-Fātiḥah (7 times) (see page 325)		الفاتحة (٧ مَرات)
Prayers on the Prophet ﷺ (ṣalawāt) (10 times):		صَلَوات (١٠ مَرات)

Allāhumma ṣalli ʿalā Muḥammadin wa ʿalā āli Muḥammadin wa sallim		أللّهُمَّ صلّ على مُحَمَّدٍ وعلى آل مُحَمَّدٍ وسلّم
O God send blessings and peace upon Muhammad and the family of Muhammad.		
Sūratu ʾl-Inshirāḥ (7 times)		سُورةُ الإنشراح (٧ مَرات)
Sūratu ʾl-Ikhlāṣ (11 times) (see page 385)		سُورةُ الإِخْلاصِ (١١ مَرّة)
Sūratu ʾl-Fātiḥah (7 times) (see page 325)		سُورةُ الفَاتحة (٧ مَرّات)
Prayers on the Prophet ﷺ (ṣalawāt) (10 times): Allāhumma ṣalli ʿalā Muḥammadin wa ʿalā āli Muḥammadin wa sallim		صَلَوات (١٠ مَرات) أللّهُمَّ صلّ على مُحَمَّدٍ وعلى آل مُحَمَّدٍ وسلّم

The remainder of the Khatm is identical to the Long Khatm (section 10) from the point the Shaykh assigns someone to recite from the Qurʾān (12:101) (see page 37).

Invoking the Masters

Yā sayyid as-sādāt wa nūr al-mawjudāt, yā man hūwa al-malja'u liman massahu ḍaymun wa ghammun wa alam. Yā aqrabu 'l-wasā'ili ilā-Allāhi taʿalā wa yā aqwā 'l-mustanad, attawasalu ila janābīka 'l-ʿaẓam bi-hādhihi's-sādāti, wa āhlillāh, wa āhli baitika 'l-kirām, li-dafʿi ḍurrin lā yudfaʿu illā bi wāsiṭatik, wa rafʿi ḍaymun lā yurfaʿu illā bi-dalālatika bi Sayyidī wa Mawlāy, yā Sayyidī yā Rasūl Allāh, yā man arsalahu 'llāhu Raḥmatan li 'l-ʿālamīn:		يا سَيِّدَ السَّاداتِ ويا نُورَ المَوْجُوداتِ، يا من هُوَ المَلْجأُ لِمَنْ مَسَّهُ ضَيْمٌ وغَمٌّ وألَمٌ، يا أقْرَبَ الوَسائِلِ إلى الله تَعالى ويا أقْوى المُسْتَنَد، أتَوَسَّلُ إلى جنابِكَ الأعْظم بِهَؤُلاءِ السَّاداتِ وأهْلِ الله وأهْلِ بيْتِكَ الكِرام لِدَفْعِ ضُرٍ لا يُدْفَعُ إلا بِواسِطتِكَ ورَفْعِ ضَيْمٍ لا يُرْفَعُ إلا بِدَلالَتِكَ بِسَيِّدي ومَوْلاي يا سَيِّدي يا رَسُولَ الله يا من أرْسَلَهُ اللهُ رَحْمَةً لِّلعالَمِين
Nabī		نَبِيْ

Ṣiddīq		صِدِّيقٌ
Salmān		سْلمانٌ
Qāsim		قَاسِمٌ
J'afar		جَعْفَرٌ
Ṭayfūr		طيفُورٌ
Abu 'l-Ḥasan		ابو الحَسَنِ
Abū 'Alī		أَبُو عليٌّ
Yūsuf		يُوسُفٌ
Abu 'l-'Abbās		أبو العبّاس
'Abd al-Khāliq		عَبْدُ الخالِقِ
'Arif		عارِفٌ
Maḥmūd		مَحْمُودٌ
'Alī		عليٌّ

Muḥammad Bābā as-Samāsī		مُحَمَّد بَابَا السَّماسِيُّ
Sayyid Amīr Kulālī		سيِّد أمير كلالي
Khwājā Bahā'uddīn Naqshband		خَواجَه بهاءُ الدّين النَقْشَبَنْد
ʿAlā'uddīn		عَلاءُ الدّينِ
Yaʿqūb		يَعْقوبُ
ʿUbayd Allāh		عُبيْدُ الله
Muḥammad Zāhid		مُحَمَّد زاهِد
Darwīsh Muḥammad		دَرْوِيش مُحَمَّدٌ
Khwājā Amkanākī		خَواجَه الامْكَناكي
Muḥammad al-Bāqī		مُحَمَّدُ الباقي
Aḥmad al-Fārūqī		أحْمَدُ الفارُوقي
Muḥammad Maʿṣūm		مُحَمَّدْ معْصومْ
Sayfuddīn		سيْفُ الدّين

Nūr Muḥammad		نورْ مُحَمَّد
Ḥabībullāh		حَبِيبُ الله
ʿAbd Allāh		عَبْدُ الله
Shaykh Khālid		الشَّيْخ خالدُ
Shaykh Ismāʿīl		الشَّيْخ إسماعيلُ
Khāṣ Muḥammad		خَاصْ مُحَمَّد
Shaykh Muḥammad Effendi al-Yarāghī		الشَّيخ مُحَمَّدْ أَفَنْدي اليراغي
Sayyid Jamāluddīn al-Ghumūqī al-Ḥusaynī		سيِّد جَمالُ الدّين الغَموقِي الحُسَيْنيّ
Abū Aḥmad aṣ-Ṣughūrī		ابو أَحْمَد الصُّغُوري
Abū Muḥammad al-Madanī		ابو مُحَمَّد المَدَني
Shaykh Sharafuddīn ad-Dāghestānī		الشَّيخ شَرَفُ الدّين الدّاغِستاني

Shaykh 'Abd Allāh al-Fā'iz ad-Dāghestānī		الشّيخ عَبْدُ الله الفائِز الدّاغستاني
Shaykh Muḥammad Nāẓim 'Adil al-Ḥaqqānī		الشّيخ مُحَمَّد نَاظِمُ الحَقّانِي

Invocation of Imam al-Mahdi and His Deputies

Sāḥibu 'z-Zamān al-Īmāmu 'l-Mahdī ﷺ		صاحِبُ الزَمانِ الإمامُ مُحَمَّد المَهْدي عليه السّلام
Shahāmatu 'l-Fardānī		شَهامَةُ الفَرْداني
Yūsufu 'ṣ-Ṣiddīq		يُوسِفُ الصّدِّيق
'Abdur-Ra'uf al-Yamānī		عَبْدُ الرَّؤوفِ اليَمَانيّ
Imāmu 'l-'Ārifīn Amānu 'l-Ḥaqq		إمامُ العارِفين أمانُ الحَقّ
Lisānu 'l-Mutakallimīn 'Awnullāhi 's-Sakhāwī		لِسانُ المُتَكَلِّمين عَوْنُ اللهِ السَّخاوي
'Ārifu 't-ṭayyār al-Mā'rūf bi Mulḥān		عارِفُ الطَّيّارِ المَعْرُوف بِمُلْحان
Burhānu 'l-Kuramā' Ghawthi 'l-Anām		بُرْهانُ الكُرَماءِ غَوْثُ الأنامِ

<table>
<tr><td>Yā Ṣāḥiba 'z-Zamān, yā Ṣāḥib al-'unṣur.</td><td></td><td>يا صاحِبَ الزَّمانِ، يا صاحِبَ العُنْصُرِ</td></tr>
<tr><td>Yā rijāl-Allāh ā'alā-llāhu ta'ala darajātihim dā'iman wa amaddanā bi-madadihim wa-nafa'nā bi-barakātihim wa anfāsihimi 'l-qudsīyya, bi-ḥurmati man lā Nabīyya ba'dahu, bi sirri Sūrati 'l-Fātiḥah (see page 325).</td><td></td><td>يا رِجالَ الله أعلى اللهُ تَعالى دَرَجاتِهُم دائِماً وأمَدَّنا بِمَدَدِهِم ونفَّعْنا ببَرَكاتِ أنْفاسِهِم القُدُسِيَّة بِحُرْمةِ من لا نَبِيَّ بَعْدَهُ وبِسرِّ سُورةِ الفاتحة</td></tr>
<tr><td colspan="3">O Master of the Period, O one of high pedigree, O men of God. May God (Exalted is He!) raise their stations always, support us with their support and benefit us through the blessings of their holy breath. By the sanctity of the one after whom there is no other prophet, and by the secret of al-Fātiḥah (see page 325).</td></tr>
</table>

Salatu-l-Maghrib

Adhan (call to prayer)		الآذان
Allāhu akbar (4 times) God is Greatest		اللهُ أَكْبَرْ، اللهُ أَكْبَرْ، اللهُ أَكْبَرْ، اللهُ أَكْبَرْ
Ash-hadu an lā ilāha ill-Allāh (2 times) I bear witness that there is no god but God		أَشْهَدُ أَنْ لا إِلَهَ إِلاَّ الله أَشْهَدُ أَنْ لا إِلَهَ إِلاَّ الله
Ash-hadu anna Muḥammadan Rasūlullāh (2 times) I bear witness that Muhammad is the Messenger of God.		أَشْهَدُ أَنَّ محمداً رَسُول الله - أَشْهَدُ أَنَّ محمداً رَسُول الله
Ḥayya ʿalā ʾṣ-ṣalāh (2 times) Hasten to the prayer		حيَّ عَلى الصلَاةُ حيَّ عَلى الصلَاةُ

Ḥayyā ʻāla 'l-falāḥ (2 times) Hasten to salvation		حيَّ عَلى الفَلاح حيَّ عَلى الفَلاح
Allāhu akbar (2 times) God is Greatest		اللهُ أَكْبَرَ اللهُ أكبَر
Lā ilāha illa-Allāh There is no god but God		لا إِلَه إلاَّ الله

AṢ-ṢALĀTU WA 'S-SALĀM (to be made aloud by the muadhdhin): Aṣ-ṣalātu wa 's-salāmu ʿalayk, yā man arsalahullāhu taʿalā raḥmatan li 'l-ʿālamīn. Aṣ-ṣalātu wa 's-salāmu ʿalayk, wa ʿalā ālika wa aṣḥābika ajmaʿīn. Aṣ-ṣalātu wa 's-salāmu ʿalaykum, yā anbiyā'Allāḥ.	الصلَاةُ والسّلام الصلَاةُ والسَّلامُ عَلَيْكَ يا مَنْ أَرْسَلَه اللهُ تعالى رحمَةً للّعالمين الصلَاةُ والسَّلامُ عَلَيْكَ وعلى آلِكَ وأَصْحَابِكَ أجمَعِين الصلَاةُ والسَّلامُ عَلَيْكُمْ، يا أَنْبِيَاءَ الله

Blessings and peace be upon you, whom God Most High sent as mercy to the Worlds.

Blessings and peace be upon you, and upon all your family and your Companions.

Blessings and peace be upon you, O Prophet of God.

INVOCATION (DU'A):

(to be made silently by all who hear the adhān):

Allāhumma rabba hādhihī 'd-da'wait 't-tāmma wa 'ṣ-ṣalāt il-qā'ima, āti Sayyidinā Muḥammadan al-wasīlata wa 'l-fadīlata wa 'd-darajati 'r-raf'īati 'l-'alīyya wab'athhu Rabbī al-maqām al-maḥmūd alladhī w'adtahu, warzuqnā shaf'atahu yawm al-qīyāma. Innaka lā tukhlifu 'l-mī'ād.

دُعاءُ:

اللَّهُمَّ رَبَّ هَذِهِ الدعْوةِ
التّامّةِ والصلَاةُ القائِمة
آتِ مُحَمَّداً الوَسِيلةَ
والفَضِيلةَ والدَّرَجةَ
الرَّفيعةَ العاليةَ وابْعَثْهُ رَبِّي
المقامَ المَحْمُودَ الذي
وَعَدْتَهُ وارْزُقْنا شَفاعَتَهُ
يَوْمَ القِيامةِإنكَ لا تُخْلِفُ
الميعاد (وزَوِّجْنا من الحُورِ
العِين)

O God! Lord of this perfect supplication and of this established prayer, grant Muhammad the Means (of nearness to You) and the excellence of the sublime and supreme rank. Raise him, O my Lord, to the Praiseworthy Station, which You promised him, and

grant us his intercession on the Day of Judgment, for You do not fail Your promise.		
2 RAKʿATS SUNNAH performed After Adhān.		رَكعَتَيْنِ سُنَّة
IQAMATU 'Ṣ-ṢALĀT		إقامةُ الصلَاةُ
Identical to Adhān with the insertion after Ḥayyā ʿāla 'l-falāḥ of: Qad qāmati 'ṣ-Ṣalāt (2 times) The prayer is beginning		مثل الآذان ولكن مع إدخال قد قامَتِ الصلَاةُ قد قامَت الصلَاةُ – بعد حي على الفلاح
3 RAKʿATS FARḌ		ثلاثُ رَكَعات فَرْض
After the final salām recite:		بعد التّسْليم
lā ilāha ill-Allāh Muḥammadur Rasūlullāh (3 times)		لا إلَهَ إلاَّ الله (ثَلاثُ مَرّات) مُحَمّد رَسُولُ الله
Astaghfirullāh 3 times I ask God's forgiveness		إسْتِغْفار (ثَلاثُ مَرّات)

Astaghfirullāh al-'Aẓīm alladhī lā ilāha illa Hūwa al-Ḥayyu 'l-Qayyūm wa atūbu ilayḥ I ask forgiveness from God Almighty, there is no god but He, the Living, the Self-Subsisting, and I turn in repentance to Him.		أَسْتَغْفِرُ اللهَ العَظِيمَ الذي لا إِلَهَ إلا هُوَ الحيُّ القَيُّوم وأَتُوبُ إليْه أَسْتَغْفِرُ الله. أَسْتَغْفِرُ الله. أَسْتَغْفِرُ الله

INVOCATION (DU'A):	دُعاء:
Allāhumma anta 's-Salām wa minka 's-salām tabārakta wa ta'ālayta yā Dhā 'l-Jalāli wa 'l-ikrām. Lā ilāha ill-Allāhu wāḥdahu lā sharīka lah, lahu 'l-mulku wa lahu 'l-ḥamd, wa Hūwa 'alā kulli shay'in qadīr. Sami'nā wa aṭa'nā, ghufrānaka, Rabbanā, wa ilayka 'l-maṣīr.	اللَّهُمَّ أنتَ السَّلامُ ومِنكَ السَّلامُ تَبارَكْتَ وتعالَيْتَ يا ذا الجَلالِ والإكْرامِ. لا إلَهَ إلاَّ اللهُ وَحْدَهُ لا شَريكَ لَهُ، لَهُ المُلْكُ ولَهُ الحَمْدُ يُحيي ويُميت وهُوَ على كُلِّ شَيْءٍ قَدير. سَمِعْنا وأطَعْنا غُفْرانَكَ رَبّنا وإلَيْكَ المَصير

O God! You are Peace and from You comes Peace. Blessed and lofty are You, O Lord of Majesty and Bounty. There is no god but God, He is One, no partner has He. His is the Kingdom and His is all praise, and He is over all things Powerful. We have heard and obeyed. Your forgiveness, O our Lord! And to Thee is the end of all journeys.

2 RAK'ATS SUNNAH		ركعتين سُنّة
'alā Rasūlinā 'ṣ-ṣalawāt. Astaghfirullāh, subḥānallāh wa 'l-ḥamdulillāh, wa lā ilāha ill-Allāh w'allāhū akbar, wa lā ḥawla wa lā quwwata illa billāhi 'l-'Alīyyi 'l-'Āẓīm.		على رَسُولِنا الصَّلَوات. أَسْتَغْفِرُ اللهَ. أَسْتَغْفِرُ اللهَ. أَسْتَغْفِرُ اللهَ سُبْحانَ الله والحَمْدُ لله ولا إِلَهَ إلاَّ اللهُ واللهُ أَكْبَرُ ولا حَوْلَ ولا قُوَّةَ إلا بالله العَلِيِّ العَظيم
Blessings upon our Prophet. I ask God's forgiveness. Glory be to God! Praise be to God! There is no god but God and God is Greatest. There is no power and no strength save in God, All-High and Almighty.		
CHAPTER 2: VERSE 163 A'ūdhu billāhi min ash-shayṭāni 'r-rajīm. Bismillāhi 'r-Raḥmāni 'r-Raḥīm.		البقرة ١٦٣ أعُوذُ بالله من الشَّيْطانِ الرَّجيم بِسْمِ اللهِ الرَّحْمنِ الرَّحيمِ

<table>
<tr><td>Wa ilāhukum ilāhun wāḥidun, lā ilāha illa Hū ar-Raḥmānu ’r-Raḥīm.</td><td></td><td>وإِلَٰهُكُم إِلَٰهٌ واحِدُ لا إِلَهَ إِلاَّ هُوَ الرَّحْمَٰنِ الرَّحِيمِ</td></tr>
<tr><td colspan="3">I seek refuge with God from Satan, the Cursed. In the name of God, the All-Beneficent, the All-Merciful. Your God is One God; there is no god but He, the All-Merciful, the All-Compassionate.</td></tr>
<tr><td>ĀYATU ’L-KURSĪ
(THRONE VERSE)</td><td></td><td>آية الكُرْسي</td></tr>
<tr><td>Allāhū lā ilāha illa Hūwa ’l-Ḥayyu ’l-Qayyūm, lā tākhudhuhū ’s-sinatun wa lā nawm, lahū mā fi ’s-samāwāti wa mā fi ’l-arḍ. Man dhā-ladhī yashfaʿu ʿindahū illā bi idhniḥ yaʿlamu mā bayna aydīhim wa mā khalfahum wa lā yuḥīṭunā bi-shay’in min ʿilmihi illā bimā shā’. Wasiʿa kursīyyuhu ’s-samāwāti wa ’l-arḍa, wa lā</td><td></td><td>اللهُ لاَ إِلَـهَ إِلاَّ هُوَ الْحَيُّ الْقَيُّومُ لاَ تَأْخُذُهُ سِنَةٌ وَلاَ نَوْمٌ لَّهُ مَا فِي السَّمَاوَاتِ وَمَا فِي الأَرْضِ مَن ذَا الَّذِي يَشْفَعُ عِنْدَهُ إِلاَّ بِإِذْنِهِ يَعْلَمُ مَا بَيْنَ أَيْدِيهِمْ وَمَا خَلْفَهُمْ وَلاَ يُحِيطُونَ بِشَيْءٍ مِّنْ عِلْمِهِ إِلاَّ بِمَا</td></tr>
</table>

ya'ūduhu ḥifẓuhumā, wa Hūwa 'l-'Alīyyu 'l-'Aẓīm. Ṣadaq-Allāhu 'l-'Aẓīm.		شَاء وَسِعَ كُرْسِيُّهُ السَّمَاوَاتِ وَالأَرْضَ وَلاَ يَؤُودُهُ حِفْظُهُمَا وَهُوَ الْعَلِيُّ الْعَظِيمُ

God! There is no god but He - the Living, the Self-subsisting, Eternal. No slumber can seize Him nor sleep. His are all things in the heavens and on earth. Who is there can intercede in His presence except as He permitteth? He knoweth what (appeareth to His creatures as) before or after or behind them. Nor shall they compass aught of His knowledge except as He willeth. His Throne doth extend over the heavens and the earth, and He feeleth no fatigue in guarding and preserving them for He is the Most High, the Supreme (in glory).

God spoke the Truth.

TASBĪḤ		تَسْبِيح
Subḥānak yā ʿAẓīm subḥānallāh, subḥānallāh (33 times)		سُبحانَكَ يا عَظيم: سُبْحانُ الله (٣٣ مرّة)
Glory be to You, O Almighty! Glory be to God.		
ʿalā nʿimati 'l-Islām wa sharafi 'l-īmān dā'iman alḥamdulillāh, alḥamdulillāh (33 times)		على نِعْمةِ الإسْلامِ وشَرَفِ الإيمانِ دائِماً: الحَمْدُ لله (٣٣ مرّة)
For the gift of Islam and the honor of faith, always, praise be to God.		
Taʿalā shā'nuhū wa lā ilāha ghayruhū, Allāhū akbar, Allāhū akbar (33 times)		تعالى شأْنهُ ولا إله غَيرُهُ: اللهُ أكْبَر (٣٣ مرّة)
Exalted is His Affair, and there is no god but He, God is Greatest.		
Allāhū akbaru kabīran wa 'lḥamdulillāhi kathīran wa subḥānallāhi bukratan wa		اللهُ أكْبَرُ كَبيرًا والحَمْدُ لله كَثيرًا وسُبْحانَ الله بُكْرةً

aṣīla. Lā ilāha illa-Allāhu wāḥdahū lā sharīka lah, lahu 'l-mulku wa lahu 'l-ḥamd yuḥīy wa yumīt wa Hūwa 'alā kulli shay'in qadīr. Subḥāna Rabbīu 'l-'Alīyyu 'l-'āla 'l-Wahhāb.		وأصيلاً لا إله إلا اللهُ وَحْدَهُ لا شَريكَ له، له المُلْكُ وله الحَمْدُ يُحِي ويُميت وهُوَ على كُلِّ شيءٍ قَديرٌ سُبْحانَ رَبِّي العَليّ الأعْلى الوهّاب
Exalted be God in His Greatness and all praise be to God. Glory be to God in the morning and the evening. There is no god but God. He is One, no partner has He. His is the Kingdom and all praise. He brings to life and makes to die, and He is over all things Powerful. Glory be to my Lord, All-High, Supreme, Most Munificent.		
SUPPLICATION (DU'A)		دُعاء شخْصي
Recite a personal invocation as one is inspired.		

AL-FĀTIHA		الفاتحة
Allāhumma ṣalli ʿalā Muḥammadin wa ʿalā āli Muḥammadin wa sallim.		اللَّهُمَّ صَلِّ على مُحَمَّدٍ وعلى آلِ مُحَمَّدٍ وسلّم
Then pray the funeral prayer		

Salatu-l-Janazah

ṢALĀT AL-JANĀZATU ʿALĀ AL-GHĀʾIB Funeral Prayer in Absentia		صلَاةُ الغائِب
Fʿātabiru yā uli ʾl-abṣār laʿallakum tufliḥūn. Inna lillāhi wa inna īlayhi rājiʿūn. Ṣalātu ʾl-janāza ʿani ʾl-ghāʾibīn alladhīna antaqalu ilā raḥmatillāhi min ummati Muḥammad ṣall-Allāhū ʿalayhi wa sallam.		فَاعْتَبِرُوا يا أولي الأَبْصار لَعَلَّكُم تُفْلِحونُ. إنَّا لله وإنَّا إِليْهِ راجِعُونَ. صلَاةُ الجَنازةِ عَنِ الغائِبينَ الّذين أنْتقلوا إلى رَحْمةِ الله من أمَّةِ

		مُحَمَّدٍ (صلّى اللهُ عليه وسلّم)
Therefore, take heed, O you who can see. Surely we belong to God and to Him we return. This is the funeral prayer for the deceased who have parted to the mercy of God from the nation of Muhammad ﷺ.		
AT-TAKBĪRATU 'L-ŪLĀ (FIRST TAKBĪR) Allāhū akbar. God is Greatest!		التكْبيرة الأولى: اللهُ أكْبر
Subḥānaka Allāhumma wa bi ḥamdika, wa tabāraka ismuka wa taʿalā jadduka, wa jalla thāna'uka, wa lā ilāha ghayruka.		سُبْحانَكَ اللَّهُمَّ وبِحَمْدِكَ، وتَبارَكَ اسْمُكَ وتَعالى جَدُّكَ وجَلَّ ثَناؤُك ولا إلهَ غَيْرُكَ
Glory and praise be to You, O my God. Great is Your Praise, and there is not god but You. (In Shāfiʿī madhab: Recite al-Fātiḥah see page 325).		

AT-TAKBĪRATU 'TH-THĀNĪYA (SECOND TAKBĪR) Allāhū akbar. God is Greatest!		التكْبيرة الثانِيَة : اللهُ أكبر
Allāhumma ṣalli ʿalā Muḥammadin wa ʿalā āli Muḥammadin, kama ṣallayta ʿalā Ibrāḥīma wa ʿalā āli Ibrāḥīma innaka ḥamīdun majīdun. Allāhumma bārik ʿalā Muḥammadin wa ʿalā āli Muḥammadin, kamā bārakta ʿalā Ibrāhīm wa ʿalā āli Ibrāhīma, innaka ḥamīdun majīdun.		اللَّهُمَّ صَّلِّ على مُحَمَّدٍ وعلى آلِ مُحَمَّدٍ كما صَّليْتَ على إبْراهيمَ وعلى آلِ إبراهيمَ إنكَ حَميدٌ مَجيدٌ. اللَّهُمَّ بارِكْ على مُحَمَّدٍ وعلى آلِ مُحَمَّدٍ كما بارَكْتَ على إبْراهيمَ وعلى آلِ إبْراهيمَ إنكَ حَميدٌ مَجيدٌ.
O God! Exalt Muhammad and the family of Muhammad, as You have exalted Abraham and the family of Abraham. Truly, You are the Praised, the Glorious. O God! Bless Muhammad and the family of		

<table>
<tr><td colspan="3">Muhammad, as You have blessed Abraham and the family of Abraham. Truly, You are the Praised, the Glorious.</td></tr>
<tr><td>AT-TAKBĪRATU TH-THĀLITHA (THIRD TAKBĪR)

Allāhū akbar.

God is Greatest!</td><td></td><td>التَّكْبِيرَة الثالثة:

اللهُ أَكْبَر</td></tr>
<tr><td>Allāhumma 'ghfir li ḥayyinā wa mayyitinā wa shāhidinā wa ghā'ibinā wa ṣaghīrinā wa kabīrinā wa dhakarinā wa unthānā. Allāhumma man aḥyaytahū minna fa aḥyihi ʿalā al-Islām wa man tawaffaytahū minnā fa tawaffahū ʿalā al-īmān. Allāhumma 'ghfir lahum wa 'rḥamhum. Allāhumma lā taḥrimnā ajrahum wa lā taftinā bʿādahum.</td><td></td><td>اللَّهُمَّ اغْفِرْ لِحَيِّنَا وَمَيِّتِنَا
وَشَاهِدِنَا وَغَائِبِنَا وَصَغِيرِنَا
وَكَبِيرِنَا وَ ذَكَرِنَا وَأُنْثَانَا.
اللَّهُمَّ مَنْ أَحْيَيْتَهُ مِنَّا فَأَحْيِهِ
عَلَى الإِسْلَامِ وَمَنْ تَوَفَّيْتَهُ
مِنَّا فَتَوَفَّهُ عَلَى الإِيمَانِ.
اللَّهُمَّ اغْفِرْ لَهُمْ وَارْحَمْهُمْ
اللَّهُمَّ لَا تَحْرِمْنَا أَجْرَهُمْ
وَلَا تَفْتِنَّا بَعْدَهُمْ</td></tr>
</table>

O God! Forgive our living and our dead, our present and our absent ones, our young and our old, our male and our female. O God! To those of us whom You have granted life, make them live according to the religion of Islam, and whosoever You cause to die, cause to die in faith. O God! Forgive them and have mercy on them. O God! Do not deny us their reward (and) do not lead us astray after them (i.e. after their death).		
AT-TAKBĪRATU 'R-RĀBIʿA (FOURTH TAKBĪR) Allāhū akbar. God is Greatest!		التَّكْبِيرَةُ الرَّابِعَةُ: اللهُ أَكْبَرُ اللَّهُمَّ لَا تَحْرِمْنَا أَجْرَهُم وَلَا تَفْتِنَّا بَعدَهُم وَاغفِرْ لَنَا وَلَهُمْ
TASLĪM (To the right) as-salāmu ʿalaykum wa raḥmatullāḥ Peace be upon you and the mercy of God.		تَسْلِيم إِلى اليَمِينِ: السَّلامُ عَلَيْكُم وَرَحْمَةُ الله

(To the left) as-salāmu 'alaykum wa raḥmatullāḥ Peace be upon you and the mercy of God.		إِلَى اليَسَار: السَّلَامُ عَلَيْكُم وَرَحْمَةُ الله
DU'A (SUPPLICATION)		دُعاء
Allāhumma 'ghfir li aḥyā'inā wa 'rḥam mawtānā washf'i marḍānā bi ḥurmati 'l-Fātiḥā.		اللَّهُمَّ اغْفِرْ لِأَحْيائِنَا وَارْحَمْ مَوْتَانَا وَاشْفِ مَرْضَانَا وَانْصُرْ سُلْطَانَنَا بِحُرْمَةِ مَنْ أَرْسَلْتَهُ رَحْمَةً لِّلْعَالَمِينَ وَبِسِرِّ سُورَةِ الفَاتِحَة
O God! Forgive the living and have mercy on our dead, and cure our sick, by the sanctity of al-Fātiḥā.		
Ṣalātu 'l-Janaza is then followed by six rak 'ats of Ṣalātu 'l-Awwābīn.		

Salatu-l-Awwabin 6 rak 'ats (3 sets of 2 Rak'āts).		صَلاةُ ٱلأَوابِين (سِتَ رَكَعات)
KALIMATU SH-SHAHĀDA (3 TIMES) Ash-hadu an lā ilāha ill-Allāh wa ash-hadu anna Muḥammadan 'abduhu wa rasūluh.		كَلِمةُ الشَهادَة (٣ مَرّات): أَشْهَدُ أَن لَا إِلٰهَ إِلَّا اللهُ وَأَشْهَدُ أَنَّ مُحَمَّدًا عَبْدُهُ وَرَسُولُهُ
I bear witness that there is no god but God, and Muhammad is His Servant and Messenger.		
ISTIGHFĀR (100 TIMES)		إِستِغْفار (١٠٠ مَرّة)
Astaghfirullāh I ask God's forgiveness.		أَسْتَغْفِرُ اللهَ

DUʿA (SUPPLICATION)		دعاء
Astaghfirullāh min kulli dhanbin wa maʿṣīyatin wa min kulli mā yukhālifu dīn al-Islām, yā arḥam ar-Rāḥimīn.		أَسْتَغْفِرُ اللهَ مِن كُلِّ ذَنْبٍ وَمَّعْصِيَةٍ وَمِن كُلِّ مَا يُخَالِفُ دِينَ اَلِإسْلَامِ يَا أَرْحَمَ الرَاحِمِين
I ask God's forgiveness for every sin and desobedience and from all that opposes the religion of Islam, O most Merciful of Merciful.		
SŪRATU S-SAJDA (PROSTRATION, PAGE 372)		سُورَةُ السَجْدَة
Aʿūdhu billāhi min ash-shayṭāni 'r-rajīm. Bismillāhi 'r-Raḥmāni 'r-Raḥīm.		أَعُوذُ بِالله من الشَّيْطانِ الرَّجيمِ. بِسْمِ الله الرَّحْمنِ الرَّحيمِ
I seek refuge with God from Satan, the Cursed. In the Name of God, the Most Merciful, the Most		

Compassionate (This will be omitted hereafter, but must be read before any Quran reading). Then, read Sūratu 'l-Fātiḥah, followed by Sūratu 's-Sajda.		
SŪRATU 'L-IKHLĀṢ (SINCERITY) (3 TIMES)		سُورةُ الإخْلاص (٣ مرات)
SŪRATU 'L-FALAQ (DAYBREAK) ONCE (SEE PAGE 386)		سُورةُ الفَلَقِ
SŪRATU 'N-NĀS (MANKIND) ONCE (SEE PAGE 387)		سُورةُ النّاسِ
TAHLĪL (10 TIMES) Lā ilāha ill-Allāh There is no god but God. (After the tenth) Muḥammadur Rasūlullāh ﷺ.		تهليل: لا إله إلا الله (١٠ مرات) (بَعْدَ العاشِرة) مُحَمَّدٌ رَّسُولُ الله صلّى اللهُ عليه وسلّم

Muhammad is the Messenger of God ﷺ.		صلوات: اللَّهُمَّ صَلِّ على مُحَمَّدٍ وعلى آلِ مُحَمَّد وسلّم (١٠ مرّة)
ṢALAWĀT (10 TIMES) Allāhumma ṣalli ʿalā Muḥammadin wa ʿalā āli Muḥammadin wa sallim.		صَلَوات (١٠ مرات) أللَّهُمَّ صلّ على مُحَمَّدٍ وعلى آل مُحَمَّدٍ وسلّم
DUʿA (INVOCATION) Ṣalli, yā Rabbī, wa sallim ʿalā jamīʿi ʾl-anbīyāʾi wa ʾl-mursalīn, wa ālin kullin ajmaʿīn wa ʾl-ḥamdulillāhi Rabbi ʾl-ʿālamīn.		دعاء صلِّ يا رَبّي وسلِّم على جَميعِ الأنبْياءِ والمُرْسَلينَ وآلِ كُلِّ أجْمَعينَ والحَمْدُ لله رَبِّ العالَمينَ
Blessings, O my Lord, and peace be upon all the prophets and messegers, and on the family of every one of them. Praise belongs to God, the Lord of the worlds.		

CHIEF OF THE PRAYERS ON PROPHET (SEE PAGE 25)		الصلَاةُ الشريفة المأثورة
IHDĀ (DEDICATION - SEE PAGE 28)		إِهدَاء

Salatu-l-Isha

Performed in the same manner as Ṣalātu 'l-Maghrib with the following changes:		
4 RAK'ATS SUNNAH		٤ رَكَعات سُنّة رَكَعات سُنّة: رَكْعَتَيْنِ سُنّة وَرَكْعَتَيْنِ نافِلة بِتَسْليم واحِد أو بتسليمين، ٤ رَكَعات فرض ثم ٤ رَكَعات سنة: رَكْعَتَيْنِ سُنّة وَرَكْعَتَيْنِ نافِلة بِتَسْليم واحِد أو بتسليمين. صلَاةُ الوِتْرِ (ثَلاثُ رَكَعات).
4 RAK'ATS FARḌ		٤ رَكَعات فَرْض

4 RAKʿATS SUNNAH		٤ رَكَعات سنة: رَكْعَتَيْنِ سُنّة ورَكْعَتَيْنِ نافِلة بِتَسْليمِ واحِد أو بتسليمين
ṢALĀTU ʾL-WITR (3 RAKʿATS)		صلَاةُ الوِتْرِ (ثَلاثُ رَكَعات)
Before the rukuʿ, or bowing, in the third rakʿat, recite:		
QUNŪT PRAYER (SEE NOTES) Allāhu akbar. Allāhumma innā nastaʿīnuka wa nastahdīka; wa nastaghfiruka wa natūbu ilayk wa nuʾminu bika, wa natawakkalu ʿalayk, wa		دعاء القنُوت (في الرَكْعةِ الثالِثة قبل الركوع على مذهب الامام ابو حنيفة)

nuthnī ʿalayk al-khayr kullahā wa nashkuruka, wa lā nakfuruka, wa nakhlaʿu wa natruku man yafjuruka. Allāhumma iyyāka naʿbudu wa laka nuṣalli wa nasjudu wa ilayka nasʿā wa naḥfidhu wa narju raḥmataka, wa nakhshā ʿadhābak, inna ʿadhābak al-jidda bil-kuffāri mulḥaq, wa ṣall-Allāhū ʿalā an-Nabī wa ʿalā ālihi wa sallam. Allāhu akbar!		اللهُ أكبَر. اللَّهُمَّ إنَّ نَسْتَعينُكَ ونَسْتَهْدِيك ونَسْتَغْفِرُكَ ونَتُوبُ إليك ونُؤْمِنُ بِكَ ونَتَوَكَّلُ عليك ونُثنِي عليكَ الخَيْرَ كَلَّهُ نَشْكُرُكَ ولا نَكْفُرُ ونَخْلَعُ ونَتْرُكُ من يَفْجُرُكَ. اللَّهُمَّ إيّاكَ نَعْبُدُ ولك نُصلّي ونَسْجُدُ إليك نَسْعى ونَحْفدُ ونَرْجو رَحْمَتَكَ ونَخْشَى عَذابَكَ إنَّ عَذابَكَ الجِدَّ بالكُفّارِ مُلحِقْ وصلّى اللهُ على النَّبي وآلِهِ وسلّم

God is Greatest! O God! To You alone we pray for succour, for guidance, and for forgiveness. And to You we return in repentance; We believe in You, and trust in You, and praise You by all that is good. We thank You and are not ungrateful. We remove and leave those who sin against You. O God! We serve only You, and to You we pray and prostrate, and towards You we strive. We hope for your mercy and fear Your chastisement, for truly, Your severe punishment will befall the disbelievers. God's blessings and peace be upon the Prophet and upon his family. God is Greatest!

Go into rukʿū

Ṣalātu 'l-Witr is followed by the customary tasbīḥ and waẓīfā (see Ṣalātu 'l-Maghrib) reciting Sūratu 'l-Mulk in place of Sūratu 's-Sajda, followed by the customary adhkār.

Salatu-l-Fajr

The adab of Ṣalātu 'l-Fajr is presented in its entirety because it differs greatly from the other prayers.		
Adhan (call to prayer)		الآذان
Allāhu akbar (4 times) God is Greatest		الله أَكْبَر، الله أَكْبَر، الله أَكْبَر، الله أَكْبر
Ash-hadu an lā ilāha ill-Allāh (2 times) I bear witness that there is no god but God		اشْهَدُ أَنْ لا إِلَهَ إِلاَّ الله اشْهَدُ أَنْ لا إِلَهَ إِلاَّ الله
Ash-hadu anna Muḥammadan Rasūlullāh (2 times) I bear witness that Muhammad is the Messenger of God.		اشْهَدُ أَنَّ محمداً رسول الله - اشْهَدُ أَنَّ محمداً رسول الله
Ḥayya ʿalā 'ṣ-ṣalāh (2 times) Hasten to the prayer		حيَّ عَلى الصلَاةُ حيَّ عَلى الصلَاةُ

Ḥayyā ʿāla ʾl-falāḥ (2 times) Hasten to salvation		حيَّ عَلى الفَلاح حيَّ عَلى الفَلاح
Aṣ-ṣalātu khayrun min an-nawm (2 times, only before Fajr) Prayer is better than sleep		الصلَاةُ خَيْرٌ مِّنَ النَّوْمْ الصلَاةُ خَيْرٌ مِّنَ النَّوْمْ
Allāhu akbar (2 times) God is Greatest		اللهُ أكْبَر اللهُ أكْبَر
Lā ilāha illa-Allāh There is no god but God		لا إلَه إلاَّ الله
AṢ-ṢALĀTU WA ʾS-SALĀM (to be made aloud by the muadhdhin): Aṣ-ṣalātu wa ʾs-salāmu ʿalayk, yā man arsalahullāhu taʿalā raḥmatan li ʾl-ʿālamīn.		الصلَاةُ والسَّلام الصلَاةُ والسَّلامُ عليك يا من أرْسَلَهُ اللهُ تَعَالى رَحْمَةً لّلعالمين الصلَاةُ والسَّلامُ عَلَيْكَ وعَلى آلِكَ وأصْحَابِكَ

<table>
<tr><td>Aṣ-ṣalātu wa ’s-salāmu ‘alayk, wa ‘alā ālika wa aṣḥābika ajma‘īn.
Aṣ-ṣalātu wa ’s-salāmu ‘alaykum, yā anbīyā’ullāḥ.</td><td></td><td>أجْمَعِين الصلاةُ والسَّلامُ
عَلَيْكُمْ، يا أنبياءَ الله</td></tr>
<tr><td colspan="3">Blessings and peace be upon you, whom God Most High sent as mercy to the Worlds.
Blessings and peace be upon you, and upon all your family and your Companions.
Blessings and peace be upon you, O prophets of God.</td></tr>
<tr><td>INVOCATION (DU‘A):
(to be made silently by all who hear the adhān):
Allāhumma rabba hādhihī ’d-da‘wat it-tāmma wa ’ṣ-ṣalāti ’l-qā’ima, āti Sayyidinā Muḥammadan al-wasīlata wa ’l-faḍīlata wa ’d-darajati ’r-raf‘īata ’l-‘alīyya w’ab‘ath-hu Rabbī al-maqām al-maḥmūd alladhī w‘adtahu, w’arzuqnā shaf‘atahu</td><td></td><td>دُعاءُ:
اللَّهُمَّ رَبَّ هَذِهِ الدعْوةِ
التّامّةِ والصلاةُ القَائِمَةِ آتِ
مُحَمَّداً الوَسيلةَ والفَضيلةَ
والدَّرَجةَ الرَّفيعةَ العاليةَ
وابْعَثْهُ رَبِّي المقامَ المَحْمودَ
الذي وَعَدْتَهُ وارْزُقْنا</td></tr>
</table>

yawm al-qīyāmati innaka lā tukhlifu 'l-mīʿad.		شَفاعَتَهُ يَوْمَ القِيامةِإنكَ لا تُخْلِفُ المِيعاد (وزَوِّجْنا من الحُورِ العِين)

O God! Lord of this perfect supplication and of this established prayer, grant Muhammad the Means (of nearness to You) and the excellence of the sublime and supreme rank. Raise him, O my Lord, to the Praiseworthy Station, which You promised him, and grant us his intercession on the Day of Judgment, for You do not fail Your promise.

2 RAKʿATS SUNNAH		٢ رَكْعتان سُنّة
KALIMATU SH-SHAHĀDA (3 TIMES) Ash-hadu an lā ilāha ill-Allāh, wa ash-hadu anna Muḥammadan ʿabduhū wa rasūluḥ.		كلمة الشَهادة: أَشْهَدُ أَنْ لا إله إلا الله وأَشْهدُ أَنَّ مُحَمَّدًا عَبْدُهُ ورَسُولُهُ (٣ مرّات)
I bear witness that there is no god but God, and Muhammad is His servant and Messenger.		
Iqāmatu 'ṣ-ṣalāt wa ītā'u 'z-zakāti wa ṣawmu ramaḍāna, wa Ḥajju 'l-bayti Ḥaqq. Āmantu billāhi wa malā'ikatihi wa kutubihi wa rusulihi wa 'l-yawmi 'l-āhkiri wa bi 'l-qadari khayrihi wa sharrihi min Allāhi taʿalā. Awdaʿnā hātayni 'l-kalimatayni 'sh-shahādatayn ʿindaka yā Rasūlullāh wa hīya lanā		إقامةُ الصلاةِ وإيتاءُ الزَّكاةِ وصَوْمُ رَمَضانَ وحَجُّ البيْتِ حَقٌّ آمَنْتُ بِالله ومَلائِكتِهِ وكُتُبِهِ ورُسُلِهِ وباليَوْمِ الآخِرِ وبالقَدَرِ خَيْرِهِ وشَرِّهِ. أَوْدَعْنا هاتَيْنِ الشَهادَتَيْنِ

wadīʿatun yawma 'l-qiyāmati ya man arsalahullāhū taʿalā raḥmatan li 'l-ʿālamīn.		عِنْدَكَ يا سيدي يا رَسُول الله وهي لنا وَديعةٌ يَوْمَ القِيامةِ يا من أَرْسَلَهُ الله تعالى رَحْمَةً للعالمينَ.

The performance of prayer, the payment of alms, the fast in Ramadān, and the Pilgrimage to the House, are true. I declare my belief in God, His Angels, His Books, His messengers, the Day of Judgment, and in Destiny—both its good and evil being from God (Exalted is He!). May the truth of what I say be accepted, O Lord.

We have commended these two testimonials to your safekeeping, O Messenger of God. They are for us a trust on the Day of Judgment, O you who were sent by God (Exalted is He!) as a mercy to the worlds.

Subḥānallāh wa bi ḥamdihi subḥānallāhi 'l-ʿAẓīm Astaghfirullāh (100 times)		سُبْحانَ الله وبحَمْدِهِ. سُبْحانَ الله العَظيمِ أَسْتَغْفِرُ الله – ١٠٠ مرة

<table>
<tr><td colspan="2">Glory be to God, and to Him be praise. Glory be to God Almighty. I ask God's forgiveness.</td></tr>
<tr><td>(after the 100th time)

Astaghfirullāh al-ʿAẓīm alladhī lā ilāha illa Hū al-Ḥayyu ʾl-Qayyūm wa atūbu ilayḥ innahu Hū at-tawābu ʾr-raḥīm min kulli dhanbin wa maʿṣīyatin wa min kulli mā yukhālifu dīn al-Islām, yā arḥam ar-Rāḥimīn, min kulli mā yukhālifu ʾsh-sharīʿah, wa min kulli mā yukhālifu ʾṭ-ṭarīqata, wa min kulli mā yukhālifu ʾl-maʿrifata, wa min-kulli mā yukhālifu ʾl-ḥaqīqata, wa min kulli mā yukhālifu ʾl-ʿazīmata, yā Arḥam ar-rāḥīmin.</td><td>بَعْدَ المئة:
أَسْتَغْفِرُ اللهَ العَظِيمَ الذي
لا إله إلا هُوَ الحيّ القَيُّوم
وأَتُوبُ إليْه إنَّهُ هو التَوّابُ
الرَحيم، من كُلِّ ذَنْبٍ
ومّعْصِيّةٍ ومِنْ كُلِّ ما
يُخالِفُ دينَ الإسْلام ومن
كُلِّ ما يُخالِفُ الشَّريعة
ومن كُلِّ ما يُخالِفُ الطَّريقةَ
ومن كُلِّ ما يُخالِفُ المَعْرِفةَ
ومن كُلِّ ما يُخالِفُ الحَقيقةَ
ومن كُلِّ ما يُخالِفُ العَزيمة
يا أرْحَمَ الرَّاحِمين.</td></tr>
</table>

I ask forgiveness from God Almighty, there is no god but He, the Living, the Self-Subsisting, and I turn in repentance to Him, verily He is the Forgiver, the Merciful, from every sin and disobedience and from all that opposes the religion of Islam, from all that opposes the Divine Law, from all that opposes the Path, from all that opposes Spiritual Realization, from all that opposes Reality, from all that opposes firm Intention, O most Merciful of the Merciful.

Astaghfirullāhu 'l-ʿAz.īm, wa atūbu ilayh (100 times)		أَسْتَغْفِرُ اللهَ العَظِيم وأَتُوبُ إليه — ١٠٠ مرة

I ask forgiveness from God Almighty and I turn to Him in repentance.

(after the 100th time) Tawbatan ʿabdin ẓālimin li nafsihi, lā yamliku li nafsihi mawtan wa lā ḥayātan wa lā nushūrā. Allāhumma anta Rabbī, lā ilāha illa Anta khalaqtanī wa anā ʿabduka wa anā ʿalā ʿahdika wa waʿdika mā		تَوْبَةَ عَبْدٍ ظالِمٍ لنَفْسِهِ لا يَمْلِكُ لنَفْسِهِ مَوْتًا ولا حَياةً ولا نُشُورًا اللَّهُمَّ رَبِّي لا إله إلا أنتَ خَلَقْتَني وأنا عَبْدُكَ وأنا على عَهْدِكَ ووَعْدِكَ ما

’staṭa‘t. A‘ūdhu bika min sharri mā ṣan‘ātu, abū’u laka bi ni‘matika ‘alayya, wa abū’u bi dhanbī faghfir lī fa innahū lā yaghfir udh-dhunūba illa Anta Yā Allāḥ.		اسْتَطَعْتُ أعُوذُ بِكَ من شَرِّ ما صَنَعْتُ وأبُوءُ لَكَ بِنِعْمَتِكَ عليّ وأبُوءُ بِذَنْبي فاغْفِرْ لي فَإنَّهُ لا يَغْفِرُ الذنوبَ إلا أنتَ يا اللهُ.

The repentance of a slave who has oppressed himself, who neither has power over his death, nor his life, nor his resurrection.

O God! You are my Lord. There is no god but You. You have created me. I am Your slave, and I hold fast to Your convenant and Your promise (as much as I am able). I take refuge in You from the evil I have done, and testify that Your Grace is upon me, and profess my sin. Forgive me, for there is none who forgives sins except You, O God!

CHAPTER 3, VERSE 8 Rabbanā lā tuzigh qulūbanā baʿda idh hadaytanā wa hab lanā min ladunka raḥmatan innaka Anta' l-Wahhāb.		سُورَةُ آل عمْران آية ٨ رَبَّنَا لاَ تُزِغْ قُلُوبَنَا بَعْدَ إِذْ هَدَيْتَنَا وَهَبْ لَنَا مِن لَّدُنكَ رَحْمَةً إِنَّكَ أَنتَ الْوَهَّابُ
Our Lord, make not our hearts to swerve after You have guided us, and give us Your Mercy; You are the Bestower.		
Yā Wahhāb. Yā Wahhāb. Yā Wahhāb. Yā Musabbib al-asbāb, yā Mufattiḥ al-abwāb, yā Muqallib al-qulūbi wa 'l-abṣār, yā Dalīl al-mutaḥayyirīn, yā Ghiyāth al-mustaghīthīn, yā Ḥayyu, yā Qayyūm, yā Dhā 'l-Jalāli wa 'l-Ikrām! Wa ufawwiḍu amrī ila-Allāh, inna-Allāha baṣīrun bi 'l-ʿibād.		يا وَهّابْ يا وَهّابْ يا وَهّابْ، يا مُسَبِّبَ الأسْبابْ. ويا مُفَتِّحَ الأبوابْ. يا مُقَلِّبَ القُلُوبِ والأبصارْ. يا دَليلَ المُتَحَيِّرينَ يا غِياثَ المُسْتَغيثينَ يا حيٌّ يا قَيُّوم. يا ذا الجَلالِ والإكْرامْ.

		وأُفَوِّضُ أمْري إلى الله. إنَّ الله بَصيرٌ بالعِباد.
O Bestower! O Bestower! O Bestower! O Originator of causes! O Opener of doors! O Turner of hearts and eyes! O Guide of the perplexed! O Succour for those who seek Your aid! O Living! O Self-Subsisting One! O (You who are) possessed of Majesty and Bounty! I entrust my affair unto God. Truly, God is aware of His servants.		
DUʿA (INVOCATION)		دُعاء
Yā man lā maljā'a minhu illa ilayhi fa lā tukhayyib rajā'anā, yā Qadīm al-iḥsān. Lā taqnaṭu min raḥmati-llāh, inna-llāha yaghfiru 'dh-dhūnuba jamīʿan, innahū Hūwa 'l-Ghafūru 'r-Raḥīm. Allāhumma innā nas'aluka 'l-ʿafwa wal ʿāfīyata fi 'd-		يَا مَنْ لا مِلْجأَ مِنْهُ إلا إلَيْه فَلا تُخَيِّبْ رَجاءَنا يا قَديمَ الإحْسانْ لا تَقْنَطُوا من رَحْمةِ الله إنَّ الله يَغْفِرُ الذُنُوبَ جَميعًا إنَّهُ هو الغَفُور الرَّحيمْ

dīni wa 'd-dunyā wa 'l-ākhira. Allahumma 'sturnā bi satrik al-jamīl. Allāhumm 'ustur ʿawratī, wa āmin rawʿatī, waqḍi lī daynī. Allāhumma inna naʿūdhu bika min jahdi 'l-balā'i, wa darki 'sh-shaqā'i, wa sūi 'l-qaḍā'i, wa shamātati 'l-āʿdā'i, bi ḥurmati man arsaltahū raḥmatan li 'l-ʿālamīn.	اللَّهُمَّ إِنآ نَسْأَلُكَ العَفْوَ والعافِيَةَ فِي الدِّينِ والدُّنْيا والآخِرَةِ اللَّهُمَّ اسْتُرْنا بِسَتْرِكَ الجَمِيل. اللَّهُمَّ اسْتُرْ عَوْرَتِي وآمِنْ رَوْعَتِي واقْضِ دَيْنِي. اللَّهُمَّ إِنّا نَعُوذُ بِكَ من جَهْدِ البَلاءِ ودَرْكِ الشَّقاءِ وسُوءِ القَضاءِ وشَماتَةِ الأعْداءِ بِحُرْمَةِ من أرْسَلْتَهُ رَحْمَةً لِلْعالَمِينَ.

O Ye whom there is no refuge except in but Ye, do not disappoint our hopes, O Eternally Beneficent.

Do not despair of the mercy of God, for God forgives every sin. Truly, He is the All-Forgiving, All-Merciful.

O God! We ask Your pardon, and ask for strength in religion, in this life and the Hereafter.

O God! Veil our shortcomings with Your Beautiful Veil.

O God! Veil my imperfection and set me rest when I fear, and settle my debts.

O God! We take refuge in You from the pangs of tribulations, from being overtaken by misfortune, and from an evil destiny, and from the gloating of mine enemies. By the sanctity of the one whom you sent as a mercy to the worlds (Sayyidinā Muhammad ﷺ).

Salatu munajiyyah		الصلَاةُ المنُجِيّة
Allāhumma ṣalli ʿalā Muḥammadin ṣalātan tunjīnā bihā min jamīʿi ʾl-ahwāli wa ʾl-āfāt, wa taqḍī lanā bihā min jamīʿi ʾl-ḥājāt, wa tuṭahhirunā bihā min jamīʿi ʾs-sayyiʾāt, wa tarfaʿunā bihā ʿindaka ʿalā ʾd-darajāt, wa tuballighunā bihā aqṣā ʾl-ghāyāt min		اللَّهُمَّ صلِّ على سَيِّدِنا مُحَمَّدٍ صلَاةً تُنْجِينا بِها من جَمِيعِ الأهْوالِ والآفاتِ وتَقْضِي لَنا بِها جَمِيعَ الحَاجَاتِ وتُطَهِّرُنا بِها من جَمِيعِ السَّيِّئاتِ وتَرْفَعُنا بِها

jamīʿi ʾl-khayrāti fi ʾl-ḥayāt wa baʿd al-mamāt.		عِنْدَكَ أعْلى الدَّرجاتِ وتُبلِّغُنا بِها أقصى الغاياتِ من جَميعِ الخَيْراتِ في الحَياة وبَعْدَ المَماتِ
O God! Blessings upon Muhammad. May they be blessings that delivers us from every fear. And appoint for us the fulfillment of every need. May we be cleansed by them (the blessings) from every sin, and by them may we be raised to the highest stations. And by them make us attain the furthest degrees in all that is good in this life and the life and after death.		
Allāhumma ʾsliḥ ummata Muḥammad.		اللَّهُمَّ أصْلِحْ أمَّةَ مُحَمَّدٍ
O God! Reconcile the nation of Muhammad.		
Allāhumma ʾrḥam ummata Muḥammad.		اللَّهُمَّ ارْحمْ أمَّةَ مُحَمَّدٍ
O God! Have mercy on the nation of Muhammad.		
Allāhūmma ʾstur ummata Muḥammad.		اللَّهُمَّ اسْتُرْ أمَّةَ مُحَمَّدٍ

O God! Veil the imperfection of the nation of Muhammad.		
Allāhūmm 'ghfir li ummati Muḥammad.		اللَّهُمَّ اغْفِرْ لأُمَّةِ مُحَمَّدٍ
O God! Forgive the nation of Muhammad.		
Allāhūmm 'aḥfaẓ ummata Muḥammad.		اللَّهُمَّ احْفَظْ أمَّةَ مُحَمَّدٍ
O God! Preserve the nation of Muhammad.		
Allāhūmma 'nṣur ummata Muḥammad.		اللَّهُمَّ أنْصُرْ أمَّةَ مُحَمَّدٍ
O God! Succour the nation of Muhammad.		
Yā arḥam ar-Rāḥīmīn arḥamnā. Yā arḥam ar-Rāḥīmīn fa'fu 'annā. Yā arḥam ar-Raḥīmīn, yā Ghaffār adh-dhūnub, Yā Sattār al-'uyūb, Yā Fattāḥ al-qulūb.		يا أرْحَمَ الرَّاحِمِينَ ارْحَمْنا. يا أرْحَمَ الرّاحِمين اعْفُ عَنّا. يا أرْحَمَ الرّاحِمين يا غفّارَ الذُّنُوب يا سَتّارَ العُيُوبْ يا فَتّاحَ القُلُوب
O Most Merciful of the Merciful! Have mercy on us. O Most Merciful of the Merciful! Forgive us. O Most		

<table>
<tr><td colspan="3">Merciful of the Merciful! O Pardoner of sins! O Veiler of our shortcomings! O Opener of hearts!</td></tr>
<tr><td>Allāhumma 'sqinā 'l-ghaytha suqyā raḥmatin wa lā taj'alnā min al-qāniṭīn. Rabb ighfir w'arḥam wa Anta khayru'r-rāḥimīn. Āmīn. Āmīn. Āmīn.</td><td></td><td>اللَّهُمَّ اسْقِنا الغَيْثَ سُقيا رَحْمَةٍ وَلَا تَجْعَلْنَا مِن القَانِطِينَ رَبِ اغْفِرْ وَارْحَمْ وَأَنْتَ خَيرُ الرَّاحِمِينَ. آمين آمين آمين</td></tr>
<tr><td colspan="3">O God give us to drink from the rain of Your Mercy. Lord, pardon and forgive, for You are the best of those who forgive. Āmīn. Āmīn. Āmīn.</td></tr>
<tr><td>Wa salāmun 'alā 'l-mursalīn, wa 'lḥamdu-lillāhi Rabbi 'l-'ālamīn.</td><td></td><td>وسَلامٌ على المُرْسَلين والحَمْدُ لله رّبِّ العالَمِين.</td></tr>
<tr><td colspan="3">Peace be upon the messengers and praise be to God, the Lord of the worlds.</td></tr>
</table>

SŪRATU 'L-IKHLĀṢ (CHAPTER 112) (3 TIMES) (SEE PAGE 385)		سُورةُ الإخْلاص – ٣ مرات
CHAPTER 37: VERSE 180 Subḥāna Rabbika Rabbi 'l-'izzati 'ammā yaṣifūn wa salāmun 'ala 'l-mursalīn wa 'l-ḥamdulillāhi Rabbi 'l-'ālamīn.		سُورة الصّافات ١٨٠ سُبْحانَ رَبِّكَ رَبِّ العَزّةَ عَمّا يَصِفُونَ وسَلامٌ على المُرْسَلينَ والحَمْدُ لله رَبِّ العالَمِينَ
Glory be to Your Lord, the Lord of Power, above what they describe! And peace be upon the Emissaries. Praise belongs to God, the Lord of the Worlds.		
Lā ilāhā ill-Allāh, wāḥdahū lā sharīka lah, lahu 'l-mulku wa lahu 'l-ḥamd, yuḥī wa yumīt, wa Hūwa Ḥāyyun dā'imun, lā yamūt, bi yadihi 'l-khayr, wa Hūwa 'alā kulli shay'in qadīr.		لا إله إلا اللهُ وَحْدَهُ لا شَريكَ له، له المُلْكُ وَلَه الحَمْدُ يُحِي ويُمِيتُ وهُوَ حيٌّ دائِمٌ لا يَمُوتُ بيَدِهِ

<table>
<tr><td></td><td></td><td>الخَيْرُ وهُوَ على كُلِّ شَيْءٍ قَدير.</td></tr>
<tr><td colspan="3">There is no god but God. He is One, no partner has He. His is the Kingdom, and His is all praise, He brings to life and causes to die. He is forever Living, never dying. In His Hands is (all) good, and He is over all things Powerful.</td></tr>
<tr><td>IHDĀ (DEDICATION - SEE PAGE 28)
Ila sharafi 'n-Nabī ṣall-Allāhū ʿalayhi wa sallama wa ālihi wa ṣaḥbih, wa ilā arwāḥi ikhwānihi min al-anbiyā'i wa 'l-mursalīn wa khudamā'i sharāʿihim wa ila arwāḥi 'l-a'immati 'l-arbaʿah wa ila arwāḥi mashāyikhinā fi 'ṭ-ṭarīqati 'n-naqshbandīyyati 'l-ʿaliyyah khāṣṣatan ila</td><td></td><td>إِهدَاء
إلى شَرَفِ النّبي وآلِهِ وصَحْبِهِ، وإلى أرْواحِ إخْوانِهِ مِن الأنْبياءِ والمُرسَلينَ وخُدَماءِ شَرائِعِهِم وإلى أَرْواحِ الأئِمَّةِ الأرْبَعَة، وإلى أرْواحِ مَشَايِخِنا في الطّرِيقَةِ النَّقْشْبَنْدِيّةِ العَلِيّةِ خاصَةً</td></tr>
</table>

rūḥi Imāmi 'ṭ-ṭarīqati wa ghawthi 'l-khalīqati Khwājā Baḥā'uddīn an-Naqshband Muḥammad al-Uwaisī 'l-Bukhārī wa ḥaḍarati Mawlanā Sulṭānu 'l-awlīyā ash-Shaykh ʿAbd Allāh al-Fā'iz ad-Dāghestanī wa sayyidunā ash-Shaykh Muḥammad Nāẓim al-Ḥaqqānī wa sa'iri sādātinā wa 'ṣ-ṣiddiqīna al-Fātiḥā	إلى رُوحِ إمامِ الطَّرِيقَةِ وغَوْثِ الخَلِيقَةِ خَواجه بَهاءُ الدِّينِ النَّقْشْبَنْد مُحَمَّدُ الأُوَيْسِيّ البُخارِيّ وإلى حَضْرَة مولانا سُلْطانُ الأَوْلِيَاءْ الشَّيْخ عَبْدُ الله ألدَّاغستَانِي وَمَولاَنَا الشَّيْخ مُحَمَّدْ نَاظِمُ الحَقَانِيّ وَإلى سَائِرِ سَادَاتِنَا وَالصِّدِّيقِين. الفَاتِحَة

Honor be to the Prophet ﷺ, and his family, and his distinguished Companions, and to our honored Shaykhs and to our Master, Sulṭānu 'l-awlīyā Shaykh ʿAbd Allāh al-Fā'izi 'd-Daghestanī and our Master ash-Shaykh Muḥammad Nāẓim al-Ḥaqqānī and to all our masters, and (those who are) the righteous al-Fātiḥah (see page 325).

<table>
<tr><td>(LIE DOWN ON RIGHT SIDE RECITING CHAPTER 20: VERSE 55)
Minhā khalaqnākum, wa fīhā nuʿīdukum, wa minhā nukhrijukum tāratan ukhrā.</td><td></td><td>اسْتَرِحْ على جَنْبِكَ الأيْمن:
سُورة طه ٥٥
مِنْهَا خَلَقْنَاكُمْ وَفِيهَا نُعِيدُكُمْ وَمِنْهَا نُخْرِجُكُمْ تَارَةً أُخْرَى</td></tr>
<tr><td colspan="3">Thereof (earth) We created you, and we shall return you unto it, and bring you forth from it a second time.</td></tr>
<tr><td>CHAPTER 2: 156
Wa innā lillāhi wa innā ilayhi rājiʿūn.</td><td></td><td>سورة البقرة ١٥٦
إِنَّا لِلَّهِ وَإِنَّا إِلَيْهِ رَاجِعونَ</td></tr>
<tr><td colspan="3">And truly we belong to God and to Him we return.</td></tr>
</table>

CHAPTER 40: 12 Fa 'l-ḥukmu lillāhi 'l-'Alīyyi 'l-Kabīr. Allāhumma thabbitnā 'alā al-īmān.	سُورة غافر ١٢ فَالْحُكْمُ لِلَّهِ الْعَلِيِّ الْكَبِيرِ. اللَّهُمَّ ثَبِّتْنَا عَلَى الْإِيمَانِ
And the decree belongs to God, Most High, Most Great. O God! Keep us steadfast in faith.	
IQĀMATU 'Ṣ-ṢALĀT (as in Ṣalātu 'l-Maghrib)	إِقامةُ الصَّلاةُ
2 RAK'ATS FARḌ	رَكْعَتَان فَرْض

QUNŪT PRAYER (SEE NOTES)

Allāhumma 'hdinā bi-faḍlika fī-man hadayt, wa 'āfinā fī-man 'āfayt, wa tawallanā fī-man tawallayt, wa bārik lanā fī-mā ā'ṭayt, wa qinā w'aṣrif 'annā sharra mā qaḍayt [palms turned down from wa qinā to qaḍayt]. Fa innaka taqḍī wa lā yuqḍā 'alayk, wa innahū lā yadhillu man wālayt, wa lā ya'izzu man 'ādayt. Tabārakta Rabbanā wa ta'ālayt, wa laka 'l-ḥamdu 'alā mā qaḍayt. Nastaghfiruk 'allāhumma wa natūbu ilayk, wa ṣalla-llāhu 'alā 'n-Nabī il-ummīyy wa 'alā ālihi wa ṣaḥbihi wa sallam.

دُعاءِ القُنُوتِ

بَعدَ سَمِعَ اللهُ لِمَنْ حَمِدَه:

اللَّهُمَّ اهْدِنا بِفَضْلِكَ فِيمَنْ هَدَيْتَ، وَعَافِنا فِيمَنْ عَافَيْتَ، وَتَوَلَّنا فِيمَنْ تَوَلَّيْتَ، وَبَارِكْ لَنا فِيما أَعْطَيْتَ، وَقِنا وَاصْرِفْ عَنّا شَرَّ مَا قَضَيْتَ، فَإِنَّكَ تَقْضِي بِالحَقِّ، وَلاَ يُقْضَى عَلَيْكَ، وَإِنَّهُ لاَ يَذِلُّ مَنْ وَالَيْتَ، وَلاَ يَعِزُّ مَنْ عَادَيْتَ تَبَارَكْتَ رَبَّنا وَتَعَالَيْتَ فَلَكَ الحَمْدُ عَلَى مَا قَضَيْتَ نَسْتَغْفِرُكَ اللَّهُمَّ مِنْ كُلِّ الذُّنُوبِ وَنَتُوبُ

		إِليكَ وَصَلّى اللهُ عَلى النَّبِيِّ الأُمِّي وَعَلى آلِهِ وَصَحْبِهِ وَسَلَّم
O God! Guide us, by Your favor, to those whom You guided, and pardon us with those whom You have pardoned. Bring us close to those whom You have brought nigh (befriended), and bless us in all that You gave us. Protect us and turn away from us the evil of what You have decreed. For it is You that decrees and there is no decree upon You. You do not humiliate the one whom You have befriended and do not increase (empower) the one whom You have taken as an enemy. Blessed and Exalted are You, our Lord. To You is all praise for what You have decreed. We ask Your forgiveness, O God, and turn in repentance to You; God's blessings and peace be upon the unlettered Prophet and on his family and his Companions.		
Allāhumma 'kshif ʿanā min al-balāya mā lā yakshifuhu ghayruk		اللَّهُمَّ اكْشِفْ عَنَّا مِن اَلبَلَايَا مَا لَا يَكْشِفُهُ غَيْرُكَ

O God! Lift from us trials which no one but You can lift.		
Allāhumma 'sqina 'l-ghaytha suqyā raḥmatin wa lā taj'alna min al-qāniṭīn. Rabbi 'ghfir warḥam wa Anta khayru 'r-rāḥimīn.		اللَّهُمَّ اسْقِنا الغَيثَ سُقْيا رَحْمةٍ وَلَا تَجْعَلْنَا مِنَ القانِطِينَ رَبِّ اغْفِرْ وَارْحَمْ وَأَنْتَ خَيْرُ الرَّاحِمِين
O God! Give us to drink from the rain of Your Mercy and let us not be of the despondent; Lord, forgive and have mercy, for You are (Most) Merciful.		
Allāhumma 'ftaḥ lanā fatḥan mubīnan wa Anta khayru 'l-fātiḥīn.		اللَّهُمَّ افْتَحْ لَنَا فَتْحاً مُبِيناً وَأَنْتَ خَيْرُ الفَاتِحِين
O God! Open for us a manifest opening for You are the best of Openers.		

<table>
<tr><td>CHAPTER 6: VERSE 45
Fa-quṭi‘a dābiru 'l-qawmi 'lladhīna ẓalamū wa 'l-ḥamdulillāhi Rabbi 'l-‘ālamīn.
(Then go to prostration without wiping face nor chest with hands.)</td><td></td><td>سُورة الأنعام ٤٥
فَقُطِعَ دَابِرُ الْقَوْمِ الَّذِينَ ظَلَمُواْ وَالْحَمْدُ لله رَبِّ الْعَالَمِينَ</td></tr>
<tr><td colspan="3">So the last remnant of the people who did evil was cut off. Praise be to God, Lord of the Worlds. God is Greatest.</td></tr>
<tr><td>(AFTER THE SALUTATIONS)
Lā ilāhā ill-Allāh (3 times)
Muḥammadur-Rasūlullāḥ</td><td></td><td>بعد التّسليم من الصلاةُ
لا إِلَهَ إلاَّ اللهُ محمدٌ رسولَ الله – ٣ مرات</td></tr>
<tr><td colspan="3">There is no god except God, Muhammad is the Prophet of God.</td></tr>
<tr><td>ISTIGHFĀR
Astaghfirullāh (3 times)
I ask God's forgiveness.</td><td></td><td>إِسْتِغفار (٣ مرّة)</td></tr>
</table>

DU'A (INVOCATION)

Allāhumma Anta 's-Salām wa minka 's-salām wa ilayka ya'ūdu 's-salām, fa ḥayyinā Rabbanā bi 's-salām, wa 'dkhilnā 'l-Jannata bi luṭfika wa karamika wa jūdika dāraka, dār as-salām. Tabārakta Rabbanā wa tā'alayta, yā Dhā 'l-Jalāli wa 'l-Jamāli wa 'l-Baqā'i wa 'l-'Aẓamati wa 'l-Ikrām. Yā Rabbanā, Yā Rabbi 'ghfir warḥam wa Anta Khayru 'r-Raḥīmīn.

دُعاء

اللَّهمَ أنتَ السَّلامُ ومِنْكَ السَّلامُ وإلَيْكَ يَعُودُ السَّلامُ فَحيِّنَا رَبنا بالسَّلامِ وادْخِلْنَاالجنَّةَ بلُطْفِكَ وكَرَمِكَ وجُودِكَ دارِكَ دارَ السَّلامِ. تَبَارَكْتَ رَبَّنَا وَتَعَالَيْتَ يَا ذَا الجَلَالِ وَالجَمَالِ وَالبَقَاءِ وَالعَظَمَةِ وَ الإِكْرَامِ. يَا رَبَّنَا يَا رَبِ اغْفِرْ وَارْحَمْ وَأنتَ خَيْرُ الرَّاحِمِين.

O God! You are Peace and from You comes Peace and to You returns Peace; Make us live in peace, our Lord. Enter us into the Garden by Your Grace and Generosity and Presence, Your Abode, the Abode of

Peace. Blessed and lofty are You, O Lord of Majesty, and Beauty, and Everlastingness, and Greatness, and Bounty. O our Lord! O Lord forgive and have mercy, for Yours is the best of Mercy.		
Lā ilāhā ill-Allāh, wāḥdahū lā sharīka lah, lahu 'l-mulku wa lahu 'l-ḥamd, yuḥī wa yūmīt, wa Hūwa 'alā kulli shay'in qadīr (9 times).		لا إِلَهَ إلاَّ الله وَحْدَهُ لا شَرِيكَ لَهُ، لَهُ المُلْكُ ولَهُ الحَمْدُ يُحْيِي ويُميتُ وهُوَ على كُلِّ شَيْءٍ قَدير (٩ مرّات).
There is no god but God. He is One, no partner has He. His is the Kingdom and His is all praise, He gives life and gives death, and He is over all things Powerful.		
Lā ilāhā ill-Allāh, wāḥdahū lā sharīka lah, lahu 'l-mulku wa lahu 'l-ḥamd, yuḥī wa yumīt, wa Hūwa Ḥāyyun dā'imun, lā yamūt, bi yadihi 'l-khayr, wa		لا إله إلا اللهُ وَحْدَهُ لا شَريكَ له، له المُلكُ وله الحَمْدُ يُحيِي ويُميت وهُوَ حيٌّ دائِمٌ لا يَمُوتُ بيَده

<table>
<tr><td>Hūwa ʿalā kulli shay'in qadīr.</td><td></td><td>الخَيْرُ وهُوَ على كُلِّ شَيْءٍ قَدير.</td></tr>
<tr><td colspan="3">There is no god but God. He is One, no partner has He. His is the Kingdom, and His is all praise, He brings to life and causes to die. He is forever Living, never dying. In His Hands is (all) good, and He is powerful over all things.</td></tr>
<tr><td>Samʿinā wa ataʿnā, ghufrānaka Rabbanā wa ilayka 'l-maṣīr.</td><td></td><td>سَمِعْنَا وَأَطَعْنَا غُفْرَانَكَ رَبَّنَا وَإِلَيْكَ المَصِير</td></tr>
<tr><td colspan="3">We have heard and obeyed, O our Lord! Yours is our destiny.</td></tr>
<tr><td>ʿAlā Rasūlinā 'ṣ-ṣalawāt (in a low voice): Allāhūma ṣalli ʿalā sayyidinā Muḥammad</td><td></td><td>عَلى رَسُولِنَا الصَّلَوَات</td></tr>
<tr><td colspan="3">On the Prophet of God, prayers. O God, bless our master Muhammad.</td></tr>
</table>

<table>
<tr><td>Astaghfirullāh, subḥānallāh wa 'l-ḥamdulillāh, wa lā ilāha ill-Allāh w'Allāhū akbar, wa lā ḥawla wa lā quwwata illa billāhi 'l-'Alīyyu 'l-'Āẓīm.</td><td></td><td>أَسْتَغْفِرُ اللهَ. أَسْتَغْفِرُ اللهَ. أَسْتَغْفِرُ اللهَ سُبْحانَ الله والحَمْدُ لله ولا إلَهَ إلاَّ الله واللهُ أَكْبَر ولا حَوْلَ ولا قُوَّةَ إلا بالله العَلِيُّ العَظِيمْ</td></tr>
<tr><td colspan="3">I ask God's forgiveness. Glory be to God! Praise be to God! There is no god but God and God is Greatest. There is no power and no strength save in God, the Most High, the Great.</td></tr>
<tr><td>CHAPTER 2, VERSE 163
A'ūdhu billāhi min ash-shayṭāni 'r-rajīm. Bismillāhi 'r-Raḥmāni 'r-Raḥīm. Wa ilāhukum ilāhun wāḥidun, lā ilāha illa Hūwa 'r-Raḥmānu 'r-Raḥīm.</td><td></td><td>البقرة ١٦٣
أعُوذُ بِالله من الشَيْطانِ الرَّجِيم. بِسْمِ الله الرَّحْمنِ الرَّحيمِ
وَإِلَـٰهُكُمْ إِلَهٌ وَاحِدٌ لاَّ إِلَهَ إِلاَّ هُوَ الرَّحْمَنُ الرَّحِيمُ.</td></tr>
</table>

I seek refuge with God from Satan, the Cursed. In the name of God, the All-Beneficent, the All-Merciful. Your God is One God; there is no god but He, the All-Merciful, the All-Compassionate.

ĀYATU 'L-KURSĪ

(THE VERSE OF THE THRONE)

Allāhū lā ilāha illa Hūwa 'l-Ḥayyu 'l-Qayyūm, lā tākhudhuhu 's-sinatun wa lā nawm, lahū mā fi 's-samāwāti wa mā fi 'l-arḍ. Man dhā-ladhī yashfa'u 'indahū illā bi idhniḥ ya'lamu mā bayna aydīhim wa mā khalfahum wa lā yuḥīṭunā bi-shay'im min 'ilmihi illā bimā shā'. Wasi'a kursīyyuhu 's-samāwāti wa 'l-arḍa, wa lā ya'uduhū ḥifẓuhuma, wa Hūwa al-'Alīyyu 'l-'Aẓīm.

Ṣadaq-Allāhu 'l-'Aẓīm.

آيةُ الكُرْسِي

اللهُ لاَ إِلَـهَ إِلاَّ هُوَ الْحَيُّ
الْقَيُّومُ لاَ تَأْخُذُهُ سِنَةٌ وَلاَ
نَوْمٌ لَّهُ مَا فِي السَّمَاوَاتِ
وَمَافِي الأَرْضِ مَن ذَا الَّذِي
يَشْفَعُ عِنْدَهُ إِلاَّ بِإِذْنِهِ يَعْلَمُ
مَا بَيْنَ أَيْدِيهِمْ وَمَا خَلْفَهُمْ
وَلاَ يُحِيطُونَ بِشَيْءٍ مِّنْ
عِلْمِهِ إِلاَّ بِمَاشَاء وَسِعَ
كُرْسِيُّهُ السَّمَاوَاتِ
وَالأَرْضَ وَلاَ يَؤُودُهُ
حِفْظُهُمَا وَهُوَ الْعَلِيُّ
الْعَظِيمُ.صَدَقَ الله العَظيم

God! There is no god but He - the Living, the Self-subsisting, Eternal. No slumber can seize Him nor sleep. His are all things in the heavens and on earth. Who is there can intercede in His presence except as He permitteth? He knoweth what (appeareth to His creatures as) before or after or behind them. Nor shall they compass aught of His knowledge except as He willeth. His Throne doth extend over the heavens and the earth, and He feeleth no fatigue in guarding and preserving them for He is the Most High, the Supreme (in glory).

CHAPTER 3, VERSE 18-19		سُورة آل عمران ١٨-١٩
Shahid-Allāhu annahū lā ilāha illa Hū. Wa 'l-malā'ikatu wa ūlu 'l-ʿilmi qā'iman bi 'l-qisṭ. Lā ilāha illa Hūwa 'l-ʿAzīzu 'l-Ḥakīm. Inna 'd-dīna ʿind Allāhi 'l-islām.		شَهِدَ اللهُ أَنَّهُ لاَ إِلَـهَ إِلاَّ هُوَ وَ الْمَلاَئِكَةُ وَأُوْلُواْ الْعِلْمِ قَآئِمَاً بِالْقِسْطِ لاَ إِلَـهَ إِلاَّ هُوَ الْعَزِيزُ الْحَكِيمُ . إِنَّ الدِّينَ عِندَ اللهِ الإِسْلاَمُ

God bears witness that there is no god but He—and

the angels and men of knowledge—upholding justice; there is no god but He, the Almighty, the Wise. The religion with God is Islam.

CHAPTER 3, VERSE 26-27 Qul ’illāhumma Mālik al-mulki. Tu‘tī ’l-mulka man tasha’u wa tanzi‘u ’l-mulka mimman tashā’u wa tu‘izzu man tashā’u wa tudhillu man tashā’u, bi yadik al-khayr, innaka ‘alā kulli shay’in qadīr. Tūliju ’l-layla fi ’n-nahāri wa tūliju ’n-nahāra fi ’l-layl, wa tukhriju ’l-ḥāyya min al-mayyiti, wa tukhriju ’l-mayyita min al-ḥāyy, wa tarzuqu man tashā’u bi ghayri ḥisāb.		سورة آل عمران ٢٦-٢٧ قُلِ اللَّهُمَّ مَالِكَ الْمُلْكِ تُؤْتِي الْمُلْكَ مَن تَشَاءُ وَتَنزِعُ الْمُلْكَ مِمَّن تَشَاءُ وَتُعِزُّ مَن تَشَاءُ وَتُذِلُّ مَن تَشَاءُ بِيَدِكَ الْخَيْرُ إِنَّكَ عَلَى كُلِّ شَيْءٍ قَدِيرٌ تُولِجُ اللَّيْلَ فِي النَّهَارِ وَتُولِجُ النَّهَارَ فِي اللَّيْلِ وَتُخْرِجُ الْحَيَّ مِنَ الْمَيِّتِ وَتُخْرِجُ الْمَيِّتَ مِنَ الْحَيِّ وَتَرْزُقُ مَن تَشَاءُ بِغَيْرِ حِسَابٍ

Say: O God, Master of the Kingdom, Thou givest the Kingdom to whom Thou wilt, and seizest the Kingdom from whom Thou wilt, Thou exaltest whom Thou wilt, and Thou abasest whom Thou wilt; in Thy hand is all good; Verily Thou art over all things Powerful. Thou makest the night to enter into the day, and Thou makest the day to enter into the night, Thou bringest forth the living from the dead, and Thou bringest forth the dead from the living, and Thou providest for whomsoever Thou wilt without reckoning.

Allāhumma lā māniʿa limā āʿṭayta, wa lā muʿṭīya limā manʿata wa lā rādda limā qaḍayta, wa lā yanfaʿu Dhā 'l-jaddi minka 'l-jaddu Rabbī wa lā ḥawla wa lā quwwata illa billāhi 'l-ʿAlīyyi 'l-ʿAẓīm.		اللّٰهُمَّ لا مانِعَ لما أَعْطَيْتَ ولا مُعْطِيَ لِما مَنَعْتَ ولا رادَّ لِما قَضَيْتَ ولا يَنْفَعُ ذا الجِدِّ مِنْكَ الجَدُّ رَبِّي لا حَوْلَ ولا قُوَّةَ إلا بِاللهِ العَلِيِّ العَظِيمِ

O God! No one can disallow the one to whom You are giving, and there is no giver to the one whom You have denied. And there is no refusing Your decree. Riches and good fortune will not profit the possessor thereof with You (for nothing will profit him but acting in obedience to You). My Lord, and there is no power and no strength save in God, the Most High, the Great.		
CHAPTER 57, VERSE 3 Hūwa 'l-Awwalu wa 'l-Ākhiru, wa 'ẓ-Ẓāhiru wa 'l-Bāṭin, wa Hūwa bi kulli shay'in 'alīm.		سُورة الحديد ٣ هُوَ الْأَوَّلُ وَالْآخِرُ وَالظَّاهِرُ وَالْبَاطِنُ وَهُوَ بِكُلِّ شَيْءٍ عَلِيمٌ
He is the First and the Last, the Outward and the Inward; He has knowledge of everything.		
SŪRATU 'L-FĀTIḤĀ		سُورة الفاتحة
SŪRATU 'L-IKHLĀṢ (SEE PAGE 385)		سُورة الإخْلاص

SŪRATU 'L-FALAQ (SEE PAGE 386)		سُورةُ الفَلَق
SŪRATU 'N-NĀS (SEE PAGE 387)		سُورةُ النّاس
TASBĪḤ Yā rabbi Dhā 'l-Jalāli wa 'l-Ikrām, Subḥānaka yā 'Aẓīm subḥānallāh, subḥānallāh (33 times)		تَسْبيح يا رَبِّيَ ذا الجَلالِ والإكْرامِ سُبحانَكَ يا عَظيم: سُبْحان الله (٣٣ مرّة)
O my Lord, Possessor of Glory and Perfection, Glory be to You, O Almighty One! Glory be to God.		
'alā n'imati 'l-Islām wa sharafi 'l-īmān dā'iman alḥamdulillāh, alḥamdulillāh (33 times).		على نِعْمةِ الإسْلامِ وشَرَفِ الإيمانِ دائِمًا: الحَمْدُ لله (٣٣ مرّة)
For the gift of Islam, the honor of faith, always, praise be to God.		

Ta'alā shā'nuhū wa lā ilāha ghayruhū, Allāhū akbar, Allāhū akbar (33 times).		تَعالَى شأْنُهُ ولا إله غَيرُهُ: اللهُ أكْبَر (٣٣ مَرّة)
Exalted is His Affair, and there is no god but He, God is Greatest.		
Allāhū akbaru kabīran wa 'lḥamdulillāhi kathīran wa subḥānallāhi bukratan wa aṣīla. Lā ilāha illa-Allāh wāḥdahū lā sharīka lah, lahu 'l-mulku wa lahu 'l-ḥamd yuḥīy wa yumīt wa Hūwa 'alā kulli shay'in qadīr. Subḥāna Rabbīu 'l-'Alīyyu 'l-'āla 'l-Wahhāb.		اللهُ أكْبَرُ كَبيرًا والحَمْدُ لله كَثيرًا وسُبْحانَ الله بُكْرَةً وَأَصِيلاً لَا إِلَهَ إِلاَّ اللهُ وَحْدَهُ لَا شَرِيكَ لَهُ، لَهُ المُلكُ وَلَهُ الحَمْدُ يُحِي وَيُمِيت وَهُوَ عَلَى كَلِّ شَيءٍ قَديرٌ. سُبْحانَ رَبِّيَ العَلِيِّ الأَعَلى الوَهَّابْ

God is most Great in His Greatness and much praise be to God. Glory be to God, early and late. There is no god but God. He is One, no partner has He. His is the Kingdom and all praise. He gives life and causes to die, and He is over all things Powerful. Glory be to my Lord, All-High, Supreme, Most Munificent.

CHAPTER 33, VERSE 56	سورة الأحزاب ٥٦
Inna-Allāha wa malā'ikatahū yuṣallūna ʿalā an-Nabī, yā ayyuh-alladhīnā āmanū, ṣallū ʿalayhi wa sallimū taslīmā. (Ṣadaq-Allāhu 'l-ʿAẓīm)	إِنَّ اللهَ وَمَلَائِكَتَهُ يُصَلُّونَ عَلَى النَّبِيِّ يَا أَيُّهَا الَّذِينَ آمَنُوا صَلُّوا عَلَيْهِ وَسَلِّمُوا تَسْلِيماً

God and His angels send blessings on the Prophet: O you who believe! Send blessings on him and greet him with all respect. (God speaks the Truth).

<table>
<tr>
<td>ṢALAWĀT (3 TIMES)
Allāhumma ṣalli ʿalā Sayyidinā Muḥammadin wa ʿalā āli Sayyidinā Muḥammad. Bi ʿadadi kulli dā'in wa dawā'in wa bārik wa sallim ʿalayhi wa ʿalayhim kathīrā
(AFTER THE 3RD TIME)
kathīran kathīra, wa 'l-ḥamdulillāhi Rabbi 'l-ʿālamīn.</td>
<td></td>
<td>صَلوات
اللَّهُمَّ صلِّ على سَيِّدِنا
مُحَمَّدٍ وعلى آلِ سَيِّدِنا مُحَمَّدٍ
بِعَدَدِ كُلِّ دَاءٍ ودَواءٍ وبارِكْ
وسَلِّمْ عليه وعليْهم كَثيرًا
في المَرَّةِ الثالثة كَثيرًا كَثيرًا</td>
</tr>
<tr>
<td colspan="3">O God! Upon Muhammad and the family of Muhammad be blessings, according to the number of every illness and cure. Bless and grant peace to him and them, many times, endlessly. And praise belongs to God, the Lord of the worlds.</td>
</tr>
<tr>
<td>TAHLĪL
Fʿālam annahū: Lā ilāha illa-Allāh, Lā ilāha illa-Allāh (100 times).</td>
<td></td>
<td>تهْليل:
فَاعْلَمْ أَنَّهُ
لا إِلَهَ إِلاَّ اللهُ (١٠٠ مرّة)</td>
</tr>
</table>

<table>
<tr><td colspan="3">Know that: There is no god but God.</td></tr>
<tr><td>ṢALAWĀT (10 TIMES)
Allāhumma ṣalli ʿalā Muḥammadin wa ʿalā āli Muḥammadin wa sallim.</td><td></td><td>صَلوات (١٠ مرات)
اللَّهُمَّ صلّ على مُحَمَّدٍ وعلى آلِ مُحَمَّدٍ وسلّم</td></tr>
<tr><td colspan="3">O God send blessings and peace upon Muhammad and the family of Muhammad.</td></tr>
<tr><td>DUʿA (INVOCATION)
Ṣalli, yā Rabbī, wa sallim ʿalā jamīʿi ʾl-anbīyāʾi wa ʾl-mursalīn, wa ālin kullin ajmaʿīn wa ʾl-ḥamdulillāhi Rabbi ʾl-ʿālamīn.</td><td></td><td>دُعاء
صلِّ يا رَبّي وسلِّم على جَميعِ الأنبْياءِ والمُرْسَلينَ وآلِ كُلٍّ أجْمَعينَ والحَمْدُ لله رَبِّ العالَمينَ</td></tr>
<tr><td colspan="3">Blessings, O my Lord, and peace be upon all the prophets and Emissaries, and on the family of every one of them. Praise belongs to God, the Lord of the worlds.</td></tr>
</table>

CHIEF OF PRAYERS ON THE PROPHET (SEE PAGE 25)		الصلاةُ الشريفة المأثورة
Subḥāna Rabbīu 'l-'Alīyyu 'l-ʿAla 'l-Wahhāb.		سُبْحانَ رَبِّيَ العَلِيِّ الأعْلى الوَهّاب
Glory be to my Lord, All-High, Supreme, Most Munificent.		
PERSONAL DUʿA (INVOCATION) FOLLOWED BY:		دُعاء شَخْصي ثم تقرأ:
CHAPTER 59, VERSE 22-24 Aʿūdhu billāhi min ash-shayṭāni 'r-rajīm. Bismillāhi 'r-Raḥmāni 'r-Raḥīm. Hūwa Allāhu 'lladhī lā ilāha illa Hū. ʿĀlimu 'l-ghaybi wa 'sh-shahādati,		سُورة الحشر ٢٢-٢٤ أعُوذُ بِالله من الشَّيْطانِ الرَّجيمِ. بِسْمِ الله الرَّحْمنِ الرَّحيمِ.

<table>
<tr>
<td>Hūwa 'r-Raḥmānu 'r-Raḥīm. Hūwa Allāh 'ulladhī lā ilāha illa Hūw al-Maliku 'l-Quddusu 's-Salāmu 'l-Mu'minu 'l-Muhaymimu 'l-'Azīzu 'l-Jabbāru 'l-Mutakabbir. Subḥānallāhi 'ammā yushrikūn. Hūw 'Allāh 'ul-Khāliqu 'l-Barī'u 'l-Musawwiru lahu 'l-asmā'u 'l-ḥusnā. Yusabbiḥu lahū mā fi 's-samāwāti wa 'l-arḍ, wa Hūwa 'l-'Azīzu 'l-Ḥakīm.</td>
<td></td>
<td>هُوَ اللهُ الَّذِي لَا إِلَهَ إِلَّا هُوَ
عَالِمُ الْغَيْبِ وَالشَّهَادَةِ
هُوَ الرَّحْمَنُ الرَّحِيمُ هُوَ اللهُ
الَّذِي لَا إِلَهَ إِلَّا هُوَ الْمَلِكُ
الْقُدُّوسُ السَّلَامُ الْمُؤْمِنُ
الْمُهَيْمِنُ الْعَزِيزُ الْجَبَّارُ
الْمُتَكَبِّرُ سُبْحَانَ اللهِ عَمَّا
يُشْرِكُونَ
. هُوَ اللهُ الْخَالِقُ الْبَارِئُ
الْمُصَوِّرُ لَهُ الْأَسْمَاءُ الْحُسْنَى
يُسَبِّحُ لَهُ مَا فِي السَّمَاوَاتِ
وَالْأَرْضِ وَهُوَ الْعَزِيزُ
الْحَكِيمُ</td>
</tr>
<tr>
<td colspan="3">I seek refuge in God from the accursed Satan. In the name of God, the Merciful, the Beneficent. God is He,</td>
</tr>
</table>

than Whom there is no other god;- Who knows (all things) both secret and open; He, Most Gracious, Most Merciful. God is He, than Whom there is no other god;- the Sovereign, the Holy One, the Source of Peace (and Perfection), the Guardian of Faith, the Preserver of Safety, the Exalted in Might, the Irresistible, the Supreme: Glory to God! (High is He) above the partners they attribute to Him. He is God, the Creator,the Evolver, the Bestower of Forms (or Colors). To Him belong the Most Beautiful Names: whatever is in the heavens and on earth, doth declare His Praises and Glory: and He is the Exalted in Might, the Wise.

CHAPTER 57, VERSE 3 Hūwa 'l-Āwwalu wa 'l-ākhiru waẓ-Ẓāhiru wa 'l-Bāṭin, wa Hūwa bi kulli shay'in 'Alīm. Ṣadaq-Allāhu 'l-'Aẓīm.		سورة الحديد ٣ هُوَ الْأَوَّلُ وَالْآخِرُ وَالظَّاهِرُ وَالْبَاطِنُ وَهُوَ بِكُلِّ شَيْءٍ عَلِيمٌ. صَدَقَ اللهُ العظيم

He is the First and the Last, the Outward and the Inward; He has knowledge of everything. (God speaks the Truth).

DU'A (INVOCATION)	دُعاءُ :
Rabbanā taqabbal minna, wa'fu 'annā, waghfir lanā, warḥamnā, wa tub 'ālaynā, wasqinā, wasliḥ shā'nanā wa shā'n al-Muslimīn, fanṣurna 'alā al-qawm il-mufsidīn, bi ḥurmati man anzalta 'alayhi Sūratu 'l-Fātiḥah (see page 325).	رَبَّنَا تَقَبَّل مِنَّا وَاعْفُ عَنَّا وَاغْفِرْ لَنَا وَارْحَمْنَا وَتُبْ عَلَيْنَا وَاهْدِنَا وَاسْقِنَا وَاصْلِحْ شَأْنَنَا وَشَأْنَ الْمُسْلِمِينَ وَانْصُرْنَا عَلى القَومِ الْكَافِرِين بِحُرْمَةِ مَن أَنْزَلْتَ عَلَيْهِ سُورَةُ الفَاتِحَة

O our Lord! Accept (this) from us and absolve us. Forgive us and have mercy on us. Accept our repentance and guide us. Quench (our thirst), and improve our condition and the condition of the Muslims. Give us success over those who falsify the Truth, by the sanctity of the one to whom You revealed Sūratu 'l-Fātiḥah (see page 325).

KALIMATU 'SH-SHAHĀDA (3 TIMES) Ash-hadu an lā ilāha ill-Allāh, wa ash-hadu anna Muḥammadan ʿabduhū wa rasūluḥ.		كَلِمَةُ الشَّهَادَة أَشْهَدُ أَنْ لا إله إلا الله وأَشْهَدُ أَنَّ مُحَمَّدًا رَّسُولُ الله (٣ مرّات) (بِصَوْتٍ خفي) صلّى اللهُ عليه وسلّم
I bear witness that there is no god but God, and Muhammad is His servant and Messenger.		
ISTIGHFĀR Astaghfirullāh (100 times) I ask God's forgiveness.		اسْتِغفار: أَسْتَغْفِرُ اللهَ (١٠٠ مَرّة)
Astaghfirullāh min kulli dhanbin wa maʿṣīyatin wa min kulli mā yukhālifu dīn al-Islām, yā arḥama 'r-Rāḥimīn.		أَسْتَغْفِرُ اللهَ مِن كُلِّ ذَنْبٍ وَمَّعْصِيَّةٍ وَمِن كُلِّ مَا يُخَالِفُ دِينَ الإِسْلَام يَا أَرْحَمَ الرَّاحِمِين

I ask God's forgiveness for every sin and disobedience and from all that opposes the religion of Islam. O Merciful of the Merciful.		
SŪRATU 'L-FĀTIḤĀ		سُورة الفاَتحة
SŪRAT YĀ SĪN (CHAPTER 36, SEE PAGE 326) CHAPTER 28, VERSE 88 Kullu shay'in hālikun illa Wajhah, lahu 'l-ḥukmu wa ilayhi turja'ūn.		سُورة يس سُورة القصص ٨٨ ثم تنتهي: كُلُّ شَيْءٍ هَالِكٌ إِلَّا وَجْهَهُ لَهُ الْحُكْمُ وَإِلَيْهِ تُرْجَعُونَ وَإِليه تُرْجَعُونَ
All things perish except His Face. His is the Judgment, and unto Him shall ye return.		

99 Beautiful Names of God

(ASMĀ'ULLAH)

A'ūdhu billāhi min ash-shayṭāni 'r-rajīm. Bismillāhi 'r-Raḥmāni 'r-Raḥīm. Hūwa Allāhu 'lladhī lā ilāha illa Hū. Ar-Raḥmānu 'r-Raḥīm (Jalla Jallāluhū). Al-Maliku 'l-Quddusu 's-Salāmu 'l-Mu'minu 'l-Muhayminu 'l-'Azīzu 'l-Jabbāru 'l-Mutakabbir (Jalla Jallāluhū). Al-Khāliqu 'l-Bāri'u 'l-Musawwiru 'l-Ghaffāru 'l-Qahhāru 'l-Wahhābu 'r-Razzāqu 'l-Fattāḥu 'l-'Alīm (Jalla Jallāluhū), al-Qābiḍu 'l-Bāsiṭu 'l-Khāfiḍu 'r-Rāf'iu

أَسْمَاءُ اللهِ الْحُسْنَى

أَعُوذُ بِاللهِ مِنَ الشَّيْطَانِ الرَّجِيمِ. بِسْمِ اللهِ الرَّحْمٰنِ الرَّحِيمِ.

هُوَ اللهُ الَّذِي لَا إِلٰهَ إِلَّا هُوَ عَالِمُ الْغَيْبِ وَالشَّهَادَةِ هُوَ الرَّحْمٰنُ الرَّحِيمُ ﷻ، الْمَلِكُ، الْقُدُّوسُ، السَّلَامُ، الْمُؤْمِنُ، الْمُهَيْمِنُ، الْعَزِيزُ، الْجَبَّارُ، الْمُتَكَبِّرُ ﷻ، الْخَالِقُ، الْبَارِئُ، الْمُصَوِّرُ، الْغَفَّارُ، الْقَهَّارُ، الْوَهَّابُ، الرَّزَّاقُ، الْفَتَّاحُ،

ʾl-Muʿizzu ʾl-Mudhillu ʾs-Samīʿu ʾl-Baṣīr, (Jalla Jallāluhū), al-Ḥakamu ʾl-ʿAdlu ʾl-Laṭīfu ʾl-Khabīru ʾl-Ḥalīmu ʾl-ʿAẓīmu ʾl-Ghafūru ʾsh-Shakūru ʾl-ʿAliyyu ʾl-Kabīr, (Jalla Jallāluhū), al-Ḥafīẓu ʾl-Muqītu ʾl-Ḥasību ʾl-Jalīlu ʾl-Karīmu ʾr-Raqību ʾl-Mujību ʾl-Wāsʿiu ʾl-Ḥakīmu ʾl-Wadūdu ʾl-Majīd, (Jalla Jallāluhū), al-Bāʿithu ʾsh-Shahīdu ʾl-Ḥaqqu ʾl-Wakīlu ʾl-Qawīyyu ʾl-Matīnu ʾl-Walīyyu ʾl-Ḥamīdu ʾl-Muḥsīyu ʾl-Mubdʿīu ʾl-Muʿīdu ʾl-Muḥīyyu ʾl-Mumītu ʾl-Ḥāyyu ʾl-Qayyūm (Jalla Jallāluhū), al-Wājidu ʾl-Mājidu ʾl-		العَلِيمُ ﷻ، القابِضُ، الباسِطُ، الخَافِضُ، الرَّافِعُ، المُعِزُّ، المُذِلُّ، السَّمِيعُ، البَصِيرُ ﷻ، الحَكَمُ، العَدْلُ، اللَّطِيفُ، الخَبِيرُ، الحَلِيمُ، العَظِيمُ، الغَفُورُ، الشَّكُورُ، العَلِيُّ، الكَبِيرُ ﷻ، الحَفِيظُ، المُقِيتُ، الحَسِيبُ، الجَلِيلُ، الكَرِيمُ، الرَّقِيبُ، المُجِيبُ، الوَاسِعُ، الحَكِيمُ، الوَدُودُ، المَجِيدُ ﷻ، الباعِثُ، الشَّهِيدُ، الحَقُّ، الوَكِيلُ، القَوِيُّ، المَتِينُ، الوَلِيُّ، الحَمِيدُ، المُحْصِي، المُبْدِئُ، المُعِيدُ،

Wāḥidu 'l-Āḥad uṣ-Ṣamadu 'l-Qādiru 'l-Muqtadir (Jalla Jallāluhū), al-Muqaddimu 'l-Mu'akhkhiru 'l-Awwalu 'l-Ākhiru 'ẓ-Ẓāhiru 'l-Bāṭinu 'l-Wālīyu 'l-Muta'ālu 'l-Barru 't-Tawwāb (Jalla Jallāluhū), al-Muntaqimu 'l-'Afuwwu 'r-Ra'uf Māliku 'l-mulki Dhā 'l-Jalāli wa 'l-Ikrām (Jalla Jallāluhū), al-Muqsiṭu 'l-Jāmi'u 'l-Ghanīyyu 'l-Mughnīyyu 'l-Mu'ṭīu 'l-Māni'u 'd-Ḍārru 'n-Nāfi'u 'n-Nūr (Jalla Jallāluhū), al-Hādīyu 'l-Bad'īu 'l-Bāqīyu 'l-Wārithu 'r-Rashīdu 'ṣ-Ṣabūr. Jalla Jallāluhū wa jallat 'āẓamatahū wa lā ilāha		المُحْيِي، المُمِيتُ، الحَيُّ، القَيُّومُ ﷻ، الوَاجِدُ، المَاجِدُ، الوَاحِدُ، الأَحَدُ، الصَّمَدُ، القَادِرُ، المُقْتَدِرُ ﷻ، المُقَدِّمُ، المُؤَخِّرُ، الأَوَّلُ، الآخِرُ، الظَّاهِرُ، البَاطِنُ، الوَالِي، المُتَعَالِ، البَرُّ، التَّوَّابُ ﷻ، المُنْتَقِمُ، العَفُوُّ، الرَّؤُوف، مالِكُ المُلْكِ، ذُو الجَلالِ وَالإِكْرَامِ ﷻ، المُقْسِطُ، الجَامِعُ، الغَنِيُّ، المُغْنِي، المُعْطِي، المَانِعُ، الضَّارُّ، النَّافِعُ، النُّورُ ﷻ، الهَادِي،

ghayruhu 'lladhī lam yalid wa lam yūlad wa lam yakun lahū kufuwan āḥad		الْبَدِيعُ، الباقِيُ، الوَارِثُ، الرَّشِيدُ، الصَّبُورُ جَلّ جَلاله وَجَلَّت عَظَمَتهُ وَلا إِلهَ غيْرُهُ الّذي لَمْ يَلِدْ وَلَمْ يُولَدْ وَلَمْ يَكُن لَّهُ كُفُواً أَحَدٌ

In the Name of God, the Most Merciful, the Most Compassionate. May He be Glorified and Exalted! He is God; there is no god but He. He is the Knower of the Unseen and Visible; He is the All-Merciful, the Compassionate, (His Greatness has become manifest). The King, the Holy, the Source of Peace, the All-Faithful, the Guardian, the Mighty, the Compeller, the Greatest, (His Greatness has become manifest). The Creator, the Maker, the Fashioner, the All-Forgiving, the Irrestible, the All-Bounteous, the Provider, the Opener, the Omniscient, (His Greatness has become manifest). The Contracter, the Expander, the Abaser, the Exalter, the Bestower of Honor, the Humiliator, the All-Hearing, the All-Seeing, (His Greatness has become manifest). The Supreme Arbiter, the Just, the Subtle, the Aware, the Forbearing, the Magnificent, the Most Forgiving, the Appreciative, the Most High, the Great, (His Greatness has become manifest). The Preserver, the Nourisher, the Reckoner, the Sublime, the Generous, the Ever-Watchful, the Responsive, the Limitless, the All-Wise, the Loving, the Glorious, (His Greatness has become manifest). The Resurrector, the Witness, the Ultimate Truth, the Trustee, the Most Strong, the Firm, the Protecting Friend, the Praiseworthy, the Reckoner, the Originator, the Restorer, the Granter of Life, the Bringer of Death, the Ever-Living, the Self-Subsisting, (His Greatness has become manifest). The Self Sufficient, the Glorified, the Unique, the Eternally Besought, the All-Powerful, the Bestower of Power, (His Greatness has become manifest). The Advancer, the Delayer, the First, the Last, the Manifest, the Hidden, the Governor, the Highly Exalted, the Beneficent, the Accepter of Repentance, (His Greatness has become manifest). The Avenger, the Eraser of Sin, the Most Compassionate, the Lord of All Dominion, the Possessor of Majesty and Bounty, (His Greatness has become manifest). The Upholder of Equity, the Gatherer, the All-Sufficient, the Enricher, the Giver,

the Preventer of harm, the Afflicter, the Creator of Good, the Light, (His Greatness has become manifest). The Guider, the Originator, the Everlasting, the Inheritor, the Guide, the Patient, (His Greatness has become manifest). His Greatness has become manifest, and there is no god but He, Who has not begotten and has not been begotten, and equal to Him is not any one.		
Yā Āḥad, Yā Ṣamad, ṣalli ʿalā Muḥammad (3 times).		يا أَحَد. يا صَمَد صلِ على محمد (٣ مرات)
O Unique One! O Eternally Besought! Bless Muhammad.		
SŪRATU 'L-IKHLĀṢ (CHAPTER 112) (11 TIMES) (SEE PAGE 385)		سُورَةُ الإخْلاصِ (١١ مرة)
SŪRATU 'L-FALAQ (CHAPTER 113) (ONCE) (SEE PAGE 386)		سُورَةُ الفَلَق

SŪRATU 'N-NĀS (CHAPTER 114) (ONCE) (SEE PAGE 387)		سُورَةُ النّاس
TAHLĪL WITH ṢALAWĀT (10 TIMES) Lā ilāhā ill-Allāh Muḥammadur Rasūlullāh, Ṣall-Allāhū ta'alā 'alayhi wa 'alā ālihi wa ṣaḥbihi wa sallam.		تهْليل: لا إله إلا الله مُحَمَّدٌ رَّسُولُ الله صلّى اللهُ تعالى عليه وعلى آلِهِ وصَحْبِهِ وسلّم (١٠ مرات)

There is no god but God. Muhammad is the Messenger of God, blessings and peace of God (Exalted is He!) be upon him, his family, and his Companions.

ṢALAWĀT (10 TIMES) Allāhumma ṣalli ʿalā Muḥammadin wa ʿalā āli Muḥammadin wa sallim.	الصَّلَواتُ الشَّريفة (١٠ مرّات) اللَّهُمَّ صلِّ على مُحَمَّدٍ وعلى آلِ مُحَمَّدٍ وسلِّم

Blessings and peace be upon Muhammad and the family of Muhammad.

DUʿA (INVOCATION) Ṣalli, yā Rabbī, wa sallim ʿalā jamīʿi 'l-anbīyāʾi wa 'l-mursalīn, wa ālin kullin ajmaʿīn wa 'l-ḥamdulillāhi Rabbi 'l-ʿālamīn.	دُعاء صلِّ يا رَبّي وسلِّم على جَميعِ الأنبياءِ والمُرسَلينَ وآلِ كُلٍّ أَجْمَعينَ والحَمْدُ لله رَبِّ العالَمينَ

Blessings, O my Lord, and peace be upon all the prophets and emissaries, and on the family of every one of them. Praise belongs to God, the Lord of the worlds.

CHIEF OF PRAYERS ON THE PROPHET (SEE PAGE 25)		الصلَاةُ الشريفة المأثورة
IHDĀ (DEDICATION - SEE PAGE 28)		إِهدَاء

Salatu-z-Zuhr

<table>
<tr><td colspan="3">Ṣalātu ’ẓ-Ẓuhr is performed in the same sequence as Ṣalātu ’l-‘Ishā, from the Adhān to the end, with the exception of Ṣalātu ’l-Witr, which is omitted.</td></tr>
<tr><td>4 RAK‘ATS SUNNAH</td><td></td><td>٤ رَكَعات سُنّة: رَكْعَتَيْنِ سُنّة ورَكْعَتَيْنِ نافِلة بِتَسْليمِ واحِد أو بتسليمين</td></tr>
<tr><td>4 RAK‘ATS FARḌ</td><td></td><td>أَرْبَعُ رَكَعات فَرْض</td></tr>
<tr><td>4 RAK‘ATS SUNNAH</td><td></td><td>أَرْبَعُ رَكَعات سُنّة</td></tr>
<tr><td>SŪRATU ’L-MULK
(CHAPTER 67, PAGE 353)</td><td></td><td>سُورةُ المُلك</td></tr>
<tr><td colspan="3">At the end of Sūratu ’l-Mulk add: Allāhu ta‘alā Rabbunā wa Rabbu ’l-‘ālamīn. Then continue with the same practices as in Ṣalātu ’l-‘Ishā with the exception of Ṣalātu ’l-Witr.</td></tr>
</table>

Salatu-l-Asr

<table>
<tr><td colspan="3">Ṣalātu ’l-‘Asr is performed exactly in the same way a Ṣalātu ’l-‘Ishā, with the exception of the final 4 rak‘āts Sunnah prayer and Ṣalātu ’l-Witr.</td></tr>
<tr><td>4 RAK‘ATS SUNNAH</td><td></td><td>٤ رَكَعات سُنّة
رَكْعَتَيْنِ سُنّة ورَكْعَتَيْنِ نافِلة
بِتَسْليم واحِد أو بتسليمين</td></tr>
<tr><td>4 RAK‘ATS FARḌ</td><td></td><td>٤ رَكَعات فَرْض</td></tr>
<tr><td>SŪRATU ’N-NABĀ
(CHAPTER 78, PAGE 364)</td><td></td><td>ثم تقرأ سُورةُ النَبأ</td></tr>
<tr><td>Continue reading with Chapter 89, Verses 24-30
Fa yawmaydhin lā yu‘adhibu ‘adhābahu āḥadun wa lā yuthiqu wathāqahu āḥad. Yā ayyatuhā ’n-nafsu ’l-muṭma’innatu ’rji‘ī ilā rabbiki rāḍīyyatan marḍīyyah. f’adkhulī fī ‘ibādī w’adkhulī jannatī.</td><td></td><td>فَيَوْمَئِذٍ لا يُعَذِّبُ عَذَابَهُ
أَحَدٌ . وَلا يُوثِقُ وَثَاقَهُ أَحَدٌ
يَا أَيَّتُهَا النَّفْسُ الْمُطْمَئِنَّةُ
ارْجِعِي إِلَى رَبِّكِ رَاضِيَةً
مَّرْضِيَّةً فَادْخُلِي فِي عِبَادِي
وَادْخُلِي جَنَّتِي</td></tr>
</table>

Then add: Razzaqanā Allāhu, yā Allāḥ, Āmannā billāhi. Ṣadaqa-Allāhu 'l-'Aẓīm.		رَزَّقْنا الله يا الله. آمنَّا بالله. صدق الله العظيم
Then continue the recitation to the end as in Ṣalātu 'l-'Ishā.		

Practices During Rajab, Shaban, Ramadan and Muharram

Practice of the Month of Rajab		أدب شهْر رجب
This Adab is performed on the day before Rajab begins between Ṣalātu 'l-'Asr and Ṣalātu 'l-Maghrib and is repeated as the daily practice of the seeker every day, beginning before Ṣalātu 'l-Fajr by an hour and a half but without the Grand Transmitted Invocation of Grandshaykh (Ad-du'āu 'l-māthūr li Sulṭān al-Awliyā on page 179) which is done only the first night. Also on the first afternoon before Rajab, the prayers of the night vigil (Ṣalātu 'n-Najāt, Ṣalātu 'sh-Shukr and Ṣalātu 't-Tasbīḥ) are not observed.		
BATHING OF PURIFICATION When the month of Rajab is entered, the murīd begins its night between Ṣalātu 'l-'Asr and Ṣalātu 'l-Maghrib		غُسل إذا دخل شهر رجب بادر المريد في ليلة ابتدائه

receiving the month of Rajab. One performs the major ritual purification (ghusl, or shower).		للغسل ما بين العصر والمغرب.
One dresses in the best clothes and (for a man) puts on a nice scent, then prays 2 rak'ats sunnat al-wuḍū'.		ثم يلبس أفضل الثياب واطهرها يتطيب ويستقبل القبلة ثم يصلي ركعتين سنة الوضوء
Recite: Yā Rabb al-'izzati wa 'l-'aẓamati wa 'l-jabbarūt		ثم يقرأ: يا رب العزة والعظمة لجبروت
O Lord of Honor and Greatness, Imposer of Thy Will.		
The murīd takes three steps in the direction of the Qiblah in his place of worship.		و يتقرب في محرابه ثلاثة اقدام نحو القبلة

NĪYYAT		النِيَّة:
Nawaytu 'l-arbāʿīn, nawaytu 'l-ʿitikāf, nawaytu 'l-khalwa, nawaytu ʿl-ʿuzla, nawaytu 'r-riyāḍa, nawaytu 's-sulūk, lillāhi taʿala fī hādhā 'l-masjid (or fī hādha al-jāmiʿ)		نَوَيْتُ الأَرْبَعين، نَوَيْتُ الإعْتِكاف نَوَيْتُ الخَلْوَة نَوَيْتُ العُزْلَة، نَوَيْتُ الرِياضَة نَوَيْتُ السُّلوك، لله تَعالى في هَذَا المَسْجِد
INTENTION: I intend the forty (days of seclusion); I intend seclusion in the mosque; I intend seclusion; I intend isolation; I intend discipline (of the ego); I intend to travel in God's Path for the sake of God in this mosque.		
100 times Yā Ḥalīm (for removing anger). O Clement One!		يا حَليمْ. يا حَليمْ. يا حَليمْ (١٠٠ مَرّة)
100 times Yā Ḥafīz (for removing affliction). O Guardian!		يا حَفيظْ. يا حَفيظْ. يا حَفيظْ (١٠٠ مَرّة)

Imagine yourself in the blessed Garden (al-Rawḍah) in front of the maqām of the Prophet ﷺ facing God's Messenger ﷺ and saying:

ṢALAWĀT 100 times Allāhummā ṣalli ʿalā Sayyidina Muḥammadin wa ʿalā āli Muḥammadin wa sallim.		صَلَوات – ١٠٠ مرة اللَّهُمَّ صلِّ على مُحَمَّدٍ وعَلى آلِ مُحَمَّدٍ وسلِّمْ

O God, pray on our master Muhammad and on his family and greet them with peace. Make the intention that God makes you to be in the spiritual Presence of God's Messenger ﷺ, Imām al-Mahdī عليه السلام, and our shaykhs.

NĪYYAT: Yā Rabbī innanī nawaytu an ataqaddama nahwa baḥri waḥdanīyyatika ilā maqāmi 'l-fanāʿi fīka. Falā tarudanī yā Rabbi, yā Allāh khā'ibān ḥatta tuwaṣṣilanī		النِيَّة: يا ربيّ إنّني نَوَيْتُ ان أتقدَّمَ نَحْوَ بَحْرِ واحْدانِيّتِكَ إلى مقامِ الفَنّاءِ فيكَ فلا تردَّني يا ربي يا الله خائبا حتى

<table>
<tr><td>ila dhāk al-maqām al-maqāmu 'l-fardānī.</td><td></td><td>تُوَصِّلَني إلى ذاك المقام – المقامُ الفَرْداني.</td></tr>
<tr><td colspan="3">INTENTION:
O my Lord, I am moving and stepping forward for the Station of Annihilation in the Divine Presence. O God—glory be to You, the Most High—I am asking you to cause me to vanish before Your Existence and, O my Lord, I am moving toward your Ocean of Unity. O my Lord, do not reject me until I reach the Unique Station.</td></tr>
<tr><td>Yā Rabbī, yā Allāh ḥaithu hādha ash-shahru hūwa shahruka, ji'tuka ḍa'ifan wa nāwī'an an 'amala 'amalan bidūn 'iwaḍun aw an yakūna fīhi ṭalaban li 'l-faḍīlati qāsidan iyyāka Ilāhī anta maqsūdī wa riḍāka maṭlūbi.</td><td></td><td>يَا ربيّ يا الله حيْثُ هذا الشَهْرُ هو شَهْرُكَ جِئتُكَ ضَيْفاً وناوِياً ان أعْمَلَ عَمَلاً بِدُونِ عُوْضٌ أو ان يَكُونَ فيه طَلَباً لِلفَضِيلةِ.قاصِداً إيَاكَ الهي</td></tr>
</table>

		أنتَ مَقْصُودي ورِضاكَ مَطْلُوبي
O my Lord, O God, since this month is your month, I came to you as a weak guest and intending to worship You without asking anything in return. My God, You are my aim, and Your good pleasure is what I seek, and that is why I am coming. Please do not reject me.		
Yā Rabbī, kullu ʿumrī qad amḍaytuhu fī 'l–maʿāsī wa 'sh-shirkil-khafī. Wa innanī uqirru bi-annanī lam ā'ti ilā bābika bi-ʿamalin maqbūlin ʿindaka anta-Allāhu 'lladhī lā yā'tī āḥadun ilā bābika bi ʿamalihi bal bi-faḍlika wa jūdika wa karamika wa iḥsānika. Anta-Allāhu 'lladhī la taruddu ʿabdan jā'a ilā bābika falā taruddanī yā Allāh.		يا ربي كُلَّ عُمُري قد أمْضَيْتُهُ في المَعاصي والشِرْكِ الخَفي وانَّني أُقِرُّ بأنَّني لم أئتِ إلى بابِكَ بِعَمَلٍ مَقْبُولٍ عِنْدَكَ أنتَ اللهُ الذي لا يأتي أحَدٌ إلى بابِكَ بعَمَلِهِ بَلْ بِفَضْلِكَ وجُودِكَ وكَرَمِكَ وإحْسانِكَ أنتَ اللهُ الذي

		لا تَرُدُّ عَبْدًا جاءَ إلى بابِكَ فلا تَرُدَّني يا اللهُ
O my Lord, I say out of abject humility that it as if I spent all my life in unbelief, polytheism, and bad behavior, and I am declaring wholeheartedly that I did not do any deed that is accepted by You. You are God, Who never threw away anyone that came to Your door. You are God, and no one came to Your door by his deeds, but (only) by Your grant and reward.		
Yā Rabbī, kullu umūrī fawwaḍtuhā ilayka, ḥayātī wa mamātī wa b'ada mamāti, wa yawmu 'l-ḥashr. Kullu umūri ḥawwaltuhā 'indaka. Wa fawwaḍtu amrī ilayka, lā amliku min amri nafsī shay-an. Lā naf'an, wa lā ḍarran, wa lā mawtan, wa lā ḥayātan, wa lā nushūran. Kullu umūri wa ḥisābī wa su'ālī wa jawābī		يا ربي كُلّ أُمُوري فَوَّضْتُها إلَيْك حَياتي ومَماتي وبَعْدَ مَماتي و يَوْمُ الحَشْرِ كُلُّ أُمُوري حَوَّلْتُها عِنْدَكَ وفَوَّضْتُ أمْري إلَيْكَ لا أمْلِكُ من أمرِ نَفْسي شَيْئاً لا نَفْعاً ولا

<table>
<tr><td>ḥawwaltuhu ʿindaka yā Rabbī yā Allāḥ. Nāṣīyatī bi-yadika wa anā ʿājizun ʿani ʾl-jawābi wa law mithqāla dharratin.</td><td></td><td>ضُرّاً ولا مَوْتاً ولا حَياة ولا نُشُوراً. كُلّ أُمُوري وحِسابِي وسُؤالي وجَوابي حَوَّلْتُهُ عِنْدَكَ يا ربي يا الله، ناصيَتي بِيَدِكَ وانا عاجِزٌ عنِ الجَوابِ ولو مِثْقالَ ذَرَّةٍ</td></tr>
<tr><td colspan="3">O my Lord, I have given everything into Your hands—my life, my death, my afterlife, and Judgment Day. All my things I have transferred to You, and You are the One Who controls me. O my Lord, I do not possess anything with my ego and my soul. I cannot give good to myself, or bad to myself, or life to myself, or death to myself, but I have transferred all my accounts, and all Your judgment on me, and all your questions to me, and all my answers I have transferred to You. Whatever You want to do with me, You do. My neck is in Your Hand. I am helpless in answering Your questions; even the smallest answer I cannot</td></tr>
</table>

give. With all this weakness, and helplessness, and hopelessness, I am coming to Your door.

Law kāna laka yā Rabbī bābayni āḥadahumā mukhaṣaṣṣun li 't-tā'ibīna min ʿibādika al-muʿminīn wa 'l-ākharu li 't-tā'ibīna min ʿibādika al-ʿaṣīn. Jiʿtuka yā Allāh naḥwu bābik alladhī yaḥtāju an yadkhula minhu ʿibāduka al-ʿaāṣīn. Wa innanī uqirru wa āaʿtarif annahu yajibu an ujaddida islāmī wa īmānī min hādha'l-bāb li-iẓhāri 'l-ʿajzi.	لو كان لَكَ ياربي بابَيْنِ أحَدَهُما مُخَصَّصٌ لِلتّائِبين من عِبادِكَ المؤمِنين والأخَرُ لِلتّائبين من عِبادِكَ العاصِين ، جِئْتُكَ يا الله نَحْوَ بابِكَ الذي يَحْتاجُ ان يَدْخُلَ مِنْهُ عِبادُكَ العاصِين وانَّني أُقِرُّ واعْتَرِفُ انَّهُ يَجِبُ ان أُجَدِّدَ إسْلامي وإيماني من هذا الباب لإظْهارِ العَجْزِ.

O my Lord, if you had two doors for Your servant to enter through—one for the believers from Your servants and one for the unbelievers from Your

<table>
<tr><td colspan="3">servants—I am coming to You from the door that the unbeliever needs to come through, and I am declaring my belief that this is the only door for me to come through. I am saying to you that I have to renew my faith and my testimony of faith from this door to show humility and helplessness.</td></tr>
<tr><td>Wa hādhā al-ʿamalu hūwa āwwalu ʿamalin lī bʿada mā shahidtu bi 'l-islāmi ḥaqqan. Yā Rabbī wa Anta wakīlī yā Wakīl ḥaithu naqūlu Allāha ʿalā mā naqūlu Wakīl wa Shahīd.</td><td></td><td>و هذا العَمَلُ هُو أوَّلُ عَمَلٍ لي بَعْدَ ما شَهِدْتُ بالإسلام حقاً يا ربيّ وأنتَ وَكِيلي يا وَكِيل حَيْثُ نَقُول الله على ما نَقُول وَكِيل وشَهِيد.</td></tr>
<tr><td colspan="3">This deed and this Shahāda is the first deed for me after I am pronouncing the Shahāda and entering Islam, and You are my Protector from whence we say: God is the Protector and Witness over what we say.</td></tr>
<tr><td>3 times Shahādah.</td><td></td><td>ثم تبدأ بكلمتي الشهادة
(٣ مرات)</td></tr>
</table>

<table>
<tr><td>Iqāmu 'ṣ-ṣalāti wa ītāu 'z-zakāt wa ṣawmu ramaḍāna, wa Ḥajju 'l-bayt.</td><td></td><td>تجديد اركان الإسلام:
إقامُ الصلَاةُ وإيتاءُ الزّكاة
وصَوْمُ رَمضان وحَجُّ
البَيْت</td></tr>
<tr><td colspan="3">Re-affirmation of Islam's five pillars:
I believe in the establishment of prayer, paying the poor-due, fasting Ramadan, and the Pilgrimage to the House of God.</td></tr>
<tr><td>Āmantu billāhi wa malā'ikatihi wa kutubihi wa rusulihi wa 'l-yawmi 'l-ākhiri wa bi 'l-qadari khayrihi wa sharrihi min Allāhi ta'alā.</td><td></td><td>تجديد الإيمان: آمَنْتُ بالله
ومَلائِكَتِهِ وكُتُبِهِ ورَسُلِهِ
وباليَوْمِ الآخِرِ وبالقَدَرِ
خَيْرِهِ وشَرِّهِ.</td></tr>
<tr><td colspan="3">Re-affirmation of the pillars of faith:
I believe in God, His Angels, His books, His Messengers, the Last Day, and that the Destiny—its good and its bad—is from God, the Most High.</td></tr>
</table>

<table>
<tr><td>Yā Rabbī, yā Allāhu, kam ẓahara minnī min adh-dhunūbi wa 'l-maʿāṣīyy ẓāhiran wa bāṭinan wa sirran min ʿahdi ījādi dharratī wa rūḥī, wa dukhūli rūḥī ilā jismī wa ẓuhūrī min al-ʿadami ilā 'l-wujūdi wa ẓuhūrī fī ʿālami 'd-dunyā ilā yawminā hādha, rajʿatu ʿani 'l-jamīʿi ilayka bi 't-tawbati wa 'l-istighfār.</td><td></td><td>يَا ربيَ يا اللهُ كَمْ ظَهَرَ مِنّي مِنَ الذُّنُوبِ والمعَاصِي ظاهِراً وباطِناً وسِرّاً مِن عَهْدِ إيجادِ ذَرَّتي ورُوحي ودُخُولِ رُوحي إلى جِسْمي وظُهُورِي مِنَ العَدَمِ إلى الوُجُودِ وظُهُوري في عَالَمِ الدُّنيا إلى يَوْمِنا هذا، رَجَعْتُ عنِ الجَمِيعِ اليْك بالتَّوْبةِ والإسْتِغْفار</td></tr>
<tr><td colspan="3">O my Lord, from the Day of Promises, whatever there was of promise from Me to You, I accept and promise to do it all.

O my Lord, O God, from the day You created my atom, my essence, and from the day You brought up</td></tr>
</table>

<table>
<tr><td colspan="3">my soul, and from the day my soul came from the absolute abstract to existence, until our day, how much of disobedience has appeared from me and my essence, and from my soul and my body, spiritually and physically! I am regretting it all, and regretting what I did, and coming back to You asking forgiveness and repentance.</td></tr>
<tr><td>Wa innanī qad dakhaltu wa salaktu fī raḥmāti shahrika hādha 'l-mubārak falā taruddnī yā Rabbī, ʿan bābika wa lā tatruknī li-aḥwāli nafsī wa law li-laḥzah wa anā astaghfiruka.</td><td></td><td>و إنَّني قد دَخَلْتُ وسَلَكْتُ في رَحْماتِ شَهْرِكَ هذا المبارَك فلا تَرُدَّني يا ربي عن بابِكَ ولا تَتْرُكْني لأحْوالِ نَفْسي ولو لَحْظة، أنا أَسْتَغْفِرُكَ</td></tr>
<tr><td colspan="3">O my Lord, I entered and I moved into the ocean of blessings of Your praised month. O my Lord, do not reject me from Your door, and do not leave me to my ego for the blink of an eye, and I am asking forgiveness of You.</td></tr>
</table>

ISTIGHFĀR 100 times Astaghfirullāh		إِسْتِغْفَار أستغفر الله (١٠٠ مرات)
I ask God's forgiveness.		
Continue with the remainder of the Naqshbandi Adab from Sūratu 'l-Fātiḥah, the verse Āmanar-Rasūl until the Ihdā at the end.		سُورةُ الفاتحةِ, آية آمَنَ الرَّسُول.....إلى الأخر الإِهدَاء
In the case of the daily practice of Rajab, continue to the Adhkār al-yawmi, the daily recitation of the wird, including "Allah, Allah" and ṣalawāt, at the level of the People of Determination (see page 22). NOTE: This is not performed on the day before Rajab.		
NOTE: The following three prayers are not performed on the day before Rajab.		
ṢALĀTU 'N-NAJĀT		صلَاةُ النّجات ركعتين

ṢALĀTU 'SH-SHUKR		صلاةُ الشّكر ركعتين
ṢALĀTU 'Ṭ-ṬASĀBĪḤ		صلاةُ التّسابيح اربع رَكَعات
In the case of the daily practice of Rajab, continue the daily recitation of the ṣalawāt, at the level of the People of Determination (see page 22).		
500 TIMES YĀ ṢAMAD		يا صَمَد.(٥٠٠ مَرة)
With the intention to eliminate the bad aspects of the ego.		
500 TIMES ASTAGHFIRULLĀH		أَسْتَغْفِرُ الله (٥٠٠ مرة)
I ask God's forgiveness. Recite with the intention of asking God to forgive your sins, from the day of creation of your soul to the present day.		

500 TIMES ASTAGHFIRULLĀH		أستغفر الله (٥٠٠ مرة)
I ask God's forgiveness. Recite with the intention that, from the present day to the last day on earth, God will protect you against sins.		
500 TIMES ALḤAMDULILLĀH		الحمدُ لله (٥٠٠ مَرة).
All praise is to God. Out of gratitude that God did not create you from the nation of other prophets.		
500 TIMES ALḤAMDULILLĀH		الحمدُ لله (٥٠٠ مَرة).
All praise is to God. Out of gratitude that God has created you from the nation of the Prophet Muḥammad ﷺ and honored you by Sayyidina Abū Bakr aṣ-Ṣiddīq ؓ, ʿAbd al-Khāliq al-Ghujdawānī, Shaykh Sayyid Sharafuddīn ad-Daghestānī, and honored you by Grandshaykh		

Shaykh ʿAbd Allāh al-Fā'iz ad-Daghestānī, and honored you by making you a follower of Mawlana Shaykh Muhammad Nāẓim al-Ḥaqqānī.

THE GRAND TRANSMITTED INVOCATION (AD-DUʿAU 'L-MĀTHŪR) OF SULṬĀN AL-AWLĪYĀ

(see page 179)

Note: only on the day before Rajab.

Daily Evening Practices in Rajab		ادب اليومي بين المغرب والعشأ في شهر رجب
1. Avoid the company of people and perform the Naqshbandi Adab in the last third of the night until sunrise, and/or between Ṣalātu 'l-'Asr and Ṣalātu 'l-Maghrib and/or between Ṣalātu 'l-Maghrib and Ṣalātu 'l-'Ishā.		
NĪYYAT:		النِيَّة:
Nawaytu 'l-arbā'īn, nawaytu 'l-'itikāf, nawaytu 'l-khalwa, nawaytu 'l-'uzla, nawaytu 'r-riyāḍa, nawaytu 's-sulūk, lillāhi ta'ala fī hādhā 'l-masjid (or fī hādha al-jāmi').		نَوَيْتُ الأرْبَعين، نَوَيْتُ الإعْتِكاف، نَوَيتُ الخَلْوَة، نَوَيْتُ العُزْلَة، نَوَيْتُ الرِّياضَة، نَوَيْتُ السُّلوك لله تَعالى في هَذَا المسجِد

INTENTION: I intend the forty (days of seclusion); I intend seclusion in the mosque; I intend seclusion; I intend isolation; I intend discipline (of the ego); I intend to travel in God's Path for the sake of God in this mosque.		
SŪRATU 'L-AN'AM Recite each day if possible.		سُورة الأنعام كل يوم (إذا امكن)
One juz' of Quran everyday (as part of daily wird)		جزء من القرآن كل يوم
DALĀ'ILU 'L-KHAYRĀT (as part of daily wird)		دلائل الخيرات
DAILY WIRD		الأوراد اليومية
FASTING		الصيام
Increase in fasting, particularly on Monday and Thursday, as well as on Raghā'ib the 7th, the middle of Rajab, and the 27th.		الإكثار من الصيام ، وخاصة صيام يوم الإثنين والخميس ونهار ليلة

		الرغائب. اي السابع من رجب ونصف شهر رجب ويوم السابع العشرين

Invocation of Rajab		دعاء رجب
Bismillāhi ’r-Raḥmāni ’r-Raḥīm. Allāhumma innī astaghfiruka min kulli mā tubtu ‘anhu ilayka thumma ‘udtu fīhi. Wa astaghfiruka min kulli mā āradtu bihi wajhaka fakhālaṭani fīhi la laysa fīhi raḍā‘uk. Wa astaghfiruka li ’n-ni‘am ’illatī taqawwaytu bihā ‘alā m‘aṣīyatik. Wa astaghfiruka min adh-dhunūb ’illati lā y‘alamuhā ghayruka, wa lā yaṭali‘u ‘alayhā aḥadun siwāk wa lā tasa‘ūhā illa raḥmatika, wa lā tunjī minhā illa maghfiratuka wa ḥilmuka. Lā ilāha illa Anta subḥānaka innī kuntu mina ’ẓ-ẓālimīn.		بسم الله الرحمن الرحيم اللّهمَّ انّي أسْتَغْفِرُكَ مِن كُلّ ما تُبْتُ عَنْهُ اليكَ ثُمَّ عُدْتُ فِيه، و أسْتَغْفِرُكَ مِن كُلّ ما أَرَدْتُ بِهِ وَجْهَكَ فَخالَطَني فِيه ما ليس فِيه رِضاكَ. و أسْتَغْفِرُكَ لِلنّعَمِ الّتي تَقَوّيتُ بِها على مَعْصِيَتِك، و أسْتَغْفِرُكَ مِنَ الذُّنوُبِ التي لا يَعْلَمُها غَيْرُكَ ولا يَطْلِعُ عليْها أحَدٌ سِواكَ ولا تَسَعُها الا رَحْمَتُكَ ولا تُنْجي مِنها الا مَغْفِرَتُكَ وحِلْمُكَ لا اله الا أنتَ

		سُبْحانَكَ اني كُنْتُ مِنَ الظّالمين
In the name of Allah, the Beneficent, the Merciful O Allah, I ask forgiveness of You for everything for which I repented to You then returned to. And I ask forgiveness of You for everything I displeased You with and all that concerns me with which You are displeased. And I ask forgiveness of You for the favors which I used for increasing my disobedience towards You. And I ask forgiveness of You for the sins which no one knows except You and no one sees except You and nothing encompasses except Your Mercy and nothing delivers from except Your forgiveness and clemency. There is no god except You alone. Glory be to You! Indeed I was an oppressor to myself.		
Allāhuma innī istaghfiruka min kulli ẓulmin ẓalamtu bihi ʿibādak. Fa ayyumā ʿabdin min ʿibādika aw amatin min imā'ika ẓalamtu fī badanihi aw ʿirdihi aw mālihi fa-āʿatihi min khazā'iniki 'llatī lā		اللهمّ انّي أسْتَغْفِرُكَ مِن كُلّ ظُلْمٍ ظَلَمْتُ بِهِ عِبادِكَ فأيُّما عَبْدٍ مِن عِبادِكَ أو أمَةٍ مِن إمائِك ظَلَمْتُ في بَدَنِهِ أو

tanquṣ. Wa as'aluka an tukrimanī bi-raḥmatiki 'llatī wasi'at kulla shay'in wa lā tuhīnanī bi-ʿadhābika wa tuʿṭīyyanī mā as'aluka fa-innī ḥaqīqun bi-raḥmatika ya arḥamu 'r-Rāhimīn. Wa ṣalla-Allāhu ʿalā Sayyidinā Muḥammadin wa ʿalā ālihi wa ṣāḥbihi ajmʿaīn. Wa lā ḥawla wa lā quwatta illa billāhi 'l-ʿAlīyyi 'l-ʿĀẓīm.	عِرْضِهِ أو مالِهِ فأعْطِهِ مِن خَزائِنِكَ التي لا تَنْقُص وأسْألُكَ ان تُكْرِمَني بِرَحْمَتِكَ التي وَسِعَتْ كُلَّ شَيءٍ ولا تُهينَني بِعَذابِكَ وتُعْطِيني ما أسْألُكَ فاني حَقيقٌ بِرَحْمَتِكَ يا أرْحَمَ الرّاحمين. وصلَّى اللهُ على سَيِّدِنا مُحَمَّدٍ وآلِهِ وصَحْبِهِ أجْمَعِين، ولا حولَ ولا قوَّةَ الا باللهِ العليّ العظيم

O Allah, I ask forgiveness of You for the injustice I committed against Your servants. Whatever of Your male or female servants whom I have hurt, physically or in their dignity or in their property, give them of Your bounty which lacks nothing. And I ask You to honor me with Your mercy which encompasses all things. Do not humble me with Your punishment but give me what I ask of You, for I am in great need of Your mercy, O Most Merciful of the merciful. May Allah send blessings upon Muhammad and upon all his companions. There is no power and no strength save in God, the Most High, the Great.

Practices of the Blessed Laylat al-Raghaib(the Night of Desires)		لَيْلَةُ الرَّغَائِبْ ادب
This *adab* is performed after the prayer of ʿIshā, on the night of the first Friday of the month of Rajab, considered by many scholars as the night when the holy light and seed of the Prophet ÿ passed from his father Abd Allah ibn Abd al-Muṭṭalib to the womb of his mother Āmina bint Wahab ﷺ. **Note:** this is the night from Thursday to Friday.		بعد صلَاةُ العشاء
NĪYYAT (INTENTION)		النِيَةَ:
Nawaytu 'l-arbāʿīn, nawaytu 'l-ʿitikāf, nawaytu 'l-khalwa, nawaytu 'l-ʿuzla, nawaytu 'r-riyāḍa, nawaytu 's-sulūk, lillāhi taʿala fī hādhā 'l-masjid (or fī hādha al-jāmiʿ).		نَوَيْتُ الأَرْبَعِين، نَوَيتُ الإعْتِكاف، نَوَيْتُ الخَلْوَة، نَوَيتُ العُزْلَة،

		نَوَيْتُ الرِّياضَة، وَيْتُ السُّلوك لله تَعالى في هَذَا المَسْجِد
I intend the forty (days of seclusion); I intend seclusion in the mosque; I intend seclusion; I intend isolation; I intend discipline (of the ego); I intend to travel in God's Path for the sake of God in this mosque.		
ADABU 'Ṭ-ṬARIQĀH		ادب الطريقة
THE GRAND TRANSMITTED INVOCATION (AD-DU'AU 'L-MĀTHŪR) OF SULṬĀN AL-AWLĪYĀ (see page 179)		الدّعاء المأثور لسلطان الأولياء
KHATMU 'L-KHWAJAGĀN (see page 31)		ختم الخواجكان مع الذكر

MAWLID		مَولِد الشَّريفةِ
ṢALĀTU 'Ṭ-ṬASĀBĪḤ		صلَاةُ التّسابيح اربع رَكَعات
It is recommended to fast that day (the day of Friday) and offer a sacrifice to Allah.		صيام نهار ليلة الرغائب. اي السابع من رجب وتقديم ذبيحة (قربان) لله.

Practices on the Night of Ascension		ادب لَيْلَةُ الإسراء والمعراج
This *adab* is performed after the prayer of Isha on the night of the 27th day of Rajab, considered the night when the Prophet made the Night Journey and Ascension.		بعد صلَاةُ العشاء
NĪYYAT (INTENTION)		النِيَةَ:
Nawaytu 'l-arbāʿīn, nawaytu 'l-ʿitikāf, nawaytu 'l-khalwa, nawaytu 'l-ʿuzla, nawaytu 'r-riyāḍa, nawaytu 's-sulūk, lillāhi taʿala fī hādhā 'l-masjid (or fī hādha al-jāmiʿ).		نَوَيْتُ الأَرْبَعين، نَوَيْتُ الإعْتِكاف، نَوَيْتُ الخَلْوَة، نَوَيْتُ العُزْلَة، نَوَيْتُ الرِّياضَة، نَوَيْتُ السُّلوك لله تَعالى في هَذَا المسجِد

I intend the forty (days of seclusion); I intend seclusion in the mosque; I intend seclusion; I intend isolation; I intend discipline (of the ego); I intend to travel in God's Path for the sake of God in this mosque.

ADAB AT-TARIQĀH		ادب الطريقة
GRAND TRANSMITTED SUPPLICATION OF SULṬĀN AL-'AWLIYĀ (SEE PAGE 179)		وتدعو بالدعاء الأعظم المأثور عن سلطان الأولياء اذا تيسر بعد
KHATMU 'L-KHWAJAGĀN (SEE PAGE 31)		ختم الخواجكان مع الذكر
MAWLID		مَولِد الشَّريفةِ
ṢALĀTU 'Ṭ-ṬASĀBĪḤ		صلَاةُ التّسابيح اربع رَكَعات
ṢALĀTU 'SH-SHUKR two rakats with Qunūt.		صلَاةُ الشّكر ركعتين مع دعاء القنوت

IHDĀ (SEE PAGE 28)		إِهدَاء
DU'Ā AND AL-FĀTIḤAH (SEE PAGE 325).		دُعاء الفاتِحة
It is recommended to fast the following day and to offer a sacrifice to Allah.		صيام نهار ليلة الإسراء اي السابع و العشرون من رجب وتقديم ذبيحة (قربان) لله.

Practices of the 15th of Shaban (nisf Sha'bān)		ادب ليلة النصف من شهر شعبان
ADAB AṬ-ṬARĪQAH		ادب الطريقة
Reading of Sūrah Yasīn three times; first with the intention of long life in Islam and faith (imān), second with the intention to ward off affliction from one's self and from the nation of Muhammad ﷺ; and the third time with the intention of receiving one's sustenance without reliance on mankind.		قراءة يس ثلاث مرات، المرة الاولى بنِيَة طول العمر بالإسلام والإيمان، والمرة الثانِيَة بنِيَة دفع البلاء عنه وعن الامة المحمدية ، والمرة الثلاثة بنِيَة الرزق والإستغناء عن الناس
After every reading recite: Allāhumma yā Dhā 'l-Manni lā yamannu 'alayhi ahad, yā Dhā 'l-Jalāli wa 'l-Ikrām yā Dhā 'ṭ-Ṭūli wa 'l-An'ām. Lā ilāha illa Anta. Ḍahara 'l-lāji'īn wa Jāru 'l-		وبعد كل مرة تدعوا بهذا الدعاء: اللهمّ يا ذا المنّ لا يَمنُّ عليْه أحَدٌ يا ذا الجَلالِ والإكْرام يا ذا الطَّولِ والأنْعام، لا إلهَ إلا

mustajirīn wa Amānu 'l-khā'ifīn.

Allāhumma in kunta katabtanī ʿindaka fī ummu 'l-Kitābi shaqīyan aw maḥrūman aw maṭrūdan aw muqataran ʿalayya mina 'r-rizq famḥu-llāhumma bi-faḍlika shaqāwatī wa ḥurmāni wa ṭurdī wa iqtāra rizqī wa thabitnī ʿindaka fī ummi 'l-kitābi saʿīdan wa marzūqan li 'l-khayrāti fa-innaka qulta wa qawluku 'l-ḥaqq fī kitābik al-munzal ʿala lisāni nabīyyika 'l-mursal: yamḥullāhu mā yashā'u wa yuthbitu wa ʿindahu Ummu 'l-Kitāb. Ilāhī bi 't-tajallī al-āʿaẓami fī lalayti 'n-niṣfi min shahri shaʿbāni 'l-muʿaẓami 'l-mukarrami 'llatī yufraqu fīhā kullu amrin ḥakīmin wa yubram, an takshifa

أنتَ ظَهَرَ اللاجِئين
وجارُ المُسْتَجِيرين وأمانُ
الخائِفِين اللهمّ ان كُنْتَ
كَتَبْتَني عَنْدَكَ في أمِّ الكِتابِ
شَقِياً أو مَحْرُوماً أو مَطْرُوداً أو
مُقَتَراً عليّ فِي الرّزْقِ فامْحُ
اللهمَ بِفَضْلِكَ شَقاوَتي
وحُرْماني وطُرْدي واقْتارَ
رِزْقي وثَبِتني عِنْدَكَ في أمّ
الكِتابِ سَعِيداً ومَرْزُوقاً
لِلخَيْراتِ فانَّكَ قُلْتَ
وقَوْلُكَ الحقّ في كِتابِكَ المُنْزَل
على لِسانِ نَبِيّكَ المُرْسَل
يَمْحُوا اللهُ ما يَشاءُ ويُثْبِتُ

'annā mina 'l-balā'i mā na'lamu wa mā lā na'lamu wa mā Anta bihi ā'alamu innaka Anta al-A'azzu 'l-Akram. Wa ṣalla-Allāhu 'alā sayyidinā Muḥammadin wa 'alā ālihi wa ṣāḥbihi wa sallam.

وَعِنْدَهُ أُمُّ الكِتَابِ. إلهي بالتّجَلّي الأَعْظَمِ في لَيْلَةِ النِّصْفِ مِن شَهْرِ شَعْبَانِ المُعَظَّمِ المُكَرَّمِ التي يُفْرَقُ فيها كُلُّ أَمْرٍ حَكِيمٍ وَيُبْرَمُ ان تَكْشِفَ عَنَّا مِنَ البَلاءِ ما نَعْلَمُ وما لا نَعْلَمُ وما أنتَ بِهِ أَعْلَمُ إنَّكَ أنتَ الأَعَزُّ الأَكْرَم. وصلى اللهُ على سَيِّدِنا محمد وعلى آلِهِ وصَحْبِهِ وسلَّم.

O God, Tireless Owner of Bounty. O Owner of Sublimity, Honor, Power, and Blessings. There is no god except You, the Support of refugees and Neighbor of those who seek nearness, Guardian of the fearful. O God, if you have written in Your Book that I be abject, deprived, banished, and tight-fisted, then erase O

God, through Your bounty, my misery, deprivation, banishment, and stinginess and establish me with You as happy, provided with blessings, for surely You have said—and Your Word is True—in Your Revealed Book on the tongue of Your Messenger, "God blots out or confirms what He pleases, and with Him is the Mother of Books." (13:39) My God, by the Great Manifestation of the Night of the middle of the Noble Month of Shaʿbān "in which every affair of wisdom is made distinct and authorized,"(44:4) remove from us calamities—those we know and those we do not know, and Thou knowest best—for surely You are the Most Mighty, the Most Generous. May God bless Muhammad and his Family and Companions.

One then invokes God with the Grand Transmitted Supplication of Sulṭān al-ʿAwliyā (see page 179) if it is easy, after each recitation, or if not, one time after the three recitations.		وتدعو بالدعاء الأعظم المأثور عن سلطان الأولياء اذا تيسر بعد كل مرة، وإلا تدعو به مرة واحدة بعد القراءة الثالثة

KHATMU 'L-KHWAJAGĀN (SEE PAGE 31)		ختم الخواجكان مع الذكر
ṢALĀTU 'Ṭ-ṬASĀBĪḤ		صلَاةُ التّسابيح اربع رَكَعات
ṢALĀTU 'SH-SHUKR two rak'ats with Qunūt.		صلَاةُ الشّكر ركعتين مع دعاء القنوت
ṢALĀTU 'T-TAHAJJUD After 'Ishā, complete 100 raka'ts of Ṣalāt at-Tahajjud. In the first raka'h after the Fātiḥah (see page 325) recite Sūrat al-Ikhlāṣ twice (see page 385) and in the second, once.		صلَاةُ التهجّد ثم بعد صلَاةُ العشاء تجتهّد ان تكمل ١٠٠ ركعة تقرأ في الرّكعة الأولى بعد الفاتحة سُورة الاخلاص مرتين تقرأ في الرّكعة الثّانِيَة بعد الفاتحة اخلاص الشريفة مرة

FASTING You are to fast its day and make a sacrifice to Allāh as a ransom for yourself and your family and distribute it to the needy.	صيام نهار ليلة النصف من شهر شعبان. اي خمسة عشرة من شعبان وتضحي قربان لله كالفدية لنفسك وعائلتك وتوزعها على المحتاجين.

The Grand Transmitted Supplication		
The Grand Transmitted Supplication From Sulṭān al-ʿAwliyā, Mawlānā ash-Shaykh ʿAbd Allāh al-Fā'iz ad-Dāghestānī, may God sanctify his secret.		الدّعاء الأعظم المأثور لسلطان الأولياء مولانا الشّيخ عبد الله الفائز الدّغستاني
Bismillāhi 'r-Raḥmāni 'r-Raḥīm. Allāhumma ṣalli ʿalā Muḥammadin an-Nabī il-mukhtār ʿadada man ṣalla ʿalayhi mina 'l-akhyār, wa ʿadada man lam yuṣalli ʿalayhi mina 'l-ashrār, wa ʿadada qaṭarāti 'l-amṭār, wa ʿadada amwāji 'l-biḥār, wa ʿadada 'r-rimāli wa 'l-qifār, wa ʿadada awrāqi 'l-ashjār, wa ʿadada anfāsi 'l-mustaghfirīna bi 'l-ashār, wa ʿadada akmāmi 'l-athmār, wa ʿadada mā kāna wa mā yakūnu ila yawmi 'l-ḥashri wa 'l-qarār, wa ṣalli		بسم الله الرحمن الرحيم اللهمّ صَلّ على محمدٍ النَّبي المُخْتار عَدَدَ مَن صَلَّى عَلَيْهِ مِنَ الأَخْيار ، وعَدَدَ مَن لم يُصَلّ عَلَيْهِ مِنَ الأَشْرَار، وعَدَدَ قَطَراتِ الأَمْطار، وعَدَدَ امْواجِ البِحار، وعَدَدَ الرّمالِ والقِفار، وعَدَدَ اوْراقِ الأَشْجار ، وعَدَدَ انْفاسِ المُسْتَغْفِرينَ

ʿalayhi mā taʿāqaba 'l-laylu wa 'n-nahāru wa ṣalli ʿalayhi mā 'khtalafu 'l-malawān wa taʿāqaba 'l-ʿasrān wa karrara 'l-jadīdān wa 'staqbala 'l-farqadān, wa balligh rūḥahu wa arwāhi āhli baytihi minnā taḥīyyatan wat-taslīm wa ʿalā jamīʿi 'l-anbīyā'i wa 'l-mursalīn wa 'l-ḥamdu lillāhi Rabbi 'l-ʿalamīn.		بالأَسْحار، وعَدَدَ أكمامِ الأَثمار، وعَدَدَ ما كانَ وما يَكُونُ إلى يَوْمِ الحَشْرِ والقَرار، وَصَلِّ عَلَيْهِ ما تَعاقَبَ اللّيْلُ والنهار، وَصَلِّ عَلَيْهِ مَا اخْتَلَفَ المَلَوان وتَعاقَبَ العَصْرَان وَكَرَّرَ الجِديدان واسْتَقْبَلَ الفَرْقَدَان، وَبَلِّغ رُوحَهُ وَأَرْوَاحَ أَهْلِ بَيْتِهِ مِنّا تَحِيَّةً وتَسْلِيماً وَعَلى جَمِيعِ الأنْبِياءِ والمُرْسلين والحَمْدُ لله رَبِّ العَالَمِين.
In the name of God, the Beneficent, the Merciful.		

God, bless Muḥammad, the Chosen Prophet as the number of those who pray on him among the righteous and as the number of those who did not pray on him among the wicked; and as the number of the drops of the rain and as the number of waves of the oceans and as the number of the grains of sand and the wastelands, as the number of the leaves of the trees and as the number of the breaths of those who seek Your forgiveness by morning and as the number of the rinds of fruit and as the number of what was and what is until the Day of Gathering and Verdict.

And Bless him (O God), as the turning of nights and days and bless him as long as the colors alternate and with the changing of time, and with the return of things renewed and with the constancy of diversity.

And convey from us to his soul and the souls of the People of his house, greetings and salutations and on all the prophets and messengers. And all Praise is due to God.

Allāhumma ṣalli ʿalā Muḥammad wa ʿalā āli Muḥammadin bi ʿadadi kulli dharratin alfa alfa marrah. Allāhumma ṣalli		اللهمّ صَلّ على محمد وعلى آلِ محمد بِعَدَدِ كُلّ ذَرَّةٍ أَلْفَ أَلفَ مَرَّة. اللهمّ صَلّ على

ʿalā Muḥammadin wa ʿalā āli Muḥammadin wa ṣaḥbihi wa sallim. Subūḥun quddūsun rabbunā wa rabbu ʾl-malāʿikati wa ʾr-Rūḥ, Rabbi ʾghfir wa ʾrḥam wa tawājaz ʿamma tʿalamu innaka Anta ʾl-Aʿazzu ʾl-Akram.		محمد وعلى آلِهِ وصَحْبِهِ وسلّم، سُبُوحٌ قُدُوسٌ رَبُّنَا وَرَبُّ الْمَلائِكَةِ وَالرُّوح، رَبِّ اغْفِرْ وَارْحَمْ وَتَجاوِزْ عَمَّا تَعْلَمُ إِنَّكَ أَنْتَ الأَعَزُّ الأَكْرَم.

O God bless Muḥammad and the Family of Muḥammad as the number of all the atoms in creation a thousand times over. O God bless Muḥammad and the Family of Muḥammad and His Companions and grant them peace. Glorified and Hallowed art Thou, our Lord and Lord of the angels and the Holy Spirit. O our Lord forgive and have mercy and pardon of what You know (best), for You are surely the Most Honored, the Most Generous.

Bismillāhi ʾr-Raḥmāni ʾr-Raḥīm. Allāhumma innī astaghfiruka min kulli mā tubtu ʿanhu ilayka thumma		بسم الله الرحمن الرحيم اللّهمَّ انّي أَسْتَغْفِرُكَ مِن كُلِّ مَا تُبْتُ عَنْهُ اِلَيْكَ ثُمَّ عُدْتُ

ʿudtu fīhi. Wa astaghfiruka min kulli mā āradtu bihi wajhaka fakhālaṭani fīhi la laysa fīhi raḍāʿuk. Wa astaghfiruka li 'n-niʿam 'illatī taqawwaytu bihā ʿalā mʿaṣīyatik. Wa astaghfiruka min adh-dhunūb 'illati lā yʿalamuhā ghayruka, wa lā yaṭaliʿu ʿalayhā aḥadun siwāk wa lā tasaʿūhā illa raḥmatika, wa lā tunjī minhā illa maghfiratuka wa ḥilmuka. Lā ilāha illa Anta subḥānaka innī kuntu mina 'ẓ-ẓālimīn.		فِيه، وَ أَسْتَغْفِرُكَ مِن كُلِّ مَا أَرَدْتُ بِهِ وَجْهَكَ فَخَالَطَنِي فِيهِ مَا لَيسَ فِيهِ رِضَائُكَ. وَ أَسْتَغْفِرُكَ لِلنِّعَمِ الَّتِي تَقَوَّيتُ بِهَا عَلى مَعْصِيَتِكَ، وَ أَسْتَغْفِرُكَ مِنَ الذُّنُوبِ الَّتِي لَا يَعْلَمُهَا غَيْرُكَ وَلَا يَطْلِعُ عَلَيْهَا أَحَدٌ سِوَاكَ وَلَا تَسَعُهَا اِلَّا رَحْمَتِكَ وَلَا تُنْجِي مِنهَا اِلَّا مَغْفِرَتُكَ وَحِلْمُكَ لَا اِلَهَ اِلَّا أَنْتَ سُبْحَانَكَ اِنِي كُنْتُ مِنَ الظَّالِمِينَ.
In the name of Allah, the Beneficent, the Merciful		

O Allah, I ask forgiveness of You for everything for which I repented to You then returned to. And I ask forgiveness of You for everything I displeased You with and all that concerns me with which You are displeased. And I ask forgiveness of You for the favors which I used for increasing my disobedience towards You. And I ask forgiveness of You for the sins which no one knows except You and no one sees except You and nothing encompasses except Your Mercy and nothing delivers from except Your forgiveness and clemency. There is no god except You alone. Glory be to You! Indeed I was an oppressor to myself.

Allāhumma innī astaghfiruka min kulli ẓulmin ẓalamtu bihi 'ibāduka fa ayyamā 'abdan min 'ibādika aw 'amatin min imā'ika ẓalamtu fī badanihi aw 'irḍhihi aw mālihi f'āṭihi min khazā'inak 'illati lā tanquṣ, wa as'aluka an tukrimanī bi raḥmatik 'illati wasi'at kulla shay'in wa lā tuhīnanī bi 'adhābika wa t'uṭiānī mā as'aluka fa innī

اللهمّ اني أَسْتَغْفِرُكَ مِن كُلِّ ظُلْمٍ ظَلَمْتُ بِهِ عِبَادِكَ فَأْتِها عَبْدٍ مِن عِبَادِكَ أَو أَمَةٍ مِن إمائكَ ظَلَمْتُ فِي بَدَنِهِ أَو عِرْضِهِ أَو مَالِهِ فَأَعْطِهِ مِن خَزَائِنِكَ التي لا تَنْقُصُ وأَسْأَلُكَ ان تُكْرِمَني بِرَحْمَتِكَ

ḥaqīqun bi-raḥmatika ya Arḥam ar-rāḥimīn. Wa ṣalla-Allāhu ʿalā sayyidinā Muḥammadin wa ālihi wa ṣāḥbihi ajmāʿīn wa lā ḥawla wa lā quwwata illa billāhi ʾl-ʿAliyyi ʾl-ʿAẓīm.	التي وَسِعَت كُلَّ شَيءٍ ولا تُهِينَني بِعَذابِكَ وتُعْطِينِي ما أسْأَلُكَ فاني حَقيقٌ بِرَحْمَتِكَ يا أرْحَمَ الرّاحمين. وصلى الله على سَيِّدِنا مُحَمَّدٍ وآلِهِ وصَحْبِهِ أجْمَعِين، ولا حولَ ولا قوَّةَ الا باللهِ العليِّ العظيم.

O God, I ask forgiveness of You for the injustice I committed against Your servants. Whatever of Your male or female servants whom I have hurt, physically or in their dignity or in their property give them of Your bounty which lacks nothing. And I ask You to honor me with Your mercy which encompasses all things. Do not humble me with Your punishment but give me what I ask of You, for I am in great need of Your mercy, O Most Merciful of the merciful. May God send blessings upon Muḥammad and upon all his companions. And there is no power and no strength save in God, the Most High, the Great.

Bismillāhi ’r-Raḥmāni ’r-Raḥīm. Bismillāhi ’n-Nūr, nūrun ‘alā nūr, wa ’lḥamdulillāhi ’lladhī khalaq as-samawāti wa ’l-arḍa wa ja‘ala aẓ-ẓulumāti wa ’n-nūr wa anzala at-tawrāta ‘alā jabali ’ṭ-Ṭūri fī kitābin masṭūr. Wa ’l-ḥamdulillāhi ’lladhī hūwa bi ’l-Ghanīyy madhkūr wa bi ’l-‘izzi wa ’l-Jalāli mashhūr, wa ’lḥamdulillāhi ’lladhī khalaqa ’s-samāwāti wa ’l-arḍi wa ja‘ala ’ẓ-ẓulumāti wa ’n-nūr thumma ’lladhīna kafarū bi-rabbihim ya‘dilūn. Kāf, Hā, ‘Ayn, Ṣād. Ḥā, Mīm, ‘Ayn, Sīn, Qāf. Īyāka n‘abudu wa Īyāka nasta‘īn. Yā Ḥayyu Yā Qayyūm. Allāhu laṭīfun bi ‘ibādihi yarzuqū man	بسم الله الرحمن الرحيم بِسْمِ الله النُّور، نُورٌ على نُور والحَمْدُ لله الذي خَلَقَ السَّمواتِ والأَرْض وجَعَلَ الظُّلُماتِ والنُّورُ وأَنْزَلَ التَّوْراةَ على جَبَلِ الطُّورِ في كِتابٍ مَسْطُور، والحَمْدُ لله الذي هُو بِالغَنِي مَذْكُور بِالعِزِّ والجَلالِ مَشْهُور، والحَمْدُ لله الذي خَلَقَ السّمواتِ والأَرْضِ وجَعَلَ الظُّلُماتِ والنُّور ثُمَّ الّذين كَفَرُوا بِرَبِهِمْ يَعْدِلُون، كهيعص، حمعسق، إياكَ

yashā'u wa Hūwa 'l-Qawiyyu 'l-'Azīz. Yā Kāfī kulla shay'in ikfinī waṣrif 'anī kulla shay'in innaka Qādirun 'alā kulli shay'in bi-yadika 'l-khayr innaka 'alā kulli shay'in Qadīr.		نَعْبُدُ وإياكَ نَسْتَعِين يا حيُّ يا قَيُّوم، اللهُ لَطِيفٌ بِعِبادِهِ يُرْزُقُ مَن يَشاءُ وهُو القَوِيُّ العَزِيز، يا كافِي كُلّ شَيءٍ إكْفِنِي واصْرِفْ عَني كُلّ شَيءٍ إنَّكَ قادِرٌ على كُلّ شَيءٍ بِيَدِكَ الخَيْر إنَّكَ على كُلّ شَيءٍ قَدِيرٌ

In the name of God, the All-Beneficent, the All-Merciful.

In the name of God, the Source of Light, Light upon Light. All praise is due to God who hath created the heavens and the earth. He created the darkness and the light and hath revealed the Torah on Mount Tūr in a Composed Book. All praise is due to God who created the heavens and the earth and created the darkness and the light.

"Yet those who reject Faith hold (others) as equal, with their Guardian-Lord." (6:1)

Kāf, Hā, ʿAyn, Ṣād. Ḥā, Mīm, Sīn, Qāf. "You alone do we worship and You alone do ask for help." (1:4)

O Ever-Living One, O Self-subsisting One.

"Gracious is Allah to His servants: He gives Sustenance to whom He pleases: and He has power and can carry out His Will." (42:19)

O Giver of all, provide me and turn from me everything that harms me. Surely You are capable over all things. In Your hands is all good and You have power over all things.

Allāhumma ya Kathīr an-nawāli wa yā Dāʿim al-wiṣāli wa yā Ḥusna 'l-fiʿāli wa yā Razzāq al-ʿibādi ʿalā kulli ḥāl.	اللهمّ يا كَثِير النَّوالِ وَيآ دَائِمَ الوِصَالِ وَيآ حُسْنَ الفِعالِ وَيَا رَازَّقَ العِبادِ عَلى كُلِّ حَال.

O God, the One who Grants plenty, O One of the Abiding Connection, O Doer of Good, O Provider of Your servants in every state.

<table>
<tr><td>Allāhumma in dakhala ’sh-shaku fī īmānī bika wa lam āʿalam bihi tubtu ʿanhu wa aqūlu lā ilāha ill-Allāh Muḥammadur-Rasūlullāh ﷺ.</td><td></td><td>اللهمّ إنْ دَخَلَ الشَّكُ في إيمَاني بِكَ وَلَمْ أَعْلَمْ بِهِ تُبْتُ عَنْهُ وَأَقُولُ لَا إِلَهَ إلاَّ الله مُحَمَّدٌ رَسُولُ الله ﷺ.</td></tr>
<tr><td colspan="3">O God, if doubt has entered my belief in You, and of which I was unaware, I repent from it and say: There is no god except God, Muḥammad ﷺ is the Prophet of God.</td></tr>
<tr><td>Allāhumma in dakhala ’sh-shakka wa ’l-kufr fī tawḥīdī īyāka wa lam āʿalam bihi tubtu ʿanhu wa aqūlu lā ilāha ill-Allāh Muḥammadur-Rasūlullāh ﷺ.</td><td></td><td>اللهمّ إنْ دَخَلَ الشَّكُ والكُفْرُ في تَوْحِيدي إياكَ ولم أَعْلَمْ بِهِ تُبْتُ عَنْهُ وأَقُولُ لَا إِلَهَ إلاَّ الله مُحَمَّدٌ رَسُولُ الله ﷺ.</td></tr>
<tr><td colspan="3">O God, if doubt and disbelief entered my affirmation of Your Oneness, and of which I was unaware, I repent from it and say: There is no god except God, Muḥammad ﷺ is the Prophet of God.</td></tr>
</table>

Allāhumma in dakhala 'sh-shubhata fī m'arifati īyāka wa lam ā'alam bihi tubtu 'anhu wa aqūlu lā ilāha ill-Allāh Muḥammadur-Rasūlullāh ﷺ.	اللهمَ إنْ دَخَلَتِ الشُّبْهَةُ في مَعْرِفَتي إياكَ ولم أَعْلَمْ بِهِ تُبْتُ عَنْهُ وأَقُولُ لَا إِلَهَ إلاَّ الله مُحَمَّدُ رَسُولُ الله ﷺ.

O God, if doubt enters my realization of You, and of which I was unaware, I repent from it and say: There is no god except God, Muḥammad ﷺ is the Prophet of God.

Allāhumma in dakhal al-'ujb wa 'r-riyā' wa 'l-kibrīyā wa 's-sum'atu fī 'ilmī wa lam ā'alam bihi tubtu 'anhu wa aqūlu lā ilāha ill-Allāh Muḥammadur-Rasūlullāh ﷺ.	اللهمّ إنْ دَخَلَ العُجْبُ والرِّياءُ والكِبْرِياءُ والسُّمْعَةُ في عِلْمي ولم أَعْلَمْ بِهِ تُبْتُ عَنْهُ وأَقُولُ لَا إِلَهَ إلاَّ الله مُحَمَّدُ رَسُولُ الله ﷺ.

O God, if vanity, affected piety, arrogance and infamy affected me and of which I was unaware, I repent from it and say: There is no god except God, Muḥammad ﷺ is the Prophet of God.

Allāhumma in jara 'l-kadhibu ʿalā lisānī wa lam āʿalam bihi tubtu ʿanhu wa aqūlu lā ilāha ill-Allāh Muḥammadur-Rasūlullāh ﷺ.		اللهمّ إنْ جَرَى الكَذِبُ على لِسَاني ولم أعْلَمْ بِهِ تُبْتُ عَنْهُ وأَقُولُ لَا إِلَهَ إلاَّ الله مُحَمَّدٌ رَسُولُ الله ﷺ.
O God, if lies run upon my tongue, of which I was unaware, I repent from it and say: There is no god except God, Muḥammad ﷺ is the Prophet of God.		
Allāhumma in dakhala an-nifāq fī qalbī min adh-dhunūbi 's-saghā'iri wa 'l-kabā'iri wa lam āʿalam bihi tubtu ʿanhu wa aqūlu lā ilāha ill-Allāh Muḥammadur-Rasūlullāh ﷺ.		اللهمّ إنْ دَخَلَ النِّفَاقُ في قَلْبي مِنَ الذُّنوبِ الصّغائِرِ والكِبائِرِ ولم أَعْلَمْ بِهِ تُبْتُ عَنْهُ وأَقُولُ لَا إِلَهَ إلاَّ الله مُحَمَّدٌ رَسُولُ الله ﷺ.
O God, if hypocrisy entered my heart from the minor and major sins, and of which I was unaware, I repent from it and say: There is no god except God, Muḥammad ﷺ is the Prophet of God.		

<table>
<tr><td>Allāhumma mā asdayta ilayya min khayrin wa lam ashkuruka wa lam āʿalam bihi tubtu ʿanhu wa aqūlu lā ilāha ill-Allāh Muḥammadur-Rasūlullāh ﷺ.</td><td></td><td>اللهمَ ما أَسْدَيْتَ إليّ مِن خَيْرٍ ولم أَشْكُرْكَ ولم أَعْلَمْ بِهِ تُبْتُ عَنْهُ وأَقُولُ لَا إِلَهَ إِلاَّ الله مُحَمَّدٌ رَسُولُ الله ﷺ.</td></tr>
<tr><td colspan="3">O Allāh, from what You have granted me of all that is good and for which I had not thanked You, and I was unaware of it, I repent from it and say: There is no god except God, Muḥammad ﷺ is the Prophet of God.</td></tr>
<tr><td>Allāhumma mā qadarta lī min amrin wa lam arḍāhu wa lam āʿalam bihi tubtu ʿanhu wa aqūlu lā ilāha ill-Allāh Muḥammadur-Rasūlullāh ﷺ.</td><td></td><td>اللهمّ ما قَدَرْتَ لي مِن أَمْرٍ ولم أَرْضاهُ ولم أَعْلَمْ بِهِ تُبْتُ عَنْهُ وأَقُولُ لَا إِلَهَ إِلاَّ الله مُحَمَّدٌ رَسُولُ الله ﷺ.</td></tr>
<tr><td colspan="3">O God, whatever You have destined for me in matters which I did not accept, and of which I was unaware, I repent from it and say: There is no god except God, Muḥammad ﷺ is the Prophet of God.</td></tr>
</table>

Allāhumma mā anʿamta ʿalayya min nʿimatin fa-ʿaṣaytuka wa ghafaltu ʿan shukrika wa lam āʿalam bihi tubtu ʿanhu wa aqūlu lā ilāha ill-Allāh Muḥammadur-Rasūlullāh ﷺ.	اللهمَّ ما أَنْعَمْتَ مِن نِعْمَةٍ فَعَصَيْتُكَ وغَفَلْتُ عَنْ شُكْرِكَ ولم أَعْلَمْ بِهِ تُبْتُ عَنْهُ وأَقُولُ لَا إِلَهَ إِلَّا الله مُحَمَّدٌ رَسُولُ الله ﷺ.

O God, from what You had conferred upon me of bounty for which I neglected to thank You, and of which I was unaware, I repent from it and say: There is no god except God, Muḥammad ﷺ is the Prophet of God.

Allāhumma mā mananta bihi ʿalayya min khayrin fa lam āḥmaduka ʿalayhi wa lam āʿalam bihi tubtu ʿanhu wa aqūlu lā ilāha ill-Allāh Muḥammadur-Rasūlullāh ﷺ.	اللهمَّ ما مَنَنْتَ بِهِ عليَّ مِن خَيْرٍ فلم أَحْمَدُكَ عليهِ ولم أَعْلَمْ بِهِ تُبْتُ عَنْهُ وأَقُولُ لَا إِلَهَ إِلَّا الله مُحَمَّدٌ رَسُولُ الله ﷺ.

O God, whatever You have bestowed on me of goodness and I did not praise You for it, and of which

<table>
<tr><td colspan="2">I was unaware, I repent from it and say: There is no god except God, Muḥammad ﷺ is the Prophet of God.</td></tr>
<tr><td>Allāhumma ma ḍayyatu min ʿumrī wa lam tarḍa bihi tubtu ʿanhu wa aqūlu lā ilāha ill-Allāh Muḥammadur-Rasūlullāh ﷺ.</td><td>اللهمّ ما ضَيَّعْتُ مِن عُمْرِي ولم تَرْضَ بِهِ ولم أَعْلَمْ بِهِ تُبْتُ عَنْهُ وأَقُولُ لَا إِلَهَ إِلاَّ الله مُحَمَّدٌ رَسُولُ الله ﷺ.</td></tr>
<tr><td colspan="2">O God, whatever I have wasted from my allotted lifetime which You were not pleased, I repent from it and say: There is no god except God, Muḥammad ﷺ is the Prophet of God.</td></tr>
<tr><td>Allāhumma bimā awjabta ʿalayya mina ʼn-naẓari min maṣnūʿātika fa-ghafaltu ʿanhu wa lam āʿalam bihi tubtu ʿanhu wa aqūlu lā ilāha ill-Allāh Muḥammadur-Rasūlullāh ﷺ.</td><td>اللهمَ بِما أَوْجَبْتَ عليّ مِنَ النَّظَرِ في مَصْنُوعاتِكَ فَغَفَلْتُ عَنْهُ ولم أَعْلَمْ بِهِ تُبْتُ عَنْهُ وأَقُولُ لَا إِلَهَ إِلاَّ الله مُحَمَّدٌ رَسُولُ الله ﷺ.</td></tr>
<tr><td colspan="2">O God, of what You have imposed upon me in the observation of the creation of Your design and of which I was heedless, and I was unaware of it, I repent</td></tr>
</table>

<table>
<tr><td colspan="3">from it and say: There is no god except God, Muḥammad ﷺ is the Prophet of God.</td></tr>
<tr><td>Allāhumma mā qaṣartu ʿanhu āmālī fī rajāʿika wa lam āʿalam bihi tubtu ʿanhu wa aqūlu lā ilāha ill-Allāh Muḥammadur-Rasūlullāh ﷺ.</td><td></td><td>اللهمّ ما قَصَرْتُ عَنْهُ آمالي في رَجائِكَ ولم أَعْلَمْ بِهِ تُبْتُ عَنْهُ وأَقُولُ لَا إِلَهَ إِلاَّ الله مُحَمَّدٌ رَسُولُ الله ﷺ.</td></tr>
<tr><td colspan="3">O God, from whatever fell short of my hope in my turning to You, and of which I was unaware, I repent from it and say: There is no god except God, Muḥammad ﷺ is the Prophet of God.</td></tr>
<tr><td>Allāhumma māʿtamadtu ʿalā aḥadin siwāka fī ’sh-shadā’idi wa lam āʿalamu bihi tubtu ʿanhu wa aqūlu lā ilāha ill-Allāh Muḥammadur-Rasūlullāh ﷺ.</td><td></td><td>اللهمَ ما اعْتَمَدْتُ على أَحَدٍ سِواكَ في الشَّدائِد ولم أَعْلَمْ بِهِ تُبْتُ عَنْهُ وأَقُولُ لَا إِلَهَ إِلاَّ الله مُحَمَّدٌ رَسُولُ الله ﷺ.</td></tr>
<tr><td colspan="3">O God, from placing dependence on other than You in the face of calamities, and of which I was unaware, I repent from it and say: There is no god except God, Muḥammad ﷺ is the Prophet of God.</td></tr>
</table>

Allāhumma mā astanaʿtu li-ghayrika fī 'sh-shadā'idi wa 'n-nawā'ibi wa lam āʿalam bihi tubtu ʿanhu wa aqūlu lā ilāha ill-Allāh Muḥammadur-Rasūlullāh ﷺ.

اللهمَ ما اسْتَعَنْتُ بِغَيْرِكَ في الشَّدائِدِ والنَّوائِبِ ولم أَعْلَمْ بِهِ تُبْتُ عَنْهُ وأَقُولُ لَا إِلَهَ إِلاَّ الله مُحَمَّدٌ رَسُولُ الله ﷺ.

O God, in what I had sought assistance from other than You in calamities and misfortune, and of which I was unaware, I repent from it and say: There is no god except God, Muḥammad ﷺ is the Prophet of God.

Allāhumma in zalla lisānī bi 's-su'āli li-ghayrika wa lam āʿalam bihi tubtu ʿanhu wa aqūlu lā ilāha ill-Allāh Muḥammadur-Rasūlullāh ﷺ.

اللهمّ إنْ زَلَّ لِساني بِالسُؤالِ لِغَيْرِكَ ولم أَعْلَمْ بِهِ تُبْتُ عَنْهُ وأَقُولُ لَا إِلَهَ إِلاَّ الله مُحَمَّدٌ رَسُولُ الله ﷺ.

O God, if my tongue has slipped by askng other than You and I was unaware of it, I repent from it and say: There is no god except God, Muḥammad ﷺ is the Prophet of God.

Allāhumma mā ṣaluḥa min shānī bi-faḍlika farā'ituhu min ghayrika wa lam ā'alam bihi tubtu ʿanhu wa aqūlu lā ilāha ill-Allāh Muḥammadu 'r-Rasūlullāh ﷺ.		اللهمّ ما صَلُحَ مِن شَأني بِفَضْلِكَ فَرَأيتُهُ مِن غَيرِكَ ولم أعْلَمْ بِهِ تُبْتُ عَنْهُ وأقُولُ لَا إِلَهَ إلاَّ الله مُحَمَّدٌ رَسُولُ الله ﷺ.
O God, whatever was rectified in my affairs through Your Grace and I saw it coming from other than You, and I was unaware of it, I repent from it and say: There is no god except God, Muḥammad ﷺ is the Prophet of God.		
Allāhumma bi-ḥaqqi lā ilāha ill-Allāh wa bi-ʿizzatih		اللهمَ بِحَقِّ لَا إِلَهَ إلاَّ الله وبِعِزَّتِهِ
O God, by the right of lā ilāha ill-Allāh and its Might;		
Wa bi-ḥaqqi 'l-ʿarshi wa ʿaẓamatihih		و بِحَقِّ العَرْشِ وعَظَمَتِهِ
And by the right of the Throne and its grandeur;		
Wa bi-ḥaqqi 'l-kursī wa saʿatih		و بِحَقِّ الكُرْسي وسَعَتِهِ
And by the right of the Chair and its vastness;		

Wa bi-ḥaqqi 'l-qalami wa jariyatih		وبِحَقِّ القَلَمِ وجَرِيَتِهِ
And by the right of the Pen and its motion;		
Wa bi-ḥaqqi 'l-lawḥi wa ḥafaẓatih		وبِحَقِّ اللَّوْحِ وحَفَظَتِهِ
And by the right of the Tablet and its preservation;		
Wa bi-ḥaqqi 'l-mīzāni wa khifatih		وبِحَقِّ المِيزانِ وخِفَتِهِ
And by the right of the Scale and its accuracy;		
Wa bi-ḥaqqi 'ṣ-Ṣirāṭi wa riqqatih		وبِحَقِّ الصِّراطِ ورِقَّتِهِ
And by the right of the Bridge and it narrowness;		
Wa bi-ḥaqqi Jibrīl wa amānatihi		وبِحَقِّ جِبْرِيل وأمانَتِهِ
And by the right of Jibrīl and his trust;		
Wa bi-ḥaqqi Riḍwān wa jannatih		وبِحَقِّ رِضْوان وجَنَّتِهِ
And by the right of Riḍwān and his paradise;		
Wa bi-ḥaqqi Mālik wa zabānīyatih		وبِحَقِّ مالِك وزَبانِيَّتِهِ

And by the right of Mālik and his angels of punishment;		
Wa bi-ḥaqqi Mīkā'īl wa shafaqatih		وبِحَقِّ مِيكائِيل وشَفَقَتِهِ
And by the right of Mīkā'īl and his compassion;		
Wa bi-ḥaqqi Isrāfīl wa nafkhatih		وبِحَقِّ إسْرافِيل ونَفْخَتِهِ
And by the right of Isrāfīl and his blowing (of the Trumpet);		
Wa bi-ḥaqqi ʿAzrā'īl wa qabḍatih		وبِحَقِّ عَزْرائِيل وقَبْضَتِهِ
And by the right of ʿAzrā'īl and his seizing (of the soul in death);		
Wa bi-ḥaqqi Ādam wa ṣafwatih		وبِحَقِّ آدم وصَفْوَتِهِ
And by the right of Ādam and his purity;		
Wa bi-ḥaqqi Shuʿayb wa nubūwwatih		وبِحَقِّ شُعَيب ونُبُوَّتِهِ
And by the right of Shuʿayb and his prophethood;		
Wa bi-ḥaqqi Nūḥ wa safīnatih		وبِحَقِّ نُوح وسَفِينَتِهِ

<table>
<tr><td colspan="3">And by the right of Nūḥ and his vessel;</td></tr>
<tr><td>Wa bi-ḥaqqi Ibrāhīm wa khullatih</td><td></td><td>و بِحَقّ إبْراهِيم وخُلّتِهِ</td></tr>
<tr><td colspan="3">And by the right of Ibrāhīm and his Friendship (to God);</td></tr>
<tr><td>Wa bi-ḥaqqi Isḥāq wa dīyānatih</td><td></td><td>و بِحَقّ إسْحاق ودِيانَتِهِ</td></tr>
<tr><td colspan="3">And by the right of Isḥaq and his belief;</td></tr>
<tr><td>Wa bi-ḥaqqi Ismāʿīl wa fidyatih</td><td></td><td>و بِحَقّ إسْماعِيل وفِدْيَتِهِ</td></tr>
<tr><td colspan="3">And by the right of Ismāʿīl and his ransom;</td></tr>
<tr><td>Wa bi-ḥaqqi Yūsuf wa ghurbatih</td><td></td><td>و بِحَقّ يُوسُف وغُرْبَتِهِ</td></tr>
<tr><td colspan="3">And by the right of Yūsuf and his estrangement;</td></tr>
<tr><td>Wa bi-ḥaqqi Mūsā wa āyātih</td><td></td><td>و بِحَقّ مُوسى وآياتِهِ</td></tr>
<tr><td colspan="3">And by the right of Mūsa and his signs;</td></tr>
<tr><td>Wa bi-ḥaqqi Hārūn wa ḥurmatih</td><td></td><td>و بِحَقّ هارُون وحُرْمَتِهِ</td></tr>
<tr><td colspan="3">And by the right of Hārūn and his sanctity;</td></tr>
</table>

Wa bi-ḥaqqi Hūd wa haybatih	وبِحَقِّ هُودٍ وهَيْبَتِهِ
And by the right of Hūd and his majesty;	
Wa bi-ḥaqqi Ṣāliḥ wa nāqatih	وبِحَقِّ صالِحٍ وناقَتِهِ
And by the right of Ṣāliḥ and his she-camel;	
Wa bi-ḥaqqi Lūṭ wa jīratih	وبِحَقِّ لُوطٍ وجِيرَتِهِ
And by the right of Lūṭ and his guests;	
Wa bi-ḥaqqi Yūnus wa daʿwatih	وبِحَقِّ يُونُسَ ودَعْوَتِهِ
And by the right of Yūnus and his invocation;	
Wa bi-ḥaqqi Dānyāl wa karāmatih	وبِحَقِّ دَنْيالَ وكَرامَتِهِ
And by the right of Danyāl and his miracles;	
Wa bi-ḥaqqi Zakariyā wa ṭahāratih	وبِحَقِّ زَكَرِيا وطَهارَتِهِ
And by the right of Zakariyā and his purity;	
Wa bi-ḥaqqi ʿIsā wa sīyāḥatih	وبِحَقِّ عِيسى وسِياحَتِهِ
And by the right of ʿIsa and his wandering;	

Wa bi-ḥaqqi sayyidinā Muḥammadin ﷺ wa shafāʿatih		و بِحَقِّ سَيِّدِنا محمد ﷺ وشَفاعَتِهِ
And by the right of Our Master Muḥammad and his Intercession;		
An taghfir lanā wa li-wālidīynā wa li-ʿulamā'inā wa an tākhudha bi-yadī wa tʿutīyanī su'āli wa tubalighanī āmālī wa an taṣrifa ʿanī kulla man ʿaādānī bi-raḥmatika yā Arḥamu 'r-Rāhimīn, wa taḥfaẓnī min kulli sū'in, lā ilāha illa Anta, subḥānaka innī kuntu min aẓ-ẓālimīn.		ان تَغْفِرِ لنا ولِوالدِيْنا ولِعُلَمائِنا وان تَأْخُذَ بيَدِى وتُعْطِيني سُؤالي وتُبَلِّغَني آمالي وان تَصْرِفَ عَني كُلِّ مَن عاداني بِرَحْمَتِكَ يا أرْحَمَ الرّاحمين وتَحْفَظَني مِن كُلِّ سُوءٍ لا إله إلا أنتَ سُبْحانَك إني كُنْتُ مِن الظّالمين
That You forgive us, our parents and our scholars and that You take me by the hand and that You grant me my asking and that You cause me to reach my		

aspirations and that You fend off all those who seek to harm me, by Your mercy, O the Most Merciful of those who give mercy. And to protect me from every vice. There is no god except You, Glory be to You! Surely I have been one of the wrong-doers.

Yā Ḥayyu, yā Qayyūm. Lā ilāha illa Anta, yā Allāh, astāghfiruka wa atūbu ilayk. Fastajabnā lahu wa najaynāhu mina 'l-ghamm wa kadhālika nanjīa 'l-mu'minīn wa ḥasbuna-llāhu wa n'ima 'l-wakīl ḥasbī Allāhu lā ilāha illa hūwa 'alayhi tawakkaltu wa Hūwa rabbu 'l-'Arshi 'l-'Aẓīm wa lā ḥawlah wa lā quwwata illa billāhi 'l-'Aẓīm.	يا حيُّ يا قَيُّوم لا إله إلا أنتَ يا الله أَسْتَغْفِرُ كَ وأَتُوبُ إلَيْكَ فاسْتَجَبْنا له ونَجَّيْناهُ مِنَ الغَمّ وكَذَلِكَ نُنْجِي المؤْمِنِين. وحَسْبُنا اللهُ ونِعْمَ الوَكيل حَسْبي اللهُ لا إلَهَ إلا هُو عليْهِ تَوَكَّلْت وهُو رَبُّ العَرْشِ العَظِيم ولا حولَ ولا قُوَّةَ إلا بِالله العليّ العَظيم

O Living, O Eternal there is no god except You. O Allāh, I seek forgiveness in You and I turn to You, So

We listened to him: and We delivered him from distress: and thus do We deliver those who have faith. God is enough for us, the best Disposer of affairs; God sufficeth me: there is no god but He: On Him is my trust,- He the Lord of the Throne (of Glory) Supreme!" And there is no power and no strength save in God, the Most High, the Great.

| Wa ṣalla-Allāhu ʿalā sayyidinā Muḥammad wa ʿalā ālihi wa ṣāḥbihi wa sallim ajmāʿīn. Subḥānā rabbika rabbi 'l-ʿIzzati ʿamā yaṣifūn wa salāmun ʿalā 'l-mursalīn wa 'l-ḥamdulillāhi rabbi 'l-ʿālamīn. | و صَلَّى اللهُ على سَيِّدِنا محمد وعلى آلِهِ وصَحْبِهِ وسلّم أَجْمَعِين. سُبْحان رَبِّكَ رَبِّ العِزَّةِ عَمَّا يَصِفُون وسَلامٌ على المُرْسَلِين والحَمْدُ لله رَبّ العالمين. |

May God bless our master Muḥammad, His Family and Companions altogether. Glory to Allah, the Lord of the Throne: (High is He) above what they attribute to Him! And Peace on the Messengers and all Praise is due to the Lord of the worlds.

| Bismillāhi 'r-Raḥmāni 'r-Raḥīm. | بسم الله الرحمن الرحيم. |

Allāhumma innī as'aluka bi mushāhadati asrāri 'l-muḥibbīn wa bi 'l-khalwati 'llatī khaṣaṣta bihā sayyid al-mursalīn ḥīna asrayta bihi laylata 's-sābʿi wa 'l-ʿishrīn an tarḥam qalbī al-ḥazīn wa tujīb dʿawatī yā Akrama 'l-Akramīn yā Arḥama 'r-Rāḥimīn. Wa ṣalla-Allāhu ʿalā sayyidinā Muḥammadin wa ʿalā ālihi wa ṣāḥbihi wa sallim ajmāʿīn.	ثُمَّ نَقُولُ اللهُمَّ اِنِّي أَسْأَلُكَ بِمُشَاهَدَةِ أَسْرَارِ المُحِبِّين وبِالخَلْوَةِ التي خَصَصْتَ بها سَيِّد المُرْسَلِين حِين أَسْرَيْتَ بِهِ لَيْلَةَ السَّابِع والعِشْرِين ان تَرْحَم قَلْبِي الحَزِين وتُجِيب دَعْوَتي يا أَكْرَم الأَكْرَمِين يا أَرْحَمَ الرَّاحِمِين وصَلَّى الله على سَيِّدِنا محمد وآلِهِ وصَحْبِهِ أَجْمَعِين.

In the name of God, the Beneficent, the Merciful.

O God, surely I beseech You by the witnessing of the secrets of the Lovers and the seclusion which you hath specified with the Master of Messengers when You raised Him on the Night of the 27th. And to pity my sorrowful heart and to answer my plea, O Most Generous of those who show generosity, O Most

<table>
<tr><td colspan="3">Merciful of those who show mercy. May God bless our master Muḥammad, His Family and all his Companions and greet them with peace.</td></tr>
<tr><td>Bismillāhi 'r-Raḥmāni 'r-Raḥīm.
Lā illāha ill-Allāh Muḥammadu Rasūlullāh yā Raḥmān yā Raḥīm yā Musta'an yā Allāh yā Muḥammad ṣalla-Allāhu 'alayhi wa sallam. Yā Abā Bakr, yā 'Umar, yā 'Uthmān, yā 'Alī, yā Ḥasan, yā Ḥusayn, yā Yahyā; yā Ḥalīm, yā Allāh, wa lā ḥawlah wa lā quwwata illa billāhi 'l-'Aliyyi 'l-'Aẓīm.</td><td></td><td>بسم الله الرحمن الرحيم
لا إله إلا الله محمد رسول الله يا رَحْمن يا رَحِيم يا مُسْتَعان ياالله يا محمد صَلّى اللهُ عليْهِ وسَلّم، يا أبا بَكْر يا عُمَر يا عُثْمان يا عَلي يا حَسَن يا حُسَيْن يا يَحْيَ يا حَلِيم يا الله ولا حولَ ولا قوَّةَ إلا بِالله العليّ العَظِيم.</td></tr>
<tr><td colspan="3">In the name of God, the Beneficent, the Merciful.
There is no god except God, Muḥammad is the Messenger of God; O Merciful, O Beneficent One, O Musta'ān, O God; O Muḥammad peace and blessings be upon him. O Abū Bakr; O 'Umar; O 'Uthmān; O 'Alī; O Ḥasan; O Ḥusayn; O Yaḥyā; O Forbearing One,</td></tr>
</table>

O God. There is no power and no strength save in God, the Most High, the Great.		
Astaghfirullāh Dhā 'l-Jalāli wa 'l-Ikrām min jamī'i 'dh-dhunūb wa 'l-āthām. Āmīn.		أَسْتَغْفِرُ الله ذُو الجَلالِ والإكْرام مِن جَمِيعِ الذُّنُوبِ والآثام آمِين.
I seek forgiveness in God, the Possessor of Majesty and Honor, from every sin and transgression. Amen.		

Greeting Ramadan		إستقبال شهر رمضان
Aʿūdhu billāhi min ash-shayṭāni 'r-rajīm Bismillāhi 'r-Raḥmāni 'r-Raḥīm		أعوذ بالله من الشيطان الرجيم بسم الله الرحمن الرحيم
I seek refuge in God from the accursed Satan In the name of God, the Merciful, the Beneficent		
Marḥaban, āhlan wa sahlan yā shahra Ramaḍān		مرحَباً أهلاً وسَهلاً يا شَهَرَ رَمَضانْ
Greetings and welcome O month of Ramaḍān		
Marḥaban, āhlan wa sahlan yā shahra 'l-Qur'ān		مَرحَباً أهلاً وسَهلاً يا شَهَرَ القرآنْ
Greetings and welcome O month of the Qur'ān		
Marḥaban, āhlan wa sahlan yā shahra 'n-nūr		مَرحَبا أهلاً وسَهلاً يا شَهَرَ النور
Greetings and welcome O month of light		

Marḥaban, āhlan wa sahlan yā shahra 'l-ijtimā'a		مَرحَباً أهلاً وسَهلاً يا شَهَرَ الإجتماعْ
Greetings and welcome O month of gathering		
Marḥaban, āhlan wa sahlan yā shahra 'l-fuqarā'		مرحباً أهلاً وسَهلاً يا شَهَرَ الفُقَراءِ
Greetings and welcome O month of the destitute		
Marḥaban, āhlan wa sahlan yā shahra 't-tawbati wa 'r-rujū'		مرحباً أهلاً وسَهلاً يا شَهَرَ التَوبةِ والرُجوع
Greetings and welcome O month of repentance and return		
Marḥaban, āhlan wa sahlan yā shahra 'd-du'ā'i wa 'l-wuqūf		مَرحَباً أهلاً وسَهلاً يا شَهَرَ الدُعاء و الوقْوفْ
Greetings and welcome O month of invocation and standing in supplication		
Marḥaban, āhlan wa sahlan yā shahra 'l-fuqarā' wa 'ḍ-ḍu'afā		مرحباً أهلاً وسَهلاً يا شَهَرَ الفُقَراءِ والضُعفاءْ

Greetings and welcome O month of the poor and the weak		
Marḥaban, āhlan wa sahlan yā shahra 'l-iḥsān		مَرحَبا أهلاً وسَهلاً يا شَهَرَ الإحسانْ
Greetings and welcome O month of doing one's best		
Marḥaban, āhlan wa sahlan yā shahra 'l-ʿuṣāt		مَرحَباً أهلاً وسَهلاً يا شَهَرَ العُصاةْ
Greetings and welcome O month of the sinners		
Marḥaban, āhlan wa sahlan yā shahra 'l-fawzi wa 'l-falāḥ		مَرحَباً أهلاً وسَهلاً يا شَهَرَ الفوزِ الفَلاحْ
Greetings and welcome O month of victory and success		
Marḥaban, āhlan wa sahlan yā shahra 'l-munājāti wa 't-tasbīḥ		مَرحَباً أهلاً وسَهلاً يا شَهَرَ الْمُناجاة والتَسبيحْ
Greetings and welcome O month of intimate discourse and glorification		

Marḥaban, āhlan wa sahlan yā shahra 'd-dʿawati wa 'l-irshād		مرحباً أهلاً وسَهلاً يا شَهَرَ الدّعوةِ والإرشادْ
Greetings and welcome O month of the call and the guidance		
Marḥaban, āhlan wa sahlan yā shahra 't-tarāwīḥi wa 'l-qiyām		مَرحَباً أهلاً وسَهلاً يا شَهَرَ التَراويح والقيامْ
Greetings and welcome O month of tarāwīḥ prayers and night vigil		
Marḥaban, āhlan wa sahlan yā shahra 'l-maṣābīḥa wa 'l-qanādīl		مَرحَباً أهلاً وسَهلاً يا شَهَرَ المَصابيحِ والقَناديلْ
Greetings and welcome O month of lanterns and lights		
Marḥaban, āhlan wa sahlan yā shahra 'l-khazā'ini wa 'l-kunūz		مَرحَباً أهلاً وسَهلاً يا شَهَرَ الخَزائن والكُنوزِ
Greetings and welcome O month of coffers and treasures		

Marḥaban, āhlan wa sahlan yā shahra 'l-malā'ikati wa 's-salām		مَرحَباً أهلاً وسَهلاً يا شَهرَ المَلائكَةِ والسَّلامْ
Greetings and Welcome to You, O month of the angels and safety		
Marḥaban, āhlan wa sahlan yā shahra 'l-ifṭāri wa 's-suḥūr		مَرحَباً أهلاً وسَهلاً يا شَهرَ الإفطارِ والسُّحورْ
Greetings and welcome O month of fast-breaking and the pre-dawn meal		
Marḥaban, āhlan wa sahlan yā shahra 'l-muthīrati wa 'l-aṣabb		مَرحَباً أهلاً وسَهلاً يا شَهرَ المُثيرةِ والأصَبْ
Greetings and welcome O month of tilling and of deafness to sin		
Marḥaban, āhlan wa sahlan yā shahra 'ḍ-ḍu'afā		مَرحَباً أهلاً وسَهلاً يا شَهرَ الضُعفاءْ
Greetings and welcome O month of the weak		

Marḥaban, āhlan wa sahlan yā shahra 'l-ajri wa 'l-jazā		مَرحَباً أهلاً وسَهلاً يا شَهَرَ الأجرِ والجَزاءْ
Greetings and welcome O month of repayment and reward		
Marḥaban, āhlan wa sahlan yā shahra 'ṣ-ṣabri wa 'ṣ-ṣiyām		مَرحَباً أهلاً وسَهلاً يا شَهَرَ الصَبرِ والصِيامْ
Greetings and welcome O month of patience and the fast		
Marḥaban, āhlan wa sahlan yā shahra 's-saʿādah		مَرحَباً أهلاً وسَهلاً يا شَهَرَ اَلسعادَة
Greetings and welcome O month of felicity		
Marḥaban, āhlan wa sahlan yā shahra 'l-miftāḥ		مرحباً أهلاً وسَهلاً يا شَهَرَ المِفتاح
Greetings and welcome O month of the key		
Marḥaban, āhlan wa sahlan yā shahra 'l-waṣli wa 'l-wiṣāl		مرحباً أهلاً وسَهلاً يا شَهَرَ الوصلِ والوِصال

Greetings and welcome O month of union and reunion		
Marḥaban, āhlan wa sahlan yā shahra 'l-wadādi wa 'l-muḥabbah		مرحباً أهلاً وسَهلاً يا شَهَرَ الَوِداد والَمحبَة
Greetings and welcome O month of friendship and love		
Marḥaban, āhlan wa sahlan yā Sayyid ash-Shuhūr		مرحَباً أهلاً وسهلاً ياسَيِد الشُهور
Greetings and welcome O master of all months.		
Lam n'arif qadraka wa 'lam naḥfaẓ ḥurmataka, yā shahra 'l-ghufrān. Fa arḍa 'annā, wa lā tashkū minnā ila 'r-Raḥmān Wa kun shāhidan lanā bi-faḍli wa 'l-iḥsān.		لَم نَعرِف قَدرَك ولَم نَحفَظ حُرمتَك يا شَهَر الغُفران، فارضَ عنا، ولا تَشكو مِنّا إلى الرَحمن وكُن شاهِداً لَنا بالفَضلِ والإحسان
We have not treated you according to your immense price nor truly sanctified you, O month of forgiveness, but be pleased with us nevertheless and do not blame		

us before The Merciful, and testify for us with grace and goodness!

Ramadan Salatu-t-Tarawih		التَّرَاوِيح في رَمَضَان
2 OR 4 RAK'ATS SUNNAH		صَلَاةُ السُّنَة ٢ أو ٤ رَكَعَات
4 RAK'ATS FARḌ 'ISHĀ		صَلَاةُ العِشَاء
2 RAK'ATS SUNNAH		وَبَعدِهَا رَكَعتَين السُنَة البَعدِيَة

INTENTION Intend to fast the obligatory fast of the next day, then intend Ṣalāt at-Tarāwīḥ (20 rakʿats).		يَنوِي الصِيَام ثُمَ يَنوِي لِصَلَاةُ التَّرَاوِيح قَائِلا: نَويتُ ان أُصَلِي ٢٠ رَكَعَات صلَاةُ التَّرَاوِيح لله تَعالَى رَبُ العَالَمِين
After each four rakʿats sit and read 3 times Sūratu 'l-Ikhlāṣ (see page 385), followed by the following: Liqā'ullāh yurjā fī 'ṣ-ṣīyām wa nūru qalbī fī 'l-qīyām, taʿal-Allāh dhu 'l-ʿarshi 'l-majīd aṣ-Ṣalātu jāmiʿa Ṣalātu't-tarāwīḥ athābakum-ullāh. An-nabī yashfaʿu liman yuṣalli ʿalayh. Allāhumma ṣalli ʿalā Muḥammadin wa ʿalā		وَبَعد كُل ٤ رَكَعات اِقرَأ سُورَةُ الِاخلَاص ٣ مَرَات أو قل: لِقَاءُ الله يُرْجَى في الصِّيَام ونُورُ القَلْبِ في القِيام تَعالى الله ذُو العَرْشِ المَجِيد، الصلَاةُ الجامِعَة صلَاةُ التّراوِيح أثابَكُمُ الله، النبي

Muḥammadin wa sallam. Allāhumma innā nas'aluka 'l-jannata wa na'ūdhu bika mina 'n-nār.	يَشْفَعُ لِمَن يُصَلِّي عَلَيْه. اَللَّهُمَّ صَلِّ عَلَى سَيِّدِنا مُحَمَّدٍ وَعَلَى آلِ سَيِّدِنا مُحَمَّدٍ. اللهمَّ إِنَّا نَسْأَلُكَ الجَنَّة وَنَعُوذُ بِكَ مِنَ النَّار
ṢALĀTU 'T-TARĀWĪḤ. (20 RAK'ATS)	صَلَاةُ التَّرَاوِيح (٢٠ رَكَعات)
ṢALĀTU 'L-WITR (3 RAK'ATS)	صَلَاةُ الوِتر (٣ رَكَعات)
Then recite: 'alā Rasūlinā 'ṣ-ṣalawāt and recitations following Ṣalāt al-'Ishā.	عَلَى رَسُولِنَا الصَّلَوَات
ĀMAN AR-RASŪLU (see page 23) 2:285- 286	آمَنَ الرَّسُولُ
SŪRATU 'L-FĀTIHĀ	الفَاتِحَة

Practices on Ashura		ادَب اعَاشُورَاء
This *adab* is performed before the prayer of Maghrib on the evening before the 10th day of Muharram, known as ʿAshūrā.		قَبْل صلَاةُ المَغْرِب
NĪYYAT (INTENTION)		النِيَّة:
Nawaytu 'l-arbāʿīn, nawaytu 'l-ʿitikāf, nawaytu 'l-khalwa, nawaytu 'l-ʿuzla, nawaytu 'r-riyāḍa, nawaytu 's-sulūk, lillāhi taʿala fī hādhā 'l-masjid (or fī hādha al-jāmiʿ).		نَوَيْتُ الأَرْبَعين، نَوَيْتُ الإعْتِكاف، نَوَيْتُ الخَلْوَة، نَوَيْتُ العُزْلَة، نَوَيْتُ الرِّياضَة، نَوَيْتُ السُّلوك لله تَعالى في هَذَا المسجِد

I intend the forty (days of seclusion); I intend seclusion in the mosque; I intend seclusion; I intend isolation; I intend discipline (of the ego); I intend to travel in God's Path for the sake of God in this mosque.

ADAB AT-TARIQĀH		ادَب الطَرِيقَة
THE GRAND TRANSMITTED INVOCATION (AD-DU'AU 'L-MĀTHŪR) OF SULṬĀN AL-AWLĪYĀ (SEE PAGE 179)		الدّعاء المأثور لِسُلطَان الأولِيَاء
KHATMU 'L-KHWAJAGĀN (SEE PAGE 31)		ختم الخواجكان مع الذكر
MAWLID		مَولِد الشَّريفةِ
IHDĀ (SEE PAGE 28)		إهدَاء
DU'Ā AND AL-FĀTIḤAH (SEE PAGE 325).		دُعاء الفاتِحة
It is recommended to fast the day of 'Ashūrā as well as the day prior (9th) and to offer a sacrifice to Allah.		صيام نهار التاسع و اعَاشُورَاء اي التاسع و

		العشرة من محرم وتقديم ذبيحة (قربان) لله.

Notes to the Guidebook

Voluntary Worship

The shaykhs of the most distinguished Naqshbandi Way have ordered the seeker at the level of the People of Determination and the Prepared to adopt himself or herself to practices of the Prophet ﷺ in daily worship, in particular:

- observing all the *Sunan* prayers accompanying the obligatory ones (*farā'id*).
- observing the night vigil (*tahajjud*).
- additionally observing the following prayers:
    - **Ṣalātu 'l-Ishrāq** – shortly after sunrise.
    - **Ṣalātu 'd-Duḥā** – two sets of four rakʿat sets in the time between mid-morning and Ṣalāt aẓ-Ẓuhr.
    - **Ṣalātu 'l-Awwābīn** – three sets of two rakʿats after Ṣalāt al-Maghrib.

Special Practices

These notes address unusual or special practices. All the practices are based on the *Sunnah* of the Prophet ﷺ and explanations of their special benefits can be found in traditional references.

The following notes are meant to clarify some of the practices which occur in the preceding pages. The perfection of them has come to us from our Master Shaykh Muhammad Nazim al-Haqqani al-Naqshbandi (may God continually raise his station). If there is any imperfection in this text, however, it comes from us, and may God be Merciful with us and forgive us.

Note: The Shaykh uses the *miswāk* (natural toothstick) before every ritual action, and before every Qur'ān reading.

Sunan Prayers

Mawlana Shaykh Nazim does not neglect one *Sunnah* prayer, whether "emphasized" (*mu'akkadah*) or voluntary rakʿats (*nāfilah*) observed by the Prophet at one time or another.

Prayer	Preceding Sunnah	Preceding Nafl	Following Sunnah	Following Nafl
Maghrib	2 rakʿats	None	2 rakʿats	6 rakʿats (al-awwābīn)
ʿIshā	2 rakʿats	2 rakʿats	2 rakʿats 3 rakʿats (al-witr)	2 rakʿats
Fajr	2 rakʿats	None	None	None
Ẓuhr	2 rakʿats	2 rakʿats	2 rakʿats	2 rakʿats
ʿAṣr	2 rakʿats	2 rakʿats	None	None

Note: In the Hanafī school the two rakʿats *Sunnah* and two rakʿats of *Nāfilah* preceding Ṣalātu 'ẓ-Ẓuhr, al-ʿAṣr and al-ʿIshā are combined in four rakʿats, whereas in the Shafiʿi school they are separate.

Salatu-l-Maghrib

The two rakʿats *Sunnah* prayer before the obligatory (*farḍ*) prayer are a "non-emphasized *Sunnah*" (*sunnah ghayr mu'akkadah*). They were quickly prayed by the Sahaba ﷺ of the Prophet ﷺ after hearing the *adhān* of Ṣalāt al-Maghrib.

Salatu-l-Janazah

The funeral prayer for those absent persons who have died without anyone praying over them is a daily *farḍ kifāyah*, a practice which only one member of the community is obliged to perform. Like the two *Sunnah* rakʿats before Ṣalātu 'l-Maghrib, we know that the great shaykhs made this a daily practice. The prayer is performed standing, facing the *Qiblah*.

Salatu-l-Awwabin

The 2-2-2 rakʿat Ṣalātu 'l-Awwābīn refers to those who turn frequently in prayer to their Lord. They constitute six rakʿats of two rakʿats each with a *taslīm* (*as-salām ʿalaykum wa raḥmatullāh* to the right and left, at the end), between every two rakʿats.

Salatu-l-Witr

The *qunūt* prayer is inserted in the third rakʿat after reading al-Fātiḥa and a sūra from the Qur'ān (the Shaykh usually reads Sūratu 'l-Ikhlāṣ), and before the *rukʿū*, or bowing. According the the Hanafī school, after you have finished reading, raise your hands to your ears—as you would to begin the prayer—and say the *takbīr, Allāhu akbar* and continue with the *duʿā* (supplication) indicated in the text. After reciting the *duʿā*, go into *rukʿū*, then continue as in a normal prayer sequence. In the Shafiʿi school the supplication is made in the standing position after *rukʿū*.

Ṣalātu 'l-witr is prayed as three rakʿats in the Hanafi school but in the Shafiʿi it is broken into two rakʿats Ṣalātu 'sh-shafʿ and one rakʿat Ṣalātu 'l-witr.

Salatu-n-Najat

One should get up at least one hour before Fajr since it is at this time that the gate of the Mercy of God, Who is Powerful and Sublime, is opened and the time when the great shaykhs look at their murīds. One should get up and perform ablution and perform two rakʿats of *Taḥīyyatu 'l-wuḍu* and then stand up, facing the *Qiblah* and ask that God, Exalted and Glorious, to purify oneself from the anger of one's *nafs* and, with this intention, one should then recite *Yā Ḥalīm* 100 times, and then one should seek protection from one's external and internal enemies, and from both heavenly and earthly misfortune, reciting *Yā Ḥafīẓ* 100 times.

Whoever wishes to reach the station of the People of Determination must keep up these practices. Our shaykhs tell us about the importance of this time and its virtues, saying: "If a person gets up one hour before Fajr and does nothing, not even praying, not even making *tasbīḥ*, but gets up to drink something, such as coffee or tea, or eat a morsel of food, then he must also be raised with the vigilant people (*ahlu ʿs-sahar*)."

Ṣalātu ’n-Najāt, the Prayer of Salvation, is prayed according to the following steps:

In the first rak‘at read Sūratu ’l-Fātiḥah as usual.		الفاتحة الشريفة
This is followed by reading the Verse of the Throne (2:255) and (3:18-19), and (3:26-27).		
ĀYATU ’L-KURSĪ (THE VERSE OF THE THRONE) CHAPTER 2, VERSE 255		آيةُ الكُرْسي البقرة ٢:٢٥٥
Allāhū lā ilāha illa Hūwa ’l-Ḥayyu ’l-Qayyūm, lā tākhudhuhū ’s-sinatun wa lā nawm, lahū mā fī ’s-samāwāti wa mā fī ’l-arḍ. Man dhā-ladhī yashfa‘u ‘indahū illā bi idhnih		اللهُ لاَ إِلَـهَ إِلاَّ هُوَ الْحَيُّ الْقَيُّومُ لاَ تَأْخُذُهُ سِنَةٌ وَلاَ نَوْمٌ لَّهُ مَا فِي السَّمَاوَاتِ وَمَا فِي الأَرْضِ مَن ذَا الَّذِي يَشْفَعُ عِنْدَهُ إِلاَّ بِإِذْنِهِ

yaʿlamu mā bayna aydīhim wa mā khalfahum wa lā yuḥīṭunā bi-shay'in min ʿilmihi illā bimā shā'. Wasiʿa kursīyyuhu 's-samāwāti wa 'l-arḍa, wa lā ya'uduhū ḥifẓuhuma, wa Hūwa 'l-ʿAlīyyu 'l-ʿAẓīm.		يَعْلَمُ مَا بَيْنَ أَيْدِيهِمْ وَمَا خَلْفَهُمْ وَلاَ يُحِيطُونَ بِشَيْءٍ مِّنْ عِلْمِهِ إِلاَّ بِمَا شَاء وَسِعَ كُرْسِيُّهُ السَّمَاوَاتِ وَالأَرْضَ وَلاَ يَؤُودُهُ حِفْظُهُمَا وَهُوَ الْعَلِيُّ الْعَظِيمُ
Ṣadaq-Allāhu ʿl-ʿAẓīm.		صدق الله العَظِيمُ

God! There is no god but He - the Living, the Self-subsisting, Eternal. No slumber can seize Him nor sleep. His are all things in the heavens and on earth. Who is there can intercede in His presence except as He permitteth? He knoweth what (appeareth to His creatures as) before or after or behind them. Nor shall they compass aught of His knowledge except as He willeth. His Throne doth extend over the heavens and the earth, and He feeleth no fatigue in guarding and preserving them for He is the Most High, the Supreme (in glory).

God speaks the Truth.

<table>
<tr><td>CHAPTER 3, VERSE 18-19
Shahid-Allāhu annahū lā ilāha illa Hū. Wa 'l-malā'ikatu wa ūlu 'l-'ilmi qā'iman bi 'l-qisṭ. Lā ilāha illa Hū al-'Azīzu 'l-Ḥakīm. Inna 'd-dīna 'ind Allāhi 'l-islām.</td><td></td><td>سورة آل عمران ١٨- ١٩
شَهِدَ اللهُ أَنَّهُ لاَ إِلَـهَ إِلاَّ هُوَ وَالْمَلاَئِكَةُ وَأُوْلُواْ الْعِلْمِ قَآئِمَاً بِالْقِسْطِ لاَ إِلَـهَ إِلاَّ هُوَ الْعَزِيزُ الْحَكِيمُ إِنَّ الدِّينَ عِندَ اللهِّ الإِسْلاَمُ</td></tr>
<tr><td colspan="3">God bears witness that there is no god but He—and the angels and men of knowledge—upholding justice; there is no god but He, the Mighty, the Wise. The religion with God is Islam.</td></tr>
<tr><td>Chapter 3, Verse 26-27
Qul 'illāhumma Mālik al-mulki. Tu'tī 'l-mulka man tasha'u wa tanzi'u 'l-mulka mimman tashā'u wa tu'izzu</td><td></td><td>سورة آل عمران ٢٦-٢٧
قُلِ اللَّهُمَّ مَالِكَ الْمُلْكِ تُؤْتِي الْمُلْكَ مَن تَشَاء وَتَنزِعُ الْمُلْكَ مِمَّن تَشَاء وَتُعِزُّ</td></tr>
</table>

man tashā'u wa tudhillu man tashā'u, bi yadika 'l-khayr, innaka 'alā kulli shay'in qadīr. Tūliju 'l-layla fī 'n-nahāri wa tūliju nahāra fī 'l-layl, wa tukhriju 'l-ḥāyya mina 'l-mayyiti, wa tukhriju 'l-mayyita mina 'l-ḥāyy, wa tarzuqu man tashā'u bi ghayri ḥisāb.	مَن تَشَاء وَتُذِلُّ مَن تَشَاء بِيَدِكَ الْخَيْرُ إِنَّكَ عَلَىَ كُلِّ شَيْءٍ قَدِيرٌ تُولِجُ اللَّيْلَ فِي الْنَّهَارِ وَتُولِجُ النَّهَارَ فِي اللَّيْلِ وَتُخْرِجُ الْحَيَّ مِنَ الْمَيِّتِ وَتُخْرِجُ الَمَيَّتَ مِنَ الْحَيِّ وَتَرْزُقُ مَن تَشَاء بِغَيْرِ حِسَابٍ

Say: O God, Master of the Kingdom, Thou givest the Kingdom to whom Thou wilt, and seizest the Kingdom from whom Thou wilt, Thou exaltest whom Thou wilt, and Thou abasest whom Thou wilt; in Thy hand is all good; Verily Thou art over all things Powerful. Thou makest the night to enter into the day, and Thou makest the day to enter into the night, Thou bringest forth the living from the dead, and Thou bringest forth the dead from the living, and Thou providest for whomsoever Thou wilt without reckoning.

In the second rakʿat, read the Fātiḥah (see page 325).		تقرأ في الركعة الثانِيَة بعد الفاتحة الشريفة
SŪRATU 'L-IKHLĀṢ (11 TIMES) (SEE PAGE 385)		سورة الاخلاص (١١ مرات)
After completing the taslīm (final salām right and left), go into prostration with the intention of asking God to rid your heart of all envy.		بعد التسليم من الصلَاةُ تدعوا بهذا الدعاء:

DU'A

Yā Rabbī, kamā tākulu 'n-nāru 'l-ḥaṭaba hākadha yākulu 'amalīyy jamī'an al-ḥasadu mutā'ṣṣila fīyya. Yā Rabbī khalliṣnī minhu wa khalliṣnī mina 'l- ghaḍabi 'n-nafsānī wa min nafsi 'ṭ-ṭifli 'l- madhmūmati wa mina 'l-akhlāqi 'dh-dhamīma yā Rabbī wa baddil akhlāqī ila akhlāqin ḥamīdatin wa af'ālin ḥasana.

دعاء:

يا رَبِّي كَما تَأْكُلُ النَّارُ الحَطَبَ هَكَذا الحَسَدُ المُتَأَصِّلُ فِيَّ يَأْكُلُ جَمِيع أَعْمالي. يا رَبِّ خَلِّصْني مِنْهُ ومِنَ الغَضَبِ النَفْساني ومِن نَفْسِ الطِّفْلِ المَذْمُومةِ ومِنَ الأَخْلاقِ الذَّمِيمَة ويا رَبِّي بَدِّلْ أَخْلاقِي إلى أَخْلاقٍ حَمِيدَةٍ وأَفْعالٍ حَسَنة

O my Lord! Just as fire consumes firewood, in the same way the envy which is rooted in me consumes all my actions. Purify me, O my Lord, from it and purify me, too, from the anger of my ego. Rid me as well, O my Lord, of the blameworthy ego of the child

and reprehensible manners. And, O my Lord, change all my manners to laudable manners and into good actions.

Salatu-t-Tasabih

In the following prayers, to keep track of any given number of recitations, it is permitted to lightly press one finger of each hand in turn, in whatever position they are (i.e., crossed or hanging at the sides). However, the *an-Najāt* and *Tasbīḥ* prayers are for the People of Determination and the Prepared; these prayers are not for beginners.		
These are four rakʿats prayed with a taslīm between them. This prayer can be done in two ways, but we have included only the one the Shaykh uses (with the taslīm at the end of the fourth rakʿat). The tasbīḥ which is recited during this prayer is:		
Subḥānallāhi wa 'l-ḥamdulillāhi wa lā illāha ill-Allāh w'allāhu akbar.		سبحان الله والحمد لله ولا إله إلا الله والله أكبر
Glory be to God! Praise be to God! There is no god but God, and God is Greatest.		

At the end of every set of 10 or 15 tasbīḥs the Shaykh adds: wa lā ḥawla wa lā quwwata illa billāhi 'l-'Alīyyi 'l-'Āẓīm.		و لا حَوْلَ ولا قُوَّةَ إلا بِالله العَلِيّ العَظيم

There is no power and no strength save in God, the Most High, the Great.

The total number of tasbīḥs recited is 300, with 75 in each rak'at. Also, the tasbīḥs is added to the regular parts of the prayer. We have observed the Shaykh using the following method:

WHEN TASBIḤ IS RECITED	NUMBER OF TIMES
After reciting the Thanā', before Sūratu 'l-Fātiḥah	15
After reciting Sūratu 'l-Fātiḥah and two Sūratu 'l-Ikhlās.	10
In ruk'u, (bowing position)	10
In qiyām (standing position), after the ruk'u	10
In the first sajda (prostration)	10

In jalsa (sitting position), after the first sajda	10
In the second sajda	10
Sub-total for first rak'at	75
The second rak'at is performed as above (no tasbīḥs is recited in the final jalsa, only tashahhud)	75
The third rak'at is performed as above	75
The fourth rak'at is performed as above (no tasbīḥs are recited in the final jalsa, only tashahhud)	75

Salatu-l-Fajr

The congregational morning prayer is a major pillar of the daily devotions.

While reading Sūrat Yā Sīn Mawlana Shaykh Nazim pauses to recite the words *Ṣalla-Allāhu 'alayhi wa sallam,* as "Yā Sīn" is one the names of the Prophet ﷺ.

After reciting Verse 36:58, he says, *razaqanā Allāh* (God grant it to us!).

After reciting Verse 36:59, he says, *ā'adhanā Allāh* (God protect us!).

The pauses in the recitation of the 99 names of God are not fixed. The Shaykh frequently changes the places of these pauses in his recitations.

Salatu-l-Ishraq

One should try to stay awake until the actual rising of the sun and then perform the two *Sunnah* rakʿats of *Ishrāq* five to ten minutes after it has risen.

Salatu-d-Duha

Ṣalātu 'ḍ-Ḍuḥā consists of two sets of four rakʿat sets in the time between mid-morning and Ṣalātu 'ẓ-Ẓuhr.

Conduct of Pilgrimage - Hajj

Hajj Obligations as per the Four Schools			
ḤANAFĪ	SHAFIʿĪ	MĀLIKĪ	ḤANBALĪ
Iḥrām	Iḥrām	Iḥrām	Iḥrām
Spending a day at ʿArafah	Spending a day at ʿArafah.	Spending a day at ʿArafah.	Spending a day at ʿArafah.
Saʿī between Ṣafā and Marwah.	Saʿī between Ṣafā and Marwah.	Saʿī between Ṣafā and Marwah.	Saʿī between Ṣafā and Marwah.
Circumam-bulation. Ṭawāf al-Ifāḍah which is done at the Yawm an-Naḥr - the day of	Circumam-bulation. Ṭawāf al-Ifāḍah which involves seven rounds of the Kaʿbah.	Circumam-bulation. Ṭawāf al-Ifāḍah which involves seven rounds of the Kaʿbah.	Circumam-bulation. Ṭawāf al-Ifāḍah which involves seven rounds of the Kaʿbah.

sacrifice - on returning from Minā. (Iḥrām is a prerequisite for the validity of Ṭawāf.)			
	Clipping some of the pilgrim's hair or shaving it all.		
	Close sequence of most rites of Ḥajj, e.g. Iḥrām must proceed all other rites and standing at ʻArafah		

	must proceed Ṭawāf.		

Restrictions of Ihram
Sexual intercourse and all matters leading to it such as kissing, caresses or talking with one's spouse about intercourse or related sexual matters.
Violating the limits ordained by Allah and disobeying His orders.
Disputing, arguing or fighting with servants, companions or others.
Wearing any sewn clothes which fit the body
It is forbidden for the Muḥrim to wear clothes dyed with a scented material that lingers with him wherever he goes. He is forbidden from using perfume on body, clothes or hair.
Abū Ḥanīfa and ath-Thawrī held that a Muḥrim may contract a marriage but he is forbidden to consummate it.

There is a consensus among the scholars that, in the state of Iḥrām, the Muḥrim is forbidden to clip his nails without any genuine excuse.
It is forbidden for a Muḥrim to cover his head with any normal headcover.
There is consensus among the scholars that hunting is forbidden to the Muḥrim even if he does not actually slaughter the animal
Summarized Steps of Hajj
On the pre-noon of the eighth Dhul-Ḥijjah enter into Iḥrām from your place and perform ghusl (total washing) if it is possible and put on the Iḥrām cloths and repeat the Talbīyah
Set out and stay at Minā to pray Ẓuhr, ʿAṣr, Maghrib, ʿIsha and Fajr prayers. Every prayer comprising of four rakʿats is to be shortened to two rakʿats only.
At ʿArafah perform Ẓuhr and ʿAṣr obligatory prayers in combination for travelers; each prayer shortened to two rakʿats. Stay there until sunset and implore God frequently facing the Qiblah.

When the sun sets, march from ʿArafah to Muzdalifah. Once at Muzdalifah you should pray Maghrib, Isha and Fajr prayers. Stay there to implore God until sunrise. If you are weak and are not able to walk and mingle with the crowd, you may go to Minā at late night. However the 49 stones must be collected by you or someone on your behalf.

When the sun is about to rise, walk from Muzdalifah to Minā; when you arrive at Minā, do the following:

A:	Stone Jamarat al-ʿAqabah which is the Stoning Site located nearest to Makkah. You have to throw seven pebbles, one by one, pronouncing Takbīr (Allāhu Akbar!) at every throw and say:		
	raghman li 'sh-Shaytan riḍan li 'r-Raḥmān 3 times, bismillāh Allāhu akbar!		رَغماً لِلشيطَان رَضاً لِلرَحمَان ٣ مَرَات بِسمِ الله الله اكبَر.
	In opposition to Satan, seeking God's good pleasure and satisfaction; God is greater!		
B:	Slaughter a sacrificial animal, eat from its meat and distribute the rest to the poor. The		

	slaughtering of a sacrificial animal is obligatory on the one doing Ḥajj Tamattuʿ or Ḥajj Qirān (combined ʿUmrah and Ḥajj).
C:	Shave or shorten the hair of your head. Shaving is recommended (women should shorten their hair equal to a fingertip length). The order of the three above-mentioned acts is: first, throwing the pebbles, second, slaughtering the sacrificial animal and third to shave or shorten the hair of the head. There is no harm if the order is interchanged. After completion of the above mentioned three acts, you can put on your normal clothes and do all the acts prohibited during the Ḥajj with the exception of sexual intercourse.

Then go to Makkah with the intention to perform Ṭawāf al-Ifāḍah (Ṭawāf al-Ḥajj) and to perform Saʿī between Ṣafā and Marwah (Saʿī al-Ḥajj).
When you reach Makkah, do circumambulation (Ṭawāf) of the Kaʿbah seven times starting from the corner of Ḥajaru 'l-Aswad (the Black Stone) and finishing by it. One then prays two rakʿats behind Maqām Ibrahīm, if possible.

After the performance of two rakʿats, go to the hillock of Ṣafā to perform Saʿī seven times commencing from Ṣafā and ending at Marwah.
After completion of Ṭawāf and Saʿī, go back to Minā in order to spend the two nights of 11th and 12th of Dhul-Ḥijjah. By completion of Ṭawāf al-Ifāḍah, every act prohibited for the pilgrim during the Ḥajj time now becomes lawful including sexual intercourse.
On the days of 11th and 12th of Dhul-Ḥijjah, after the sun declines, throw the pebbles at the three Stoning Sites (Jamarahs). Start with the furthest from Makkah and then the middle one and finally Jamarat al-ʿAqabah. Throw seven pebbles at each Stoning Site and pronounce the Takbīr every time a stone is thrown. After throwing at the first and the middle Stoning Site, implore God facing the Qiblah; it is a must that throwing of the stones in these two days (i.e. 11th and 12th) be after zawāl (noon).
When you complete throwing the pebbles on the 12th of Dhul-Ḥijjah, you may go out of Minā before sunset. If you want to delay going out it is better to spend the night of the 13th of Dhul-Ḥijjah at Minā and repeat

throwing pebbles at the three Stoning Sites after the sun reaches its noon peak (zawāl) as before.
If you want to go back home, you have to perform a Farewell Circumambulation (Ṭawāf al-Wida‘) (seven turns around the Ka‘bah). There is no Ṭawāf al-Wida‘ enjoined on a woman in the post-partum state or one in her menses.
Summarized Steps of Umrah
‘Umrah technically means paying a visit to Ka'bah, performing circumambulation (Ṭawāf) around it, walking between Ṣafā and Marwah seven times (Sā‘ī). A performer of ‘Umrah puts off his Iḥrām by having his hair shaved or cut. If you want to perform ‘Umrah, make the intention (niyyah) for ‘Umrah, first perform ghusl (shower). Next put on the Iḥrām clothes. Pray two rakats Sunnatu 'l-Iḥrām. Then pronounce the Talbīyah.
When you reach Makkah, do circumambulation (Ṭawāf) of the Ka‘bah seven times for ‘Umrah starting from the corner of Ḥajaru 'l-Aswad (the Black Stone) and finishing by it. One then prays two rak‘ats behind Maqām Ibrahīm, if possible.

After the performance of two rakʿats, go to the hillock of Ṣafā to perform Saʿī seven times commencing from Ṣafā and ending at Marwah.
After completion of Saʿī you may shorten your hair. By this, your ʿUmrah is complete and you may disengage from Iḥrām clothes and put on normal clothes.
Detailed Steps of Hajj and Umrah
Here we present details of some but not all aspects of the rites of Ḥajj and ʿUmrah for which the shaykhs of the Naqshbandi Way have given particular recitations and or methodologies, to be observed in addition to all the normal steps performed by the pilgrim in following his or her particular madhhab and the guide assigned to his or her group.

PREPARATION FOR ḤAJJ

Imam Nawawī said according to the consensus of scholars it is from the adab of Ḥajj, that the essential intention of Ḥajj is to repent. Such repentance has the following conditions:
1. to leave all manner of sins;
2. to never return to these sins;
3. to regret the sins you have committed;
4. to ask forgiveness of anyone you have harmed, upset or made angry. If you owe someone money but you are unable pay them back at the time, you should inform them of your intention to make Ḥajj and give them a faithful promise to repay them in the future.
5. to write a will, since one does not knows if he will return from Ḥajj alive;
6. to use only money from licit means (ḥalāl) to go for Ḥajj, as God said:

The pilgrim visits his family, neighbors and friends, informs them he is leaving and asks them to pray for him.
One states the intention to go for Ḥajj before the 8th of Dhul-Ḥijjah, or before arriving at the location (al-mīqāt) for dressing in the Iḥrām, whichever comes first. Intention should normally be made before starting one's trip, or at least one hour by plane from arrival at Jeddah. If coming by land from outside the Ḥijāz, it is recommended to make intention before setting out.
Before you enter into travel, take a shower and pray two rak'ats niyyatu 'l-Ḥajj,
If more than two are travelling together should choose one among them as a leader.
Make intention to undertake a great deal of supplication (du'a) and to give generously in the way of God for the poor.

Ihram
Types of Iḥrām For men, Iḥrām consists of two pieces of white, unsewn and plain cloth; for women no special form of dress is required.
There are three types of Iḥrām:
1. Ifrād (single) One intends only the Ḥajj and maintains Iḥrām up to the Day of Sacrifice. No offering is required from the mufrid.
2. Qirān (combined) One intends the Ḥajj and ʿUmrah combined. ʿUmrah is done and Ḥajj is followed immediately in the same Iḥrām. Only after pelting the Jamrah of al-ʿAqabah, and shaving the hair for men or trimming the hair (men and women) can the pilgrim take off Iḥrām. The condition is to slaughter an animal, or if one is unable, to fast three days during Ḥajj and seven upon returning home.
3. Tamattuʿ (interrupted)

One intends 'Umrah and Ḥajj separately. One performs 'Umrah in Iḥrām, then return to a normal state and dress and remains like that until the Yawm al-tarwīyya, which is the 8th of Dhul-Ḥijjah, when he again dresses in Iḥrām from the mīqāt with the intention of Ḥajj and performs the Ḥajj. After fulfilling the Ḥajj rituals, one should offer a sacrificial animal.

INTENTION

Correct intention is crucial when putting on Iḥrām for Ḥajj or 'Umrah. The intention is made based on the type of Ḥajj/'Umrah being performed.

1. Ḥajj Ifrād One intends: Allāhuma innī nawaytu al-Ḥajja, fa-yassirhu lī wa taqabalhu minnī.		نِيَّةُ الحَجِّ: اَللّهُمَّ إِنِّي نَوَيْتُ الحَجَّ فَيَسِّرْهُ لِي وتَقَبَّلْهُ مِنِّي

O God I intend to make the pilgrimage so make it easy for me and accept it from me.

2. 'Umrah		نِيَّةُ العُمْرَةِ:

<table>
<tr><td>For ʿUmrah alone one intends:
Allāhuma innī nawaytu al-ʿUmrata, fa-yassirhā lī wa taqabalhā minnī.</td><td></td><td>اللهمّ إنّي نَوَيْتُ العُمْرَةَ
فَيَسّرْهَا لِي وتَقَبَّلْها مِنّي</td></tr>
<tr><td colspan="3">O God I intend to make the lesser pilgrimage so make it easy for me and accept it from me.</td></tr>
<tr><td>3. Qirān
For Ḥajj and ʿUmrah combined one intends:
Allāhuma innī nawaytu al-ʿumrata wal-Ḥajja, fa-yassirhumā lī wa taqabalhumā minnī.</td><td></td><td>نِيّةَ الحَج وَالعُمرَة:
اللهمَ إنّي نَوَيْتُ الحَجَّ
والعُمْرَةَ فَيَسّرْهُمَا لِي
وتَقَبَّلْهما مِنِي</td></tr>
<tr><td colspan="3">O God I intend to make both the lesser pilgrimage and the greater pilgrimage so make them both easy for me and accept them both from me.</td></tr>
<tr><td>One then says:
Nawaytu ’l-arbāʿīn, nawaytu ’l-ʿitikāf, nawaytu ’l-khalwah,</td><td></td><td>نَويتُ الأَرْبَعِين، نَويتُ
الإعْتِكاف نَويتُ الخَلْوَة</td></tr>
</table>

<table>
<tr><td>nawaytu 'l-ʿuzlah, nawaytu 'r-riyāḍa, nawaytu 's-sulūk, lillāhi taʿalā al-ʿAẓīm.</td><td></td><td>نَوَيْتُ العُزْلَة، نَويتُ الرِّيَاضَة نَويتُ السُّلوك، لله تعالى</td></tr>
<tr><td colspan="3">For the sake of blessing (barakah) I intend the forty (days of seclusion); I intend isolation; I intend discipline (of the ego); I intend to travel in God's Path; for the sake of God, the Exalted.
I am intending to perform Ḥajj on behalf of myself and my family and on behalf of the entire Nation of the Prophet ﷺ. If God with His Favor, honors me by accepting my Ḥajj, I gift the rewards of this worship (faḍīlat), to the Prophet ﷺ, to all 124,000 prophets and messengers, to the Sahabah, to the saints, to Imam Mahdi and to my Shaykh. I am sharing all the rewards that He is granting me in His Mercy with the entire Nation of the Prophet ﷺ, without leaving one person behind.</td></tr>
</table>

TALBĪYAH Recite three times: Labaik allāhumma labaik, labaika lā sharīka laka labaik. Then: Inna al-ḥamda w'an-ni'mata laka wal-mulk, lā sharīka laka labaik.	التَلبِيَة لَبَّيْكَ اللهمّ لَبَّيْك لَبَّيْك لَا شَرِيكَ لَكَ لَبَّيْك، إنَّ الحَمْدَ والنِّعْمَةَ لَكَ والمُلْك لَا شَرِيكَ لَكَ

At Your service O my God, at your service. At Your service, there is no partner to You, at Your service. Verily all praise, and all bounty belongs to You, as does the Kingdom. There is no partner to You, at Your service.

Then sit and recite the Naqshbandi Adab up to the first Ihdā. (see page 17)

ABANDONING ANGER AND SMOKING

Then from that time onwards, do not speak unnecessarily. Two things must be avoided at all costs

during Ḥajj: anger and smoking. Anger must be abandoned completely. Know that that there will be a lot of testing to see if you have truly eliminated anger. Know that God, His Angels, the Prophet ﷺ and the inheritors of the Prophet ﷺ the awliya and the Abdāl are observing you. Even on the last moment of your pilgrimage, you might face a disliked situation that incites your anger, so you must be careful. If your anger emerges; if you complain or fight, your Ḥajj will be brought to nought, so beware of anger.
Anger in Ḥajj is utterly unacceptable. If you sense that you are likely to get angry, do not go for Ḥajj, but rather work to eliminate this bad characteristic from yourself.
Avoid smoking.

CONDUCT OF TRAVEL As soon as you enter the vehicle of travel recite: 100x Bismillāhi 'r-Raḥmāni 'r-Raḥīm. Dhālika taqdīru 'l-'Azīzi 'l-'Alīm (36:38)		ادب السفر (١٠٠ مرة) بِسْمِ اللهِ الرَّحْمٰنِ الرَّحِيمِ. ذَٰلِكَ تَقْدِيرُ الْعَزِيزِ الْعَلِيمِ
In the name of God the Beneficent, the Merciful. That is the decree of (Him), the Exalted in Might, the All-Knowing.		

From that time on, occupy the time on your journey with whatever comes to your heart of dhikr, praise of the Prophet ﷺ, reading Quran, reading Dalā'il al-Khayrāt or making any kind of glorification (tasbīḥ) until you reach your destination.

When one approaches Madīnah (if flying, this is about an hour and a half before arriving at Jeddah), you pay respect towards the Prophet ﷺ by praising and seeking his intercession to accept you to be from his Ummah, and to facilitate your Ḥajj and your

Visitation (ziyārah) to him. Then call upon the Men of God (rijālullāh) of Makkah and Madīnah to support you in that intention.
Praise the Prophet ﷺ excessively one hour before landing, five hundred or one thousand times continuously until you reach your first entry point or destination in Ḥijāz.
When you reach the entry point (the airport at Jeddah or the border, if coming by land), you will go through some formalities after which your guide will take you to either Makkah or Madīnah depending on your date of arrival.
CONDUCT OF ARRIVAL IN MAKKAH
When you arrive in Makkah, proceed directly to the accommodations assigned to you, whether it be a hotel room, a room in a house or any other form of lodging. Do not fight with other members of your Ḥajj group by demanding special treatment or accommodations, but rather go directly to whatever

accommodations have been assigned to you or is available.		
If you are tired rest. Then shower (ghusl), pray two rakʿats, then proceed to Masjid al-Ḥarām for making ʿUmrah, if you are doing Ḥajj tamattuʿ. Intend to make your ʿUmrah immediately after you enter Masjid al-Ḥarām.		
Before entering the Sanctuary (ḥaram), recite a greeting for the Kaʿbah:		
GREETING KAʿBAH		تَحِيةَ الكَعبَة
Allāhumma anta ʿs-Salām wa minka ʿs-salām wa ilayka yāʿūdu ʾs-salām, fa ḥayyinā Rabbanā bi ʾs-salām, wa adkhilnā ʾl-Jannata bi luṭfika wa karamika wa jūdika dāraka, dār as-salām. Tabārakta Rabbanā wa tāʿalayta, yā Dhā ʾl-Jalāli		اللهمّ أَنّتَ السَّلَام ومِنْكَ السَّلام وإلَيْكَ يَعُودُ السَّلام فَحَيّنا رَبّنا بِالسّلَام وادْخُلْنَا الجَنَّةَ بِلُطْفِكَ وكَرَمِكَ وجُودِكَ دارَكَ دار السّلام. تَبارَكْتَ رَبّنا

<table>
<tr>
<td>wa 'l-Jamāli wal-Baqā'i wa 'l-ʿAẓamati wa 'l-Ikrām. Kulluna laka ʿabdun. Wa aḥaqqu mā yaqūl al-ʿabd Allāhumma lā māniʿa limā āaʿṭayta, wa lā muʿṭiya limā manʿata wa lā rādda limā qaḍayta, wa lā yanfaʿu Dhā 'l-jaddi minka al-jaddu. Rabbī lā ḥawla wa lā quwwata illa billāhi 'l-ʿAlīyyi 'l-ʿAẓīm.</td>
<td></td>
<td>وتَعالَيْتَ يَا ذَا الجَلالِ والجَمالِ والبَقاءِ والعَظَمَةِ الإكْرام. كُلَّنا لَكَ عَبْد وأَحَقّ ما يَقُولُ العَبْدُ اللَّهُمَّ لَا مانِعَ لِمَا أَعْطَيْتَ ولَا مُعْطِي لِمَا مَنَعْتَ ولَا رادَّ لما قَضَيْتَ ولَا يَنْفَعُ ذا الجِدِّ مِنْكَ الجَدُّ رَبِّي لَا حَوْلَ ولَا قُوَّةَ إِلا بِالله العَلِيّ العَظِيم.</td>
</tr>
<tr>
<td colspan="3">O God! You are Peace and from You comes Peace. Blessed and lofty are You, O Lord of Majesty and Bounty. There is no god but God, He is One, no partner has He. His is the Kingdom and His is all praise, and He is over all things Powerful. We have heard and obeyed. Your forgiveness, O our Lord! And to Thee is the end of all journeys. All of us are servants to You, and the most true of what a servant may say</td>
</tr>
</table>

is: O God! No one can disallow the one to whom You are giving, and there is no giver, to the one whom You have denied. And there is no refusing Your decree. Riches and good fortune will not profit the possessor thereof with You (for nothing will profit him but acting in obedience to You). My Lord, and there is no power and no strength save in God, the Most High, the Great.
That is greeting for Makkah and the Kaʿbah. You ask the spiritual servants of God, His angels and the inheritors of the Prophet ﷺ to direct you as you perform your Ḥajj/ ʿUmrah. When you enter, it is recommended to enter from the Bābu 's-salām – the Gate of Peace. Bābu 's-salām is below where adhān is called, as you enter the Ḥaram, there is a line of sight direct to the Kaʿbah where you recite greetings to the Kaʿbah, raising your two hands towards the Ḥajaru 'l-Aswad or if it is possible to approach it without scuffling, one should do so and kiss it, otherwise raise both hands towards it and say:

Face the Ḥajaru 'l-Aswad and say: Bismillāh Allāhu Akbar (3 times) As-salāmu ʿalayki yā Kaʿbatallāh		بسم الله الله اكبر (٣ مرات) السلام عليك يا كعبة الله
Peace be upon you, O Kaʿbah of God.		
As-salāmu ʿalayka yā Baytallāh		السّلَام عَلَيْكَ يا بَيْتَ الله
Peace be upon you, O House of God.		
If God wants, you will hear the Kaʿbah return the greeting to you, as many saints hear. If you have not yet reached that level, the Kaʿbah will return your greeting but you will not hear anything.		
Tawaf al-Qudum		
Before ʿUmrah or Ḥajj, the Ṭawāf al-qudūm is required (wājib). First make intention, depending on whether doing Ḥajj or ʿUmrah:		

Intention (Ḥajj) Nawaytu Ṭawāf al qudūm.		نَوَيْتُ طَوَافَ القُدُوم
I intend the preliminary circumambulation.		

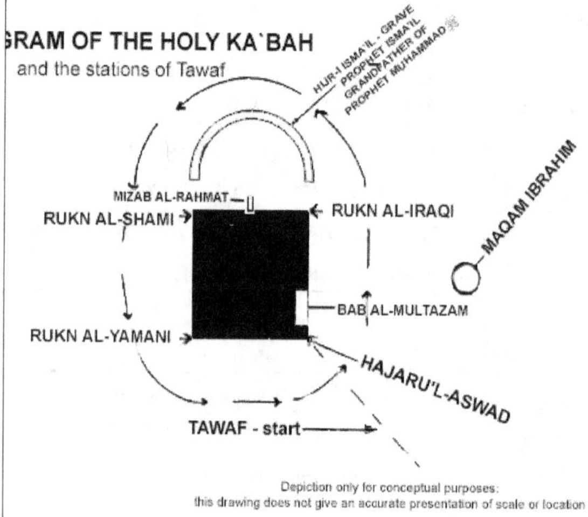

Intention (ʿUmrah) Nawaytu Ṭawāf al ʿumrāh.		نَوَيْتُ طَوافَ العُمْرَة
I intend the circumambulation of the lesser pilgrimage.		
Raise hands towards the Black Stone and say: Bismillāh, Allāhu Akbar three times.		بسم الله أكْبَر (٣ مرات)
During circumambulation talbīyah is not done, until after complete sāʿī.		
When in front of the door of the Kaʿbah say: Allāhumma inna ʾl-bayta baytuk, wa ʾl-ḥaramu ḥaramuk, wa ʾl-amnu amnuk wa hadhā maqāmu ʾl-ʾāʿidhi bika mina ʾn-nār.		امام باب الكعبة: اللهُمّ إنّ البَيْتَ بَيْتُكَ والحَرَمُ حَرَمُكَ والأَمْنُ أَمْنُك وهذا مقامُ العائِذِ بِكَ مِنَ النّار
O God, this house is Thy house, this sacred territory is Thy sacred territory, this security is Thy security, and		

this is the place for one who seeks protection with Thee against the hell fire.		
(ii) At the corner of the second wall by the opening of the ḥijr (semi-circular wall): Allāhumma innī ʿaūdhu bika mina 'sh-shakki wa 'sh-shirki wa 'sh-shiqāqi wa 'n-nifāqi wa sū 'il-akhlāqi wa sū 'il-munqalabi fī 'l-āhli wa 'l-māli wa 'l-walad.		(ب) أمام باقي الجدار من باب الكعبة: اللهُمّ أعُوذُ بِكَ مِنَ الشَّكِ والشّرْكِ والشّقاقِ والنّفاقِ وسُوءِ الأَخْلاقِ وسُوءِ المُنْقَلَّبِ في الأَهْلِ والمالِ والوَلَد.
O God I take refuge in You from doubt, from ascribing partners to You, from discord, hypocrisy, evil traits, and bad turns of fortune in family, property and children.		
(iii) While passing the second wall, in front of the drainspout of Mercy (mīzāb ar-raḥmah):		(ج) عند الجدار الثاني:

Allāhumma aẓillanī fī ẓillika yauma lā ẓilla illā ẓillu ʿarshik. W'asqinī bi-kā'si sayyidinā Muḥammadin sallallāhu ʿalayhi wa sallam, sharbatan hanī'atan ma-rī'atan lā aẓmā'u bʿadahā abadan yā Dhā 'l-Jalāli wa 'l-Ikrām.		اللّهُمّ أظِلَّني في ظِلّكَ يَوْمَ لا ظِلَّ إلا ظِلُّ عَرْشِكَ واسْقِني بِكَأْسِ سَيّدِنا محمد صلى الله عليه وسلَم شَرْبَة هَنِيئَة مَرِيئَة لا أظْمَأُ بَعْدَها أبَداً، يا ذا الجَلالِ والإكْرام.
O God, put me under Thy shadow on the day when there will be no shadow except the shadow of Thy Throne and give me to drink from the cup of our master Muhammad a delicious and sating drink after which I shall never get thirsty, O Thou full of Majesty and Bounty.		
(iv) When crossing the third wall between the third corner and the Yamānī corner (and according to whether it is		(د) عند الجدار الثالث حسب الحج او العمرة:

during the Ḥajj or the 'Umrah): Allāhum 'aj'alhu Ḥajjan mabrūrā/ (aj'alhā 'umratam-mabrūra) wa dhanban maghfūran wa sā'īyan mashkūrān wa tijāratan lan tabūra yā 'Azīzu yā Ghafūr.		اللّهُمَّ اجْعَلْهُ حَجّاً مَبْرُوراً (أو عُمْرَة مَبْرُورة) وذَنْباً مَغْفُوراً وسَعْياً مَشْكُوراً وتِجارَة لنْ تَبُورَ يا عَزِيزُ يا غَفُور

O God, make that this be a Ḥajj/'Umrah which is accepted, with (my) sin which is pardoned, an accepted work, a commerce which is not lost, O Thou the Powerful, the Forgiving.
When one reaches the Yamānī corner do not kiss it, but touch it if possible and then kiss one's hand.

(v) While crossing the fourth wall: Rabbanā ātinā fī 'd-dunyā ḥasanatan wa fī 'l-ākhirati ḥasanatan wa qinā 'adhāb an-nār.		(هـ) عند الجدار الرابع: رَبّنا آتِنا في الدُّنْيا حَسَنَة وفي الآخِرَةِ حَسَنَة وقِنا عَذابَ النَّار.

O our Lord, give us good in this world and good in the Hereafter, and protect us from the punishment of the hell fire.

Once one reaches the Black Stone a single round (ṭawāf) has been completed. It is Sunnah for men to trot in the first three rounds and to bare their right shoulders, except in the Farewell Ṭawāf. However if this means leaving any women without menfolk to accompany, this should not be done, or some men should remain with the women.

After completing the circumambulation until you finish seven turns (ṭawāf), reciting what you are able of the above invocations then you go to Bāb al-Multazam and make du'a there. If it is difficult due to crowds, do not fight, but step back and go to Maqām Ibrāhīm and from far away make the invocation. Then pray two raka'at at Maqām Ibrāhīm. It is often not possible for ladies to pray there, so they should pray two raka'ats in the ladies section.

Sai		
Then you go to do Sa'ī. At this portion of 'Umrah/Ḥajj one should keep in mind the struggle of Lady Hajar, searching desperately for water for her baby, the Prophet Isma'īl .		
CONDUCT OF SA'Ī		ادب السعي
Begin saying: Bismillāhi 'r-Raḥmāni 'r-Raḥīm In the name of God the Beneficent, the Merciful.		بِسْمِ اللهِ الرَّحْمنِ الرَّحيمِ
Then invoke God (du'a): Ya Rabbī, Ya Allāh, I am making Sa'ī I am seeking the means of support through the Prophet ﷺ and the inheritors of his spiritual states, the saints. O God, if You favor me by accepting my 'Umrah/Ḥajj, all the rewards that I receive I will share with all your servants on this earth.		

After completing Sa'ī, present your 'Umrah, or Ḥajj to the Presence of the Prophet ﷺ, by saying, "Ya Rasulullāh, I performed that 'Umrah/Ḥajj by trying to follow your footsteps, I am requesting that it be accepted and be changed from imitational to real worship and that you O Prophet of God, present it to the Presence of God."

You then ask from God whatever you want for this life and the hereafter.

You return to your lodging if you are making 'Umrah. In the case of Ḥajj at-Tamattu', after completing the 'Umrah, the pilgrim trims his or her hair, showers, and changes into everyday clothes.

These steps complete the 'Umrah portion of the Ḥajj at-Tamattu'. All restrictions of the Iḥrām are temporarily lifted. The pilgrim waits until the 8th of Dhul-Ḥijjah to start the rites of Ḥajj and return to Iḥrām.

INTENTION AND IḤRĀM FOR ḤAJJ TAMATTU'

If doing Ḥajj at-Tamattu', on the 8th of Dhul-Ḥijjah, the pilgrim pronounces a new intention (nīyyah) at the place to perform Ḥajj. There is no need to go to the mīqāt for this. The pilgrim changes into Iḥrām in the prescribed manner and proceeds to Minā soon after the Fajr Prayers.

Then perform the rites of Ḥajj, by going to 'Arafah, Minā and Muzdalifa and Minā and observing all the details following one's Ḥajj guide.

Standing at Arafah

> *It is no crime in you if ye seek of the bounty of your Lord (during pilgrimage). Then when ye pour down from (Mount) Arafah, celebrate the praises of God at the Sacred Monument, and celebrate His praises as He has directed you, even though, before this, ye went astray.* (2:198).

There is consensus among Muslim scholars that spending the Day of ʿArafah is the most important part of Ḥajj.
Standing as much as possible is very much recommended, especially around the plains of Jabal ar-Raḥmah (Mount of Mercy) where the Prophet ﷺ delivered his last sermon.
On that day the pilgrims should spend most of their time reading the Qur'an, making remembrance of God (dhikr), supplication (duʿa), praising the Prophet (ṣalawāt) ﷺ, and most importantly asking Allah for forgiveness.

Stoning the Jamarat

One pelts the Stoning Sites on the four days of Eid. On the first day you throw seven stones at the Jamarat al-ʿAqabah only. On the remaining three days you must throw 21 stones altogether each day, seven at each Jamarah, one-by-one pronouncing the formula below. Some people take the stones and throw them altogether - this is not accepted. Similarly, it is

unacceptable to use your slippers or other objects to stone the sites. Ladies can appoint someone to throw stones for them if the Stoning Sites are very crowded.		
CONDUCT OF STONING Take one pebble at a time and with each one say: Raghman li 'sh-shaiṭān, riḍan li 'r-Rahman, 3 times, Bismillāh, Allāhu Akbar. And then throw it at the Jamarah.		ادب الرجم رَغْماً لِلشَّيْطان رِضاً لِلرَّحمن (٣) مراتٍ بسم الله الله اكبر.
In opposition to Satan, seeking God's good pleasure and satisfaction; In opposition to Satan, seeking God's good pleasure and satisfaction; God is greater!		
Stay at Mina		
During one's stay at Minā, the pilgrim should engage in much remembrance (dhikr, tasbiīḥ), praise of the		

Prophet ﷺ (ṣalawāt), recitation of Qur'an, invocation (duʿa) and supererogatory prayers.

ṬAWĀF AL-WADAʿ

This is the Ṭawāf of farewell, which is unrelated to either the ʿUmrah or Ḥajj. One makes this before leaving with the intention not to return.

This concludes the essential conduct of Ḥajj. Keep in mind this contains only a summarized version of the Ḥajj rites. The main intent here is to present the spiritual aspects of the intention and recitations at various point in the pilgrimage. However, to observe the Ḥajj correctly it is essential to follow the instructions and details that your Ḥajj guide directs you to do.

Zamzam

It is recommended to do much of drinking the water of the well of Zamzam for whatever intention one wishes, religious or other-worldly, and it is Sunnah to face the Kaʿbah standing while drinking, to breathe three times and say, "Bismillāh" each time one drinks and "alḥamdulillāh," drinking one's fill of it. People often take bottles of Zamzam water home from pilgrimage to share as a blessing (barakah) with family and friends. The same adab is observed when drinking it.

It is recommended to look at the Ka'bah, for it is the locus of the Divine Gaze, and it is said that God sends down one hundred and twenty mercies day and night upon the House of God: sixty for those circumambulating; forty for those praying there and twenty for those looking at it.

DAILY ṬAWĀF

When you enter the Sacred Mosque, it is preferred to make a Ṭawāf as it is the greeting for the Ka'bah (Taḥīyyatul Ka'bah). Use the same steps mentioned above, leaving out the wording "al-qudūm" from the intention. If it is not possible to do the Ṭawāf, pray first, and when it is less crowded make Ṭawāf if you are able.

When you leave the Sacred Mosque, it is not necessary to make Ṭawāf.

SHOPPING AND DAILY ACTIVITY

During pilgrimage it is permitted to shop, but one should not spend excessive time doing so. Similarly, excessive time should not be spent in restaurants and coffee shops. Rather, keep oneself busy in praying, remembrance (dhikr) and praise of the Prophet (ṣalawāt) ﷺ.

Holy Places of Visitation in Makkah

JANNAT AL-MU'ALLA

Also known as al-Ḥājūn, this is a general cemetery in existence from before the time of the Prophet ﷺ and in which his first wife, the Mother of the Believers (Umm al-mu'minīn) Sayyida Khadījat al-Kubrā ﵂ is buried. Buried there too are many member of the Family of the Prophet ﷺ, his Companions, Successors, Successors of the Successors, saints and scholars. The Prophet ﷺ used to visit it frequently. It is the second holiest graveyard after al-Baqi' in Madīnah.

Those buried here include:

Grave of 'Abd Manāf: Great, great-grandfather of the Holy Prophet ﷺ

Grave of Hāshim: Great-grandfather of the Holy Prophet ﷺ

Grave of 'Abd al-Muṭṭalib: Grandfather of the Holy Prophet ﷺ, who raised him in his early childhood.

Grave of Sayyidah Āmina bint Wahb: Mother of the Holy Prophet ﷺ who died when he was only 5 years old. According to another source, Sayyidah Āmina is buried in Abwā (between Makkah and Madīna).

Grave of Sayyidinā 'Abd Allāh ibn 'Abd al-Muṭṭalib: The blessed father of our Holy Prophet ﷺ, who died and was buried in Madīna. Later his body was disinterred and found to be intact. It was transferred to Makkah and buried in Jannat al-Mu'alla.

Grave of Abū Ṭālib: The uncle of the Prophet ﷺ who raised him after the passing of his grandfather 'Abd al-Muṭṭalib. He was father of 'Alī ibn Abī Ṭālib, Ja'far and 'Aqīl.

Grave of Khadīja: First wife of the Holy Prophet ﷺ and mother of his daughters.

Grave of Qāsim: son of the Holy Prophet ﷺ who died in his infancy.

BAYT MAWLID AN-NABĪ ﷺ

The house where the Prophet ﷺ was born. The house belonged to the grandfather of our Prophet ﷺ 'Abd al-Muṭṭalib, from whom it passed to the Prophet ﷺ and was later turned into a mosque and visitation by the mother of two Ummayyad caliphs, al-Hādī and Hārūn ar-Rashīd. Despite numerous recent attempts to demolish the structure, its foundations remain intact under a library built above it.

MASJID AL-JINN

A group of Jinn were passing by, when they heard the Prophet ﷺ reciting the Holy Quran. They were so moved that they came to the Prophet ﷺ, repented and accepted Islam. A masjid was later built at the location and named Masjid al-Jinn.

CAVE OF THAWR

During the Hijrah the Prophet ﷺ stayed here for three days during the Migration from Makkah. The miraculous incident took place here, in which a spider spun a web and a pigeon laid eggs at the mouth of this cave causing the trackers sparing the Prophet ﷺ and his companion Abū Bakr aš-Šiddīq from being found and harmed by the pursuing Makkans.

CAVE OF HIRĀ

The cave in which the Prophet ﷺ used to seclude himself before the first revelation, and in which the first revelation, the Surah "The Clot" was revealed to him by the archangel Gabriel.

MOUNT OF MERCY (JABAL RAḤMAH)

This is a mountain in the plain of ʿArafah. It is highly recommended to pray two rakʿats Prayer of Need (ḥājah) here.

MUZDALIFAH

Pilgrims on Ḥajj are required to spend the night here. It is here they collect 70 pebbles for lapidating the pillars representing Satan in Minā.

MINĀ

This is a city that comes to existence for three days during the year. All pilgrims are required to spend the night in Minā, to stone the three pillars representing Satan each day and to sacrifice an animal for the sake of God, whose meat is distributed to the indigent. Men must shave their heads or cut their hair, while women are required only to cut the hair.

MASJID KHAYF

It is highly recommended to pray six rak'ats of prayer in this Masjid in Minā and that has great reward as it is said that many prophets of God prayed here.

MASJID HUDAYBĪYYAH

This is the location where the Prophet ﷺ gave a special initiation (baya') to the Companions that were with him seeking to make pilgrimage, after Quraysh captured our master 'Uthmān ibn 'Affān and held him.

Visiting Madinat al-Munawwarah

The merits of Madīnah, of prayer in Madīnah, of visiting the Masjid al-Nabawī, of living in Madīnah, of not cutting trees there, etc. are all based on the fact that the Prophet ﷺ is there.

Thus in Madīnah, you must keep even more respect than in Makkah, because there you are in the presence of the Prophet ﷺ. Make continuous ṣalawāt in your heart, in unison with fellow pilgrims if you are on a bus, until you reach Madīnah. Whether you enter Madīnah by bus or by plane, after you clear the checkpoints, you will travel four or five miles before you begin to see the Sanctuary of the Prophet's Holy Mosque (ḥaram) in the distance. When you do, ask permission from the Prophet ﷺ to enter into his territory.

Etiquette in the Rawdah

A visitor should not raise his voice in the Mosque as a sign of politeness with the Messenger of God's ﷺ.

Lowering one's voice is also a sign of obedience to God the Almighty.

The Prophet ﷺ said, "Between my grave and my pulpit lies a grove from the groves of Paradise." [Bukhari and Muslim]

CONDUCT OF ENTERING THE MOSQUE OF THE HOLY PROPHET ﷺ

When you enter al-Ḥaram ash-Sharīf, take your miswāk and make Sunnat al-istiyāk saying, Allāhumma ṭāhir qalbī mina 'sh-shirki wa 'n-nifāq (O God, purify my heart from the lesser association with You and from hypocrisy). For men it is preferred to enter from Bāb ar-Rahmah (Door of Mercy), the door of Sayyidinā Abū Bakr ؓ, Bāb as-Salām (Door of Peace), Bāb Jibrīl ؑ (Door of Archangel Gabriel), Bāb Fāṭimata 'z-Zahrah ؓ (Door of Fāṭima, daughter of the Prophet ﷺ). For women there is no choice, they have to enter through one special door. Before entering stand still and recite greetings on the Prophet ﷺ and his caliphs, his children, the Sahaba of the

Prophet ﷺ and on awlīyāullāh, especially your shaykh, in the following manner:		
Aṣ-ṣālatu wa 's-salāmu 'alayka yā Sayyidī yā Rasūlullāh		الصَّلوةُ والسَّلامُ عليْك يا رَسُولَ الله
Blessings and peace be upon you, O Prophet of God.		
Aṣ-ṣālatu wa 's-salāmu 'alayka yā Ḥabībāllāh		الصَّلوةُ والسَّلامُ عليْكَ يا حَبِيبَ الله
Blessings and peace be upon you, O Beloved of God.		
As-salāmu 'alayka yā Sayyidanā Abā Bakr aṣ-Ṣiddīq		السَّلامُ عليْكَ يا سَيِّدَنا أبا بَكْر الصِّدّيق
Peace be upon you, O our master Abū Bakr aṣ-Ṣiddīq.		
As-salāmu 'alayka yā Sayyidanā 'Umar al-Fārūq		السَّلامُ عليْكَ يا سَيِّدَنا عُمَر الفارُوق
Peace be upon you, O our master 'Umar al-Fārūq.		
As-salāmu 'alayka yā Sayyidanā 'Uthman wa yā Sayyidanā 'Alī		السَّلامُ عليْكَ يا سَيِّدَنا عُثْمان وسَيِّدَنا عَلِي

Peace be upon you, O our master 'Uthman and our master 'Alī.		
As-salāmu 'alayki yā Sayyidatanā Fāṭimata 'z-Zahrah		السَّلامُ عليْكِ يا سَيِّدَتَنا فاطِمَةَ الزَّهْرَة
Peace be upon you, O our Lady Fāṭimat az-Zahrah.		
As-salāmu 'alaykum yā Āhla Jannati 'l-Baq'i		السَّلامُ عَلَيْكُم يا أَهْلَ جَنَّةِ البَقِيع
Peace be upon you, O inhabitants of the Garden of Baq'i.		
As-salāmu 'alayka yā Sayyidanā Ḥamzah		السَّلامُ عليْكَ يا سَيِّدَنا حَمْزَة
Peace be upon you, O our master Ḥamzah.		
As-salāmu 'alaykum yā Shuhadā Uḥud.		السَّلامُ عَلَيْكُم يا شُهُداءَ أُحُد
Peace be upon you, O martyrs of Uḥud.		

You then enter the Prophet's Mosque with your right foot saying: Aʿūdhu billāhi 'l-ʿAẓīm wa wajhihi 'l-karīm wa sulṭānahu 'l-qadīm mina 'sh-shayṭāni 'r-rajīm. Allāhuma 'ftaḥ abwāba raḥmatik. I seek refuge with the Mighty God. I seek protection in His Generous Countenance and His Everlasting Authority against the cursed Devil. In the Name of God. O God! Bless Muhammad and his family. O God! Forgive my sins, and open the gates of Your mercy to me.	إذا وصلت إلى المسجد النبوي فقدم رجلك اليمين عند دخوله وقل أَعُوذُ بِاللهِ العَظِيمِ وَوَجْهِهِ الكَرِيمِ وسُلْطَانَهُ القَدِيمِ مِنَ الشَّيْطانِ الرَّجِيمِ اللَّهُمَّ افْتَحْ لِي أَبْوابَ رَحْمَتِك.

<table>
<tr><td>One then says:
Nawaytu 'l-arbāʿīn, nawaytu 'l-ʿitikāf, nawaytu 'l-khalwah, nawaytu 'l-ʿuzlah, nawaytu 'r-riyāḍa, nawaytu 's-sulūk, lillāhi taʿalā al-ʿAẓīm fī ḥarami 'n-Nabi ﷺ.
Then enter the Mosque.</td><td></td><td>نويتُ الأَرْبَعِين، نويتُ الإعْتِكاف، نَوَيْتُ الخَلْوَة نَوَيْتُ العُزْلَة، نويتُ الرّياضة نَويتُ السُّلوكَ لله تَعالى في حَرَمِ النَّبي صَلّى اللهُ عَلَيْهِ وسَلّم</td></tr>
<tr><td colspan="3">For the sake of blessings (barakah) I intend the forty (days of seclusion); I intend isolation; I intend discipline (of the ego); I intend to travel in God's Path; for the sake of God, the Exalted in the Holy Place of the Prophet ﷺ.</td></tr>
<tr><td colspan="3">If it is not possible to visit the Prophet ﷺ immediately because it is crowded, or it is time for congregational prayer, then pray two rakʿat greeting the Mosque (taḥiyyat al-masjid). However, if you are able to do so, go directly to make your visit. When you visit the Prophet ﷺ, try to enter from the door of Sayyidinā Abū Bakr ؓ or Bāb as-Salām, opposite the grave. Move all</td></tr>
</table>

the way across the space to arrive at the Prophet's ﷺ Muwājihatu 'sh-Sharīfah. If you are coming at the time of prayer, enter the Mosque from any door, pray first with the congregation, then make your visit to the Prophet ﷺ after finishing the prayers.

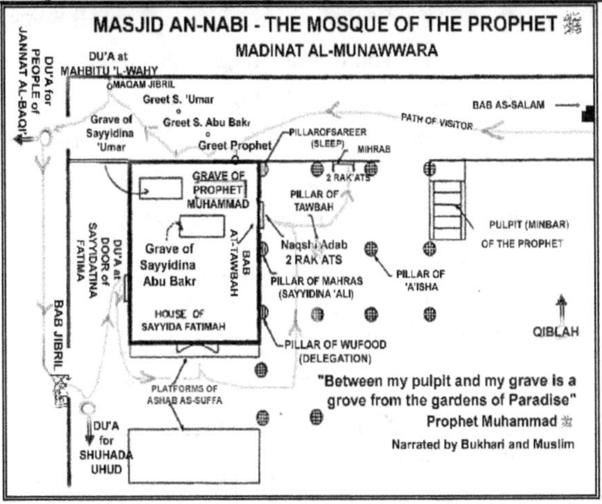

CONDUCT OF ZIYĀRAH

At the Muwājihatu 'sh-Sharīfah face the holy grave of the Prophet ﷺ. Be careful, as many people mistakenly think that the first door with a hole is the door of the Prophet ﷺ. The first two doors, with two small holes, contain nothing. The one in the middle which has a large hole and two small holes is the grave of Sayyidinā Muhammad ﷺ and directly behind his grave, at his feet is the grave of Sayyidinā Abu Bakr ؓ; Sayyidinā Umar ؓ is buried at the feet of Sayyidinā Abu Bakr ؓ.

Greeting the Prophet ﷺ

Stand in front of the middle door a bit far away behind where there are two pillars, and say:

O Prophet of God, I came to your presence, please accept me.		

Aṣ-ṣālatu wa 's-salāmu 'alayka yā Sayyidī yā Rasūlullāh		الصَّلوةُ والسَّلامُ عليْكَ يا سَيّدي يا رَسُولَ الله
Blessings and Peace be upon you, O Prophet of God.		
Aṣ-ṣālatu wa 's-salāmu 'alayka yā Ḥabīballāh		الصَّلوةُ والسَّلامُ عليْكَ يا حَبِيبَ الله
Blessings and Peace be upon you, O Beloved of God.		
Aṣ-ṣālatu wa 's-salāmu 'alayka yā Shāfi'an li 'l-muslimīn		الصَّلوةُ والسَّلامُ عليك يا شافَعاً لِلمُسْلِمِين
Blessings and Peace be upon you, O Intercessor of the Muslims.		
Aṣ-ṣālatu wa 's-salāmu 'alayka yā Rasūla rabbi' l-'alamin		الصَّلوةُ والسَّلامُ عليْكَ يا رَسُولَ رَبِّ العالَمِين
Blessings and Peace be upon you, O Messenger of the Lord of the Worlds.		
Then add to that whatever comes to your heart of greetings to the Prophet ﷺ.		

<table>
<tr><td>Testification of Faith (Shahāda)
3 times: ash-hadu an lā ilāha illa-Allāh wa ash-hadu anna Muḥammadan ʿabduhu wa rasūluh;</td><td></td><td>كَلِمةُ الشَّهادتين (٣ مرات)
أَشْهَدُ أَنْ لا إله إلا الله وأَشْهَدُ أَنَّ مُحَمَّدًا عَبْدُهُ ورَسُولُهُ</td></tr>
<tr><td colspan="3">I testify that there is no god but God and I testify that Muḥmmad is His Servant and Messenger.</td></tr>
<tr><td colspan="3">The first Testification of Faith (Shahādah) is for one's self, bringing to mind the Presence of the Prophet ﷺ and saying in one's heart, "Yā Sayyidī Yā Rasūlullāh, you are my witness; Allah is my witness; all angels are my witness; all Ṣaḥābah are my witness; all Prophets are my witness; everyone in creation is my witness; and my Shaykh is my witness," then pronounce the Shahādah, for you are renewing your Islam. Then pronounce the second Shahādah on behalf of yourself, your parents, your children, your family, your brothers and sisters, your relations, friends and neighbors and all Muslim people. The third Shahādah</td></tr>
</table>

is on behalf of unbelievers with the intention that they become believers.		
Istighfār: 3x Astaghfirullāh		أستغفر الله (٣ مرات)
I ask forgiveness of God. The first Istighfār is for yourself; the second is for your family and for whoever asked you to pray (make du'ā) for them and the third is for the Community of the Prophet ﷺ.		
Yā Rabbī, yā Allāh, kam ẓahara minnī mina 'dh-dhunūbi wa 'l-ma'āṣīyy ẓāhiran wa bāṭinan wa sirran min ẓuhūrī fī 'ālami 'd-dunyā ilā yawminā hādha, raj'atu 'ani 'l-jamī'i bi 't-tawbati wa 'l-istighfār wa as'aluka an taghfira lī bi-jāhi Nabīyyika Muḥammad.		يا ربي يا اللهُ كَمْ ظَهَرَ مِنّي مِنَ الذُّنُوبِ والمعاصِي ظاهِراً وباطِناً وسِرّاً مِن عَهْدِ إيجادِ ذَرَّتي ورُوحي ودُخُولِ رُوحي إلى جِسْمي وظُهُوري مِنَ العَدَمِ إلى الوُجُودِ وظُهُوري في عالَمِ الدُّنيا إلى يَوْمِنا هذا، رَجَعْتُ

		عنِ الجَميع اليْك بالتَّوْبةِ والإسْتِغْفار وأسْألكَ ان تَغْفِرَ لي(يا الله) بجاهِ نَبيّكَ محمد

O My Lord, O God, from the day of my appearance in creation until our day, how much of disobedience has appeared from me spiritually or physically - I am regretting them all coming and asking forgiveness and repentance, and I am asking you to forgive me for the sake of the Prophet.

Kamā qāl Allāhu taʿala fī 'l-Qur'ān: wa mā arsalnā min rasūlin illā liyuṭāʿa bi-idhnillāhi wa law annahum idh dhalamū anfusahum jā'ūka fastaghfarū'llāha wastaghfara lahumu 'r-		كما قال الله تعالى في القرآن: وَمَا أَرْسَلْنَا مِن رَّسُولٍ إِلاَّ لِيُطَاعَ بِإِذْنِ اللّهِ وَلَوْ أَنَّهُمْ إِذ ظَّلَمُواْ أَنفُسَهُمْ جَآؤُوكَ فَاسْتَغْفَرُواْ اللّهَ وَاسْتَغْفَرَ

rasūlu la-wajadū'llāha tawwāban rahīmān.		لَهُمُ الرَّسُولُ لَوَجَدُواْ اللَّهَ تَوَّابًا رَّحِيمًا

As God said in the Holy Quran:

> *We sent not a messenger, but to be obeyed, in accordance with the will of God. If they had only, when they were unjust to themselves, come unto thee and asked God's forgiveness, and the Messenger had asked forgiveness for them, they would have found God indeed Oft-returning, Most Merciful.* (4:64)

Then you invoke God, asking for whatever you need or desire, seeking a good life for yourself, your family and for your Shaykh, for the Muslims in general, and mercy and peace for all mankind.

Then you move on (it is not necessary to move physically) to give greetings to Sayyidinā Abu Bakr as-Siddiq ﷺ. Follow the same adab as with the Prophet ﷺ. Then move on to give greetings to Sayyidinā 'Umar ﷺ, again following the same adab.

Then, before leaving, give greetings in your heart to to Sayyidinā 'Uthman ﷺ, Sayyidinā 'Alī ﷺ, all the

Companions, all 124,000 prophets and messengers, all 124,000 saints because their souls too, have a spiritual presence in that holy place. Finally, send greetings to Sayyidinā al-Ḥasan ؓ and Sayyidinā al-Ḥusain ؓ.

As-salāmu ʿalayka yā Sayyidanā Abā Bakr aṣ-Ṣiddīq	السَّلامُ عليكَ يا سيّدَنا أبا بَكْرٍ الصّدّيق
Peace be upon you, O our master Abā Bakr aṣ-Ṣiddīq.	
As-salāmu ʿalayka yā Sayyidanā ʿUmar al-Fārūq	السَّلامُ عليكَ يا سيدَنا عُمَر الفارُّوق
Peace be upon you, O our master ʿUmar al-Fārūq.	
As-salāmu ʿalayka yā Sayyidanā ʿUthmān wa yā Sayyidanā ʿAlī	السَّلامُ عليْكَ يا سيدَنا عُثْمان وسَيِّدُنا علي
Peace be upon you, O our master ʿUthmān and our master ʿAlī.	
As-salāmu ʿalaykum yā aṣḥābi 'n-Nabī	السَّلامُ عليكُم يا أصْحابَ النّبي
Peace be upon you, O Companions of the Prophet.	

As-salāmu ʿalaykum yā awlīyā'ullāh.		السَّلامُ عليْكُم يا أوْلِياءَ الله
Peace be upon you, O saints of God.		
Then, on the right side before the exit door is a large wall covered with ceramic ornamention/calligraphy. There is the Maḥbitu ʿl-waḥī, where Gabriel عليه السلام used to come to bring revelation to the Prophet. In the past, one could make a turn inside, but it is now blocked with a fence, so you have to go outside. But before you go outside, make duʿā at the Maḥbitu ʿl-waḥī. From this station, you face Qiblah and say:		
Ya Rabbi' l-ʿizzati wa 'l-ʿaẓamati wa 'l-jabarūt.		يا رَبَّ العِزَّةِ والعَظِيمَةِ والجَبَرُوت
O Lord of Honor and Greatness, Imposer of Thy Will.		
As-salāmu ʿalayka yā Sayyidanā Jibrīl.		السَّلامُ عليْكَ يا سيدَنا جِبْرِيل
Peace be upon you, O our master Gabriel.		

As-salāmu 'alayka yā Sayyidanā Mikā'īl.		السَّلامُ عليْكَ يا سيدَنا مِيكَائِيل
Peace be upon you, O our master Michael.		
As-salāmu 'alayka yā Sayyidanā Izrā'īl.		السَّلامُ عليْكَ يا سيدَنا عَزْرائِيل
Peace be upon you, O our master Izra'īl.		
As-salāmu 'alayka yā Sayyidanā Isrāfīl.		السَّلامُ عليْكَ يا سيدَنا لإسْرافِيل
Peace be upon you, O our master Isrāfīl.		
As-salāmu 'alayka yā Sayyidanā Riḍwān.		السَّلامُ عليْكَ يا سيدَنا رِضْوان
Peace be upon you, O our master Riḍwān.		
As-salāmu 'alayka yā Sayyidana Mālik.		السَّلامُ عليْكَ يا سيدَنا مالِك
Peace be upon you, O our master Mālik.		

As-salāmu 'alaykum yā Malāi'kata 's-samāwati al-'aẓīm.		السَّلام عليْكُم يا مَلائِكَة السَّمَواتِ والأَرْض
Peace be upon you, O Angels of the Tremendous Heavens.		
As-salāmu 'alaykum yā Malā'ikata 'l-karībiyyūn.		السَّلامُ عليْكُم يا مَلائِكَة الكَرِبيُون
Peace be upon you, O Cherubim.		
As-salāmu 'alaykum yā Ḥamalata 'l-'Arsh.		السَّلامُ عليْكُم يا حَمَلَة العَرْش
Peace be upon you, O our master O Bearers of the Throne.		
As-salāmu 'alaykum yā Malā'ikata Anwārillāh		السَّلامُ عليْكُم يا مَلائِكَة أَنْوار الله
Peace be upon you, O Angels of God's Light.		
You beseech God there saying: 'Yā Rabbī for the sake of the Prophet ﷺ, for the sake of his Sahaba and his caliphs; for the sake of Mahdī and for the sake of all		

saints, Yā Rabbī Yā Allāh…", and then invoke God in duʿa for whatever you like.

And then after reciting these greetings to the angels you make whatever duʿa you like, and then pray two rakʿat. You exit from that door, at which point you will be facing Jannat al-Baq'i. You make a Fatiha for all who are buried there. You go left and go down, then enter the door of Sayyidatina Fāṭimatu 'z-Zahrā and go left in there to an empty area, just before reaching the Platforms of Aṣḥāb aṣ-Ṣuffah. It is reported historically that the angels have transferred Sayyidatina Fāṭimat az-Zahra from Jannat al-Baqʿi to this grave. So you approach the grave and say:

As-salāmu ʿalaykī ya Sayyidatanā Fāṭimata 'z-zahrā.		السَّلامُ عليْكَ يا سَيِّدَتَنا فاطِمَةَ الزَّهْرَة

Peace be upon you, O our Lady Fāṭimah, the Pure Blossom.

As-salāmu ʿalaykī yā Umma 'l-Ḥasani wa 'l-Ḥusain		السَّلام عليْكِ يا سَيِّدَتَنا أمَّ الحَسَنِ والحُسَيْن

<table>
<tr><td colspan="3">Peace be upon you, O mother of al-Ḥasan and al-Ḥusain.</td></tr>
<tr><td>As-salāmu ʿalaykī yā Sayyidata nisā'i āhli 'l-jannah.</td><td></td><td>السَّلامُ عليْكِ يا سَيِّدَةَ
نِسَاءِ أَهْلِ الجَنَّة</td></tr>
<tr><td colspan="3">Peace be upon you, O Noble Chief of the ladies of the People of Paradise.</td></tr>
<tr><td colspan="3">You then go around and come to the Blessed Garden (Rawḍat ash-Sharīfah) if you are able. If you are not able to, you come anywhere adjacent to Rawḍat ash-Sharīfah. There is Bāb at-Tawbah which is the last closet of Quran's, near the Rawḍah. Try to reach there, but if you cannot stand at a distance, face the Qiblah and say:</td></tr>
<tr><td>Law kāna laka yā Rabbī bābayni āḥadahumā mukhaṣaṣṣun li 't-tā'ibīna min ʿibādika 'l-muʿminīn wa 'l-ākharu li 't-tā'ibīna min ʿibādika 'l-mudhinibīn. Jiʿtuka yā Allāh naḥwu</td><td></td><td>لو كان لَكَ ياربي بابَيْنِ
أَحَدَهُما مُخَصَّصٌ لِلتّائِبين
من عِبادِكَ المُؤْمِنين
والأَخَرُ لِلتّائبين من عِبادِكَ
العاصِين ، جِئْتُكَ يا الله</td></tr>
</table>

bābik alladhī yaḥtāju an yadkhula minhu ʿibāduka ʾl-mudhinibīn. Wa innanī uqirru wa āaʿtarif annahu yajibu an ujaddida islāmī wa īmānī min hādha ʾl-bāb iẓhāran li ʾl-ʿajzi.		نَحْوَ بابِكَ الذي يَحْتاجُ ان يَدْخُلَ مِنْهُ عِبادُكَ العاصِين إنَّني أُقِرُّ واعْتَرِفُ انَّهُ يَجِبُ ان أُجَدِّدَ إسْلامي وإيماني من هذا الباب لإظْهارِ العَجْزِ.

O my Lord, O God, I am coming to your door, the door of repentance. Yā Rabbi, if you had two doors for Your servant to enter through; one for the believers from Your servants and one for the sinner from Your servants, I am coming to You from the door that the sinner needs to come through and I am declaring that believing that this is the only door for me to come through. I am saying to you that I have to renew my faith from this door to show humility and helplessness.

Recite Shahādah three times and the remainder of the adab of the Naqshbandi Order, leaving out the dhikr.

This will take from ten minutes. Following the adab pray two rak'at, and then to invoke God seeking whatever you like.

DAILY CONDUCT

It was the custom of Mawlana Shaykh Nazim to perform these devotions a half-hour after Fajr prayer, when it would be less crowded. During the Ḥajj season, however, it is always crowded. Still, there are some times that are better than others. One of these is the period after Duḥā (mid-day), until the time of Ẓuhr prayer (9 a.m. to noon). The other is the period between Ẓuhr and 'Aṣr prayers, because people then go to eat and take an afternoon nap. During that time, ladies—but not men—can enter the Rawḍah, so this is the best time for them to perform these devotions.

The murīd should try to hold fast to as much as of the above aspects of adab as possible, but should not worry if some parts of it are missed.

Finally keep in mind you must control your ego as much as possible. If you get angry quickly take a shower and ask forgiveness from God and seek the Prophet's ﷺ asking forgiveness on your behalf.

FAREWELL VISITATION

When the time comes for you to leave Madīnah, on your last day in the city, you make ziyārah and you ask permission from the Prophet ﷺ to travel.
Perform the Farewell Visitation of the Prophet ﷺ (ziyāratu 'l-wada') and then you set forth.

Holy Places of Visitation in Madinah

SEEKING BLESSINGS BY MEANS OF PLACES THE PROPHET ﷺ VISITED (TABARRUK)

Thus to visit any location where the Prophet's ﷺ blessed feet touched the earth, was touched by his holy hand or his breath entered is to take blessings. For that reason, the entire earth of Madīnah, its air and its water are blessed.

As the Prophet ﷺ asked God's Blessings on the city and its fruits, then Madīnah must be full of blessing, as his supplication is an or answered prayer (du'a mustajāb). Therefore, it is common practice for pilgrims to purchase dates from Madīnah for the blessings, and to bring them back home to share among those who could not make the pilgrimage. It is said that there remain living some of the date palms planted by the Holy Prophet ﷺ himself.

THE GRAVEYARD BAQI' AL-GHARQAD

It is desirable that one go daily to the cemetery of Baqi', but particularly on Friday; before the visit, one should first pronounce greetings on the Prophet ﷺ.

When one arrives at Baqi', say:

as-Salāmu 'alaykum dāra qawmin mu'minīna wa innā inshā-Allāhu bikum lāhiqūn, Allāhumma ighfir li āhli Baqi' al-gharqad, Allāhumma ighfir lanā wa lahum.		السَّلاَمُ عَلَيْكُمْ دَارَ قَوْمٍ مُؤْمِنِينَ وَإِنَّا إِنْ شَاءَ اللهُ بِكُم لَلاَحِقُونَ اللَّهُمَّ اغْفِرْ لأَهْلِ بَقِيعِ الْغَرْقَد اللَّهُمَّ اغْفِرْ لَنَا وَلَهُمْ

Peace be upon ye, abode of the believing folk. And indeed we will soon be meeting with ye. O God forgive the people of Baqi' al-gharqad, O God forgive us and them.

Then he visits the visible graves there, such as that of Ibrahīm, 'Uthmān, al-'Abbās, al-Ḥasan the son of 'Alī, 'Alī the son of al-Ḥusayn, Muḥammad ibn 'Alī, Ja'far ibn Muḥammad, and others ❧. The last stop would be the grave of Ṣafiyya ❧, the Aunt of God's Messenger ❧. It has been established in numerous sound hadiths that there is merit in the graves of the Baqī' and in visiting them.

THE QUBĀ MOSQUE

It was the first mosque to be built in Madīnah. God praised this Mosque and those who maintained it. It is recommended to visit the well of Ārīs, which is located by the mosque of Qubā, and drink from its water and perform ablution with it.

It is desirable that one visit all the sites of significance in Islam. There are approximately thirty such places, and they are known to the inhabitants of Madīnah. The pilgrim should visit as many as possible.

SEVEN MOSQUES

Masjid Qiblatain: In this mosque, God directed Prophet Muhammad ﷺ, who was in the middle of prayers along with his Companions, to turn his face from Islam's first Qiblah (Baitu 'l-Maqdis) towards the Ka'bah in Masjid al-Ḥarām in the verse:

"Verily! We have seen the turning of your face towards the heaven. Surely, We shall turn you to a Qiblah that shall please you, so turn your face in the direction of al-Masjid al-Ḥarām...." (2:144).

That is why this mosque is known as a mosque with two Qiblas.

Masjid Jum'ah: This mosque was built at a place where the Prophet offered his first Jum'ah prayer in Madīnah.

Masjid Ghamāmah: This mosque is not far from Masjid an-Nabī. The Prophet ﷺ used to offer his the prayers of the two Eids here. Once the Prophet ﷺ led prayer for rain (istasqā) in it and suddenly clouds appeared and it started raining, hence the name ghamāma (clouds).

Masjid Fatima, Masjid Abū Bakr, Masjid Umar Farūq and Masjid 'Alī: These four mosques are near Masjid Ghamāmah.

BADR

The plain and dune of Badr is 32 kilometers southwest of Madīnah where the first battle between 313 Muslims and 1,000 Quraish of Makkah took place in 624 A.D. The Muslims had 70 camels and two horses whereas the Quraish had a cavalry of 200 horses and 700 camels. They were superior in weapons as well, but Muslims were victorious because they were strong in morale and strategy due to the presence of the Holy Prophet's ﷺ leadership.

UḤUD MOUNTAIN

About seven kilometers to the north of Madīnah, the famous battle of Uḥud was fought here. Sayyidina Hamza ؓ, the Holy Prophet's uncle and other companions are buried at the foot of the mountain.

SALAʻA MOUNTAIN

This is the site for the battle of the Trench was fought in 5 A.H. Now there are six mosques at this location.

WATER-WELLS OF THE PROPHET ﷺ

It is a blessing to visit the wells where the Prophet ﷺ used to perform ablution and wash. There are seven such wells.

Additionally the visitor can ask the muṭawaf to assist you in Madīnah to visit the seven mosques, the many cemeteries, wells and other locations of historical significance.

Funeral Procedures

Approach of Death

When a Muslim is approaching death, it is Sunnah to instruct him or her to repeat the phrase of Oneness lā ilāha illa-Allāh Muḥammadun Rasūlullāh, as the Prophet instructed, "Put on the tongue of your dying ones lā ilāha illa-Allāh." This is known as talqīn.

It is Sunnah to direct the dying one's face towards the qiblah.

It is Sunnah to recite Sūrah YāSīn because the Prophet said, "YāSīn is the heart of the Qur'ān: if someone reads it seeking Allāh and the hereafter, Allāh will forgive him his sins." And the Prophet said, "Read YāSīn over your dead/dying ones."

It is preferred to bury the deceased within 24 hours, observing all guidelines of Islamic law (see *Reliance of the Traveller*, translated by Shaykh Nuh Ha Mim Keller, for full details). A summary from this books is presented here.

Washing the Dead
WHO SHOULD WASH THE BODY
Male: his Muslim male relatives beginning with father; father's father; son; son's son; brother; father's brother; son of the father's brother; other males related to the deceased through father or son; any men related to the deceased; men not related to the deceased; the deceased's wife and finally his unmarriageable female relatives (mahram).
Female: her female relatives such as her daughter or mother; other women; her husband; and then a member of her unmarriageable male relatives (mahram).
It is recommended that the washer be trustworthy.
HOW TO WASH THE BODY
It is obligatory for the washer to keep the nakedness of the deceased covered while washing.

It is Sunnah that no one be present except the washer and an assistant.
It is preferable that the body be washed while clothed in an ankle-length shirt into which the washer inserts his hand from the sleeve or a tear in the seam, pouring water over the garment and washing the body under it. It is obligatory that the body be covered from naval to knees.
It is best to wash the body under a roof, and that cold water be used, except when necessary (or to heat it, such as to clean away filth that could not otherwise be removed, or when the weather is cold, since the deceased suffers from it just as a living person would).
It is unlawful to look at the nakedness of the deceased or touch it, except with a cloth or other material. It is recommended not to look at or directly touch the other parts of the body save with a cloth.
It is recommended to:
1- force out waste from the stomach; 2- clean the private parts of filth;

3- give the body ablution (wuḍ'u) like the ablution of a living person, turning the head when rinsing the mouth and nostrils so that no water reaches the stomach;

4- make the intention of performing the purificatory bath (ghusl), and then to wash the head, beard, and body each three times with water infused with sidr (lote) tree leaves, taking care each time to press the hand on the stomach in a downward stroke, leaning on it to force its contents out, but gently. The hair and beard should be gently combed with a wide-toothed comb so as not to pull any out. Any hair which comes out should be placed in the shroud.

It is Sunnah:

1- that the place of washing be on an incline so the head is highest and the water flows down away from it;

2- that incense be burned in a burner;

3- to put one's right hand on the shoulder of the deceased with the thumb on the nape of the neck so that the head does not loll, and brace the back up against one's right knee;
4- to have the helper pour abundant water during the process to obviate offensive odors from waste leaving the body;
5- to stroke the stomach firmly and effectively with one's left hand;
6- and when finished, to lay the deceased down again on his back with the feet towards the direction of prayer (qiblah).

If the body is not clean after three times, wash it an additional odd number of washings. It is Sunnah to add a little camphor to the water.

The obligatory minimum for this purificatory bath (ghusl) is that water reach all external parts of the body and it is obligatory to remove any filth (najasa), if present. The body should be dried with a cloth afterwards.

If anything leaves the body after washing, only the affected area need be washed.
SHROUDING THE BODY
Male: recommended he be wrapped in three washed (not new) white shrouds, without an ankle-length shirt or turban, each shroud covering the whole body (unless the deceased was in a state of iḥrām, in which case the head of the male or face of the female must be left uncovered).
Female: recommended she be dressed in a wraparound, headcover, and a shift, and that she be wrapped in two shrouds like those used for men in being white and washed, each of which covers her entire body.
The obligatory minimum for shrouding a man or woman is to completely cover their nakedness. For a man it is obligatory to cover the navel, the knees, and what lies between them, and for a woman, her entire body.
It is recommended:

1- to scent the shrouds with incense from aloes;
2- to sprinkle them with ḥunuṭ (an aromatic compound of camphor, reed perfume, and red and white sandalwood) and camphor;
3- to place cotton and ḥunuṭ on the seven apertures of the head and on the eight places that touch the ground in prostration;
4- and it is commendable to perfume the entire body.

If a person dies while in a state of iḥrām, the conditions of iḥrām remain on the body (no sewed cloth for men, no perfume).

The Funeral Prayer

The communal obligation is fulfilled if a single mature Muslim male prays over the deceased, but it is recommended to pray it in a group.

WHO SHOULD LEAD THE FUNERAL PRAYER

The person best suited to lead the funeral prayer as imam is the one who is best suited to wash the deceased from the males of the family and is given preference in leading the prayer even over the mosque's imam.

PLACING THE BODY FOR THE FUNERAL PRAYER

In the funeral prayer itself, the enshrouded deceased is placed on a bier in front of the imam lying on the right side facing the direction of prayer (qiblah). It is recommended that the imam stand by the head of the deceased, if male, and by the posterior, if female.

The prayer is performed as described at page 70

After the third takbīr one supplicates for the deceased. In addition to the standard supplication mentioned on page 75, it is recommended to say:

Allāhuma hādhā ʿabduka wa 'bnu ʿabdika, kharaja min rawḥi 'd-dunyā wa saʿatihā, wa maḥbūbuhu wa aḥibbā'uhu fīhā ilā ẓulmati 'l-qabri wa mā hūwa lāqīh. Kāna yashadu an lā ilāha illa		اللَّهُمَّ هذا عَبدُكَ وَابنُ عَبدِكَ، خَرَجَ مِن رَوحِ الدُّنيَا وسعَتِهَا، ومَحبُوبُهُ وأحِبَّاؤُهُ فِيهَا إلى ظُلمَةِ القبرِ ومَا هُوَ لاَقِيهِ، كَانَ يَشهَدُ أن لاَ إلَه

Anta waḥdaka lā sharīka laka wa anna sayyīdinā muḥammadan ʿabduka wa rasūluka wa Anta Āʿalamu bihi minnā. Allāhuma innahu nazala bika wa Anta khayru manzūlin bihi wa aṣbaḥa faqīran ilā raḥmatika wa Anta ghanīyyun ʿan ʿadhābihi wa qad j'ināka rāghibīna 'ilayka shufaʿāun lahu. Allāhuma in kāna muḥsinan fa zid fī iḥsānihi. Wa in kāna musīyyan fatajāwaz ʿanhu wa laqqihi bi-raḥmatika riḍāka wa qihi fitnata 'l-qabri wa ʿadhābahu wa afsaḥ lahu fī qabrihi. Wa jāfī 'l-arḍa ʿan janbayih wa laqqahi bi-raḥmatika al-amna min

إلاَّ أنتَ وَحدَكَ لاَ شَريكَ
لَكَ، وأنَّ سيدنا مُحَمَّداً ﷺ
عَبدُكَ ورَسُولُكَ، وأنتَ
أعلَمُ بِهِ مِنَّا، اللَّهُمَّ إنَّهُ نَزَلَ
بِكَ، وأنتَ خيرُ مَنزُولٍ بِهِ،
وأصبَحَ فَقِيراً إلى رَحمَتِكَ،
وأنتَ غَنِيٌّ عَن عذابِهِ، وقَد
جِئنَاكَ راغبينَ إلَيكَ شُفَعاءَ
لَهُ، اللَّهُمَّ إن كَانَ مُحسِناً فَزِد
في إحسانِهِ، وإن كَانَ مُسيئاً
فَتَجاوَز عَنهُ، ولَقِّهِ بِرَحمَتِكَ
رِضَاكَ، وقِهِ فِتنَةَ القَبرِ
وعَذابَهُ، وأفسَح لَهُ في قَبرِهِ؛
وجَافِ الأرضَ عَن جَنبَيهِ،

ʿadhābika ḥatā tabʿathhu āminan ilā jannatika bi-raḥmatika yā Arḥama 'r-Rāḥimīn.		ولَقِّهِ بِرَحمَتِكَ الأَمنَ مِن عَذَابِكَ حَتَّى تَبعَثَهُ آمِناً إلى جَنَّتِكَ بِرَحمَتِكَ يا أَرحَمَ الراحِمينَ

O Allah, this is Your slave, and son of Your slave. He has left the zephyr of this world and its spaciousness, in which were the things and people he loved, for the darkness of the grave and that which he will meet. He testified that there is no god but You alone without a partner, and that Muhammad is Your slave and messenger. You know him better than we. O Allah, he has gone to remain with You, and You are the best to remain with. He is now in need of Your mercy, and You have no need to torment him. We come to You in desire for You, interceding for him. O Allah, if he did well, treat him the better, and if he did wrong, disregard it and through Your mercy show him Your good pleasure and protect him from the trial and torment of the grave. Make his grave spacious for him and distance the earth

from his sides, and through Your mercy protect him from Your torment until You raise him and send him safely to Your paradise, O Most Merciful of the Merciful.		
If it is the funeral of a child, one may add to this:		
Allāhuma aja'ālhu faraṭān li abawayhi wa salafan wa dhukhran wa 'iẓatan wa i'tibāran wa shafīyy'an wa thaqil bihi mawāzīnahumā wa afrigha 'ṣ-ṣabra 'alā qulūbihimā.		اللَّهُمَّ اجعَلهُ فَرَطاً لأبويهِ، وسَلَفاً وذُخراً وعِظَةً واعتِبَاراً وشَفِيعاً، وثَقَّل بِهِ مَوَازينَهُما، وأفرِغِ الصَّبرَ على قُلوبِهِما
O Allah, send him ahead to smoothe the way for his parents, and make him a reason for reward, a treasure, admonition, reflection, and intercessor. Make the scales of their good deeds heavy through him, and fill their hearts with patience.		
When the imam finishes with Salams, a latecomer goes on to complete the remaining number of times of saying takbīr and the other spoken elements, and then finishes with his own Salams.		

LATECOMERS
It is recommended that the body not be lifted until the latecomers finish their prayer. Someone who has missed praying a funeral prayer until after the deceased has been buried may pray it at the grave.
Burial should proceed immediately after the funeral prayers and not be delayed, except for the responsible family member.
Funeral Procession
It is Sunnah to follow the bier and scholars recommend reciting the tahlīl (lā ilāha illa-Allāh) in a loud voice in unison. It is best if the bier is carried by its poles sometimes by four men and sometimes by five, the fifth being between the two forward poles and they walk faster than usual but they should not trot
The Grave
The grave should be the height of an average man with his arm fully extended upward.

The grave is dug so the deceased will lie with his/her face to qiblah when placed on his/her right side, which is obligatory.

It is preferred to shape the grave not as a straight trench, but with a parallel lateral hollow large enough for the body to fit (lahd).

It is disliked to bury the deceased in a coffin, unless the earth is soft or moist.

Burial

Men should bury the dead, whether male, or female, in which case the most suited is the husband, if able and then those listed in the funeral prayer preference.

It is preferable to conceal the grave with a cloth while placing the body in it. The head of the deceased is placed at the foot of the grave and the body is slid from the bier headfirst until the feet come to rest at the foot of the grave.

It is recommended for the person burying the deceased, who is standing in the grave receiving the body to say:

Bismillāh wa ʿalā millati rasūlillāh.		بِسم الله وَ على مِلّةِ رَسُولِ الله

In the name of Allāh and according to the religion of the Messenger of Allāh.

He also should supplicate on behalf of the deceased. He should place a block as a pillow for the deceased and pull back the shroud enough for the deceased's cheek to rest on the block.

If the grave is of lahd shape, then the lateral hollow containing the body is walled with blocks. If a trench is used, block walls are raised along the sides and after the deceased is interred, a ceiling is built with blocks.
The person at the graveside then sprinkles three scoops of earth into the grave saying according to the Sunnah:

1. Minhā khalaqnākum 2. wa fīhā nuʿīdukum 3. wa minhā nukhrijukum tāratan ukhrā.		١ مِنْهَا خَلَقْنَاكُمْ ٢ وَفِيهَا نُعِيدُكُمْ ٣ وَمِنْهَا نُخْرِجُكُمْ تَارَةً أُخْرَى

With the first scoop: "Of it we created you all," with the second: "to it we shall make ye return," and with the third: "and from it we shall bring ye forth again." (20:55)
The grave is then filled in after which one stays for some time to: • instruct the deceased on the answers he/she will need to give the questioning angels, Munkir and Nakīr as to his Lord, his religion and his Prophet in the following manner:
Coaching the Deceased

Talqīn al-mayt Yā fulān ibn/ibnata fulān 3x or Yā fulān ibn/ibnata Ḥawwā 3x.		تلقين الميت: فليقم أحدكم على رأس قبره، ثم ليقل :يا فلان بن فلانة ٣ مرات، او فإن لم يعرف أمه فقل يا فلان بن حواء ٣ مرات

<table>
<tr><td colspan="2">One person will stand at the head of the grave and say aloud to the deceased: O such-and-such son/daughter of [mother's name]! If the mother's name is unknown, then say: O such-and-such son/daughter of Ḥawwā:</td></tr>
<tr><td>Idhkur mā kharajta ʿalayhi min ad-dunyā shahādata an lā ilāha ill-Allāh wa anna Muḥammadan ʿabduhu wa rasūluh, wa annaka raḍīta billāhi rabban wa bi 'l-islāmi dīnan wa bi-Muḥammadin nabīyan, wa bi 'l-qurān īmāman.</td><td dir="rtl">اذْكُرْ مَا خَرَجْتَ عَلَيْهِ مِنَ الدُّنْيَا شَهَادَةَ أَنْ لا إِلَهَ إِلا اللهُ، وَأَنَّ مُحَمَّدًا عَبْدُهُ وَرَسُولُهُ، وَأَنَّكَ رَضِيتَ بِاللهِ رَبًّا، وَبِالإِسْلامِ دِينًا، وَبِمُحَمَّدٍ نَبِيًّا، وَبِالْقُرْآنِ إِمَامًا،</td></tr>
<tr><td colspan="2">Remember the covenant by which you exited this world: the testification that there is no God but Allah and that Muhammad is the messenger and slave of Allah, and that you have accepted Allah as your Lord, Islam as your religion, and Muhammad as Prophet, and the Qur'an as your guide.</td></tr>
</table>

After this one stays for some time to: • supplicate for the deceased; • ask forgiveness for the deceased; • recite a portion of Qur'ān gifting its reward to the deceased.
Finishing the Grave
One should raise the surface of the grave one span above the ground. It is recommended to sprinkle water on the grave and to put pebbles on it.

Quranic Readings

Sūrat al-Fātiḥah: The Opening (1)		سُورَةُ الفَاتِحَة
1. Bismillāhi ’r-Raḥmāni ’r-Rahīm		بِسْمِ اللَّهِ الرَّحْمَنِ الرَّحِيمِ
In the Name of Allah, the Most Beneficent, the Most Merciful.		
2. Alḥamdu lillāhi Rabbi ’l-‘ālamīn		الْحَمْدُ لله رَبِّ الْعَالَمِينَ
all Praise is for Allāh the Lord and Cherisher of the worlds		
3. ar-Raḥmāni ’r-Raḥīmi		الرَّحْمَـنِ الرَّحِيمِ
The Beneficent, the Merciful		
4. Māliki yawmi ’d-dīni		مَـالِكِ يَوْمِ الدِّينِ
Master of the Day of Judgment		
5. iyyāka na‘budu wa ’ iyyāka nasta‘īnu		إِيَّاكَ نَعْبُدُ وإِيَّاكَ نَسْتَعِينُ
we worship You alone and seek Your help alone		

6. ihdina ' ṣ-ṣirāṭa ' l-mustaqīma		اهدِنَا الصِّرَاطَ المُستَقِيمَ
guide us to the straight path		
7. sirāṭa 'Lladhīna an'amta 'alayhim ghayri 'l-maghḍūbi 'alayhim wa lā 'ḍ-ḍāllīn		صِرَاطَ الَّذِينَ أَنعَمتَ عَلَيهِمْ غَيرِ المَغضُوبِ عَلَيهِمْ وَلاَ الضَّالِّينَ
the path of those whom Thou hast favored, not of those who earn Thine anger nor of those who go astray.		

Sūrah **Yā Sīn (36)**		سورة يس
Read after Ṣalāt al-Fajr.		
Bismillāhi 'r-Raḥmāni 'r-Rahīm		بسم الله الرحمن الرحيم
In the Name of Allah, the Most Beneficent, the Most Merciful.		
1. Yā Sīn		يس
Yā Sīn.		
2. Wa 'l-qur'āni 'l-ḥakīm		وَالْقُرْآنِ الْحَكِيمِ
By the wise Quran,		
3. Innaka la-mina 'l-mursalīn		إِنَّكَ لَمِنَ الْمُرْسَلِينَ
Lo! thou art of those sent		
4. 'alā ṣirāṭin mustaqīm		عَلَى صِرَاطٍ مُّسْتَقِيمٍ
On a straight path,		
5. Tanzīla 'l-'Azīz 'r-Raḥīm		تَنزِيلَ الْعَزِيزِ الرَّحِيمِ

A revelation of the Mighty, the Merciful,		
6. Li-tundhira qawman mā undhira ābāū'hum fa-hum ghāfilūn		لِتُنذِرَ قَوْمًا مَّا أُنذِرَ آبَاؤُهُمْ فَهُمْ غَافِلُونَ
That thou mayst warn a folk whose fathers were not warned, so they are heedless.		
7. Laqad haqqa 'l-qawlu ʿalā aktharihim fa-hum lā yu'minūn		لَقَدْ حَقَّ الْقَوْلُ عَلَى أَكْثَرِهِمْ فَهُمْ لا يُؤْمِنُونَ
Already hath the word proved true of most of them, for they believe not.		
8. Inna jaʿalnā fī ʿanāqihim aghlālan fa-hīya ila 'l-adhqāni fa-hum muqmaḥūn		إِنَّا جَعَلْنَا فِي أَعْنَاقِهِمْ أَغْلاَلاً فَهِيَ إِلَى الأَذْقَانِ فَهُم مُّقْمَحُونَ
Lo! we have put on their necks carcans reaching unto the chins, so that they are made stiff necked.		
9. Wa jaʿalnā min bayni aydīhim saddan wa min khalfihim saddan fa-		وَجَعَلْنَا مِن بَيْنِ أَيْدِيهِمْ سَدًّا وَمِنْ خَلْفِهِمْ سَدًّا

aghshaynāhum fa-hum lā yubṣirūn		فَأَغْشَيْنَاهُمْ فَهُمْ لاَ يُبْصِرُونَ
And We have set a bar before them and a bar behind them, and (thus) have covered them so that they see not.		
10. Wa sawā'un 'alayhim ā-andhartahum am lam tundhirhum lā yu'minūn		وَسَوَاء عَلَيْهِمْ أَأَنذَرْتَهُمْ أَمْ لَمْ تُنذِرْهُمْ لاَ يُؤْمِنُونَ
Whether thou warn them or thou warn them not, it is alike for them, for they believe not.		
11. Innamā tundhiru mani 'ttaba'a 'dh-dhikra wa khashīya 'r-Raḥmāna bi 'l-ghaybi fa-bashshirhu bi-maghfiratin wa ajrin karīm		إِنَّمَا تُنذِرُ مَنِ اتَّبَعَ الذِّكْرَ وَخَشِيَ الرَّحْمَن بِالْغَيْبِ فَبَشِّرْهُ بِمَغْفِرَةٍ وَأَجْرٍ كَرِيمٍ
Thou warnest only him who followeth the Reminder and feareth the Beneficent in secret. To him bear tidings of forgiveness and a rich reward.		

<table>
<tr><td>12. Inna naḥnu nuḥyī ’l-mawta wa naktubu mā qaddamū wa āthārahum wa kulla shay’in aḥṣaynāhu fī imāmin mubīn</td><td></td><td>إِنَّا نَحْنُ نُحْيِي الْمَوْتَى
وَنَكْتُبُ مَا قَدَّمُوا وَآثَارَهُمْ
وَكُلَّ شَيْءٍ أَحْصَيْنَاهُ فِي
إِمَامٍ مُبِينٍ</td></tr>
<tr><td colspan="3">Lo! We it is Who bring the dead to life. We record that which they send before (them), and their footprints. And all things We have kept in a clear register.</td></tr>
<tr><td>13. W ’adrib lahum mathalan aṣḥāba ’l-qarīyati idh jā’ahā ’l-mursalūn</td><td></td><td>وَاضْرِبْ لَهُم مَّثَلًا
أَصْحَابَ الْقَرْيَةِ إِذْ جَاءَهَا
الْمُرْسَلُونَ</td></tr>
<tr><td colspan="3">Coin for them a similitude: The people of the city when those sent (from Allah) came unto them;</td></tr>
<tr><td>14. Idh arsalnā ilayhimu ’thnayni fa-kadhdhabūhuma fa ‘azzaznā bi-thālithin fa qālū innā ilaykum mursalūn</td><td></td><td>إِذْ أَرْسَلْنَا إِلَيْهِمُ اثْنَيْنِ
فَكَذَّبُوهُمَا فَعَزَّزْنَا بِثَالِثٍ
فَقَالُوا إِنَّا إِلَيْكُم مُّرْسَلُونَ</td></tr>
</table>

<table>
<tr><td colspan="3">When We sent unto them twain, and they denied them both, so We reinforced them with a third, and they said; Lo! we have been sent unto you.</td></tr>
<tr><td>15. Qālū mā antum illa basharun mithlunā wa mā anzala ’r-Raḥmānu min shay’in in antum illa takdhibūn</td><td></td><td>قَالُوا مَا أَنتُمْ إِلاَّ بَشَرٌ مِّثْلُنَا وَمَا أَنزَلَ الرَّحْمَن مِن شَيْءٍ إِنْ أَنتُمْ إِلاَّ تَكْذِبُونَ</td></tr>
<tr><td colspan="3">They said: Ye are but mortals like unto us. The Beneficent hath naught revealed. Ye do but lie!</td></tr>
<tr><td>16. Qālū rabbunā ya‘lamu inna ilaykum la-mursalūna</td><td></td><td>قَالُوا رَبُّنَا يَعْلَمُ إِنَّا إِلَيْكُمْ لَمُرْسَلُونَ</td></tr>
<tr><td colspan="3">They answered: Our lord knoweth that we are indeed sent unto you,</td></tr>
<tr><td>17. Wa mā ‘alaynā illa ’l-balāghu ’l-mubīn</td><td></td><td>وَمَا عَلَيْنَا إِلاَّ الْبَلاَغُ الْمُبِينُ</td></tr>
<tr><td colspan="3">And our duty is but plain conveyance (of the message).</td></tr>
</table>

18. Qālū innā taṭayyarnā bikum la'in lam tantahū la-narjumannakum wa la-yamassannakum minnā ʿadhābun alīm		قَالُوا إِنَّا تَطَيَّرْنَا بِكُمْ لَئِن لَّمْ تَنتَهُوا لَنَرْجُمَنَّكُمْ وَلَيَمَسَّنَّكُم مِّنَّا عَذَابٌ أَلِيمٌ
(The people of the city) said: We augur ill of you. If ye desist not, we shall surely stone you, and grievous torture will befall you at our hands.		
19. Qālū ṭa'irukum maʿakum a'in dhukkirtum bal antum qawmun musrifūn		قَالُوا طَائِرُكُم مَّعَكُمْ أَئِن ذُكِّرْتُم بَلْ أَنتُمْ قَوْمٌ مُّسْرِفُونَ
They said: Your evil augury be with you! Is it because ye are reminded (of the truth)? Nay, but ye are froward folk?		
20. Wa jā'a min aqsa 'l-madīnati rajulun yasʿa qāla yā qawmi 'ittabiʿū 'l-mursalīn		وَجَاءَ مِنْ أَقْصَى الْمَدِينَةِ رَجُلٌ يَسْعَى قَالَ يَا قَوْمِ اتَّبِعُوا الْمُرْسَلِينَ

And there came from the uttermost part of the city a man running. He cried: O my people! Follow those who have been sent!		
21. 'Ittabiʿū man lā yas'alukum ajran wa-hum muhtadūn		اتَّبِعُوا مَن لَّا يَسْأَلُكُمْ أَجْرًا وَهُم مُّهْتَدُونَ
Follow those who ask of you no fee, and who are rightly guided.		
22. Wa-mā līya lā ʿabudu 'l-ladhī faṭaranī wa ilayhi turjaʿūn		وَمَا لِيَ لَا أَعْبُدُ الَّذِي فَطَرَنِي وَإِلَيْهِ تُرْجَعُونَ
For what cause should I not serve Him Who hath created me, and unto Whom ye will be brought back?		
23. A'attakhidhu min dūnihi ālihatan in yuridni 'r-Raḥmānu bi-ḍurrin lā tughni ʿannī shafāʿatuhum shay'an wa lā yunqidhūn		أَأَتَّخِذُ مِن دُونِهِ آلِهَةً إِن يُرِدْنِ الرَّحْمَٰنُ بِضُرٍّ لَّا تُغْنِ عَنِّي شَفَاعَتُهُمْ شَيْئًا وَلَا يُنقِذُونِ

Shall I take (other) gods in place of Him when, if the Beneficent should wish me any harm, their intercession will avail me naught, nor can they save?		
24. Innī idhan lafī ḍalālin mubīn		إِنِّي إِذًا لَّفِي ضَلَالٍ مُّبِينٍ
Then truly I should be in error manifest.		
25. Innī āmantu bi-rabbikum fa ʼsmaʻūn		إِنِّي آمَنتُ بِرَبِّكُمْ فَاسْمَعُونِ
Lo! I have believed in your Lord, so hear met		
26. Qīla ʼdkhuli ʼl-jannata qāla ya layta qawmī yaʻlamūna		قِيلَ ادْخُلِ الْجَنَّةَ قَالَ يَا لَيْتَ قَوْمِي يَعْلَمُونَ
It was said (unto him): Enter Paradise. He said: Would that my people knew		
27. Bi-mā ghafara lī rabbī wa jaʻalanī mina ʼl-mukramīn		بِمَا غَفَرَ لِي رَبِّي وَجَعَلَنِي مِنَ الْمُكْرَمِينَ
With what (munificence) my Lord hath pardoned me and made me of the honored ones!		

<table>
<tr><td>28. Wa-mā anzalnā ʿalā qawmihi min baʿdihi min jundin mina ʼs-samāʼi wa mā kunnā munzilīn</td><td></td><td>وَمَا أَنزَلْنَا عَلَى قَوْمِهِ مِن
بَعْدِهِ مِنْ جُندٍ مِّنَ السَّمَاء
وَمَا كُنَّا مُنزِلِينَ</td></tr>
<tr><td colspan="3">We sent not down against his people after him a host from heaven, nor do We ever send.</td></tr>
<tr><td>29. In kānat illa ṣayḥatan waḥidatan fa idhā hum khāmidūn</td><td></td><td>إِن كَانَتْ إِلاَّ صَيْحَةً
وَاحِدَةً فَإِذَا هُمْ خَامِدُونَ</td></tr>
<tr><td colspan="3">It was but one Shout, and lo! they were extinct.</td></tr>
<tr><td>30. Yā ḥasratan ʿalā ʼl-ʿibadi ma yāʼtīhim min rasūlin illa kānū bihi yastahziʼūn</td><td></td><td>يَا حَسْرَةً عَلَى الْعِبَادِ مَا
يَأْتِيهِم مِّن رَّسُولٍ إِلاَّ كَانُوا
بِهِ يَسْتَهْزِئُونَ</td></tr>
<tr><td colspan="3">Ah, the anguish for the bondmen! Never came there unto them a messenger but they did mock him!</td></tr>
</table>

31. Alam yaraw kam ahlaknā qablahum mina 'l-qurūni annahum ilayhim la yarjiʿūn		أَلَمْ يَرَوْا كَمْ أَهْلَكْنَا قَبْلَهُم مِّنَ الْقُرُونِ أَنَّهُمْ إِلَيْهِمْ لَا يَرْجِعُونَ
Have they not seen how many generations We destroyed before them, which Indeed return not unto them;		
32. Wa in kullun lammā jamīʿūn ladayna muḥḍarūn		وَإِن كُلٌّ لَّمَّا جَمِيعٌ لَّدَيْنَا مُحْضَرُونَ
But all, without exception, will be brought before Us.		
33. Wa āyatun lahumu 'l-arḍu 'l-maytatu aḥyaynāhā wa akhrajnā min-hā ḥabban fa minhu ya'kulūn		وَآيَةٌ لَّهُمُ الْأَرْضُ الْمَيْتَةُ أَحْيَيْنَاهَا وَأَخْرَجْنَا مِنْهَا حَبًّا فَمِنْهُ يَأْكُلُونَ
A token unto them is the dead earth. We revive it, and We bring forth from it grain so that they eat thereof;		

<table>
<tr><td>34. Wa ja‘alnā fī-hā jannātin min nakhīlin wa ‘anābin wa fajjarnā fī-hā mina ’l-‘uyūn</td><td></td><td>وَجَعَلْنَا فِيهَا جَنَّاتٍ مِن نَّخِيلٍ وَأَعْنَابٍ وَفَجَّرْنَا فِيهَا مِنَ الْعُيُونِ</td></tr>
<tr><td colspan="3">And We have placed therein gardens of the date palm and grapes, and We have caused springs of water to gush forth therein.</td></tr>
<tr><td>35. Li yā’kulū min thamarihi wa mā ‘amilathu aydīhim afalā yashkurūn</td><td></td><td>لِيَأْكُلُوا مِن ثَمَرِهِ وَمَا عَمِلَتْهُ أَيْدِيهِمْ أَفَلَا يَشْكُرُونَ</td></tr>
<tr><td colspan="3">That they may eat of the fruit thereof, and their hand made it not. Will they not, then, give thanks?</td></tr>
<tr><td>36. Subḥāna ’l-ladhī khalaqa ’l-azwāja kullahā mimmā tunbitu ’l-arḍu wa min anfusihim wa mimmā lā ya‘lamūn</td><td></td><td>سُبْحَانَ الَّذِي خَلَقَ الْأَزْوَاجَ كُلَّهَا مِمَّا تُنبِتُ الْأَرْضُ وَمِنْ أَنفُسِهِمْ وَمِمَّا لَا يَعْلَمُونَ</td></tr>
</table>

Glory be to Him Who created all the sexual pairs, of that which the earth groweth, and of themselves, and of that which they know not!		
37. Wa āyatun lahumu 'l-laylu naslakhu minhu 'n-nahāra fa-idhā hum muẓlimūn		وَآيَةٌ لَّهُمْ اللَّيْلُ نَسْلَخُ مِنْهُ النَّهَارَ فَإِذَا هُم مُّظْلِمُونَ
A token unto them is night. We strip it of the day, and lo! they are in darkness.		
38. Wa 'sh-shamsu tajrī li-mustaqarrin lahā dhālika taqdīru 'l-ʿazīzi 'l-alīm		وَالشَّمْسُ تَجْرِي لِمُسْتَقَرٍّ لَّهَا ذَلِكَ تَقْدِيرُ الْعَزِيزِ الْعَلِيمِ
And the sun runneth on unto a resting place for him. That is the measuring of the Mighty, the Wise.		
39. Wa 'l-qamara qaddarnāhu manāzila ḥattā aʿāda ka 'l-ʿurjūni 'l-qadīm		وَالْقَمَرَ قَدَّرْنَاهُ مَنَازِلَ حَتَّى عَادَ كَالْعُرْجُونِ الْقَدِيمِ
And for the moon We have appointed mansions till she return like an old shrivelled palm leaf.		

<table>
<tr><td>40. Lā 'sh-shamsu yanbaghī lahā an tudrika 'l-qamara wa lā 'l-laylu ṣābiqu 'n-nahāri wa kullun fī falakin yasbaḥūn</td><td></td><td>لا الشَّمْسُ يَنبَغِي لَهَا أَن تُدْرِكَ الْقَمَرَ وَلا اللَّيْلُ سَابِقُ النَّهَارِ وَكُلٌّ فِي فَلَكٍ يَسْبَحُونَ</td></tr>
<tr><td colspan="3">It is not for the sun to overtake the moon, nor doth the night outstrip the day. They float each in an orbit.</td></tr>
<tr><td>41. Wa āyatun lahum annā ḥamalnā dhurrīyyatahum fī 'l-fulki 'l-mashḥūn</td><td></td><td>وَآيَةٌ لَّهُمْ أَنَّا حَمَلْنَا ذُرِّيَّتَهُمْ فِي الْفُلْكِ الْمَشْحُونِ</td></tr>
<tr><td colspan="3">And a token unto them is that We bear their offspring in the laden ship,</td></tr>
<tr><td>42. Wa khalaqnā lahum min mithlihi mā yarkabūn</td><td></td><td>وَخَلَقْنَا لَهُم مِّن مِّثْلِهِ مَا يَرْكَبُونَ</td></tr>
<tr><td colspan="3">And have created for them of the like thereof whereon they ride.</td></tr>
</table>

43. Wa in nashā' nughriqhum fa-lā ṣarīkha lahum walā hum yunqadhūn	وَإِن نَّشَأْ نُغْرِقْهُمْ فَلَا صَرِيخَ لَهُمْ وَلَا هُمْ يُنقَذُونَ

And if We will, We drown them, and there is no help for them, neither can they be saved;

44. Illa raḥmatan minnā wa matāʿan ilā ḥīn	إِلَّا رَحْمَةً مِّنَّا وَمَتَاعًا إِلَىٰ حِينٍ

Unless by mercy from Us and as comfort for a while.

45. Wa idha qīla lahumu 'ttaqū mā bayna aydīkum wa mā khalfakum laʿallakum turḥamūn	وَإِذَا قِيلَ لَهُمُ اتَّقُوا مَا بَيْنَ أَيْدِيكُمْ وَمَا خَلْفَكُمْ لَعَلَّكُمْ تُرْحَمُونَ

When it is said unto them: Beware of that which is before you and that which is behind you, that haply ye may find mercy (they are heedless).

46. Wa mā tā'tīhim min āyatin min āyāti rabbihim illā kānū ʿanhā mʿuridīn		وَمَا تَأْتِيهِم مِّنْ آيَةٍ مِّنْ آيَاتِ رَبِّهِمْ إِلا كَانُوا عَنْهَا مُعْرِضِينَ
Never came a token of the tokens of their Lord to them, but they did turn away from it!		
47. Wa idhā qīla lahum anfiqū mimmā razaqakum-ullāhu qāla 'l-ladhīna kafarū lil-ladhīna amanū anuṭʿimu man law yashā'u 'llāhu aṭʿamahu in antum illā fī ḍalālin mubīn		وَإِذَا قِيلَ لَهُمْ أَنفِقُوا مِمَّا رَزَقَكُمْ اللهُ قَالَ الَّذِينَ كَفَرُوا لِلَّذِينَ آمَنُوا أَنُطْعِمُ مَن لَّوْ يَشَاءُ اللهُ أَطْعَمَهُ إِنْ أَنتُمْ إِلا فِي ضَلالٍ مُّبِينٍ
And when it is said unto them: Spend of that wherewith Allah hath provided you. those who disbelieve say unto those who believe: Shall we feed those whom Allah, if He willed, would feed? Ye are in naught else than error manifest.		

<table>
<tr><td>48. Wa yaqūlūna matā hadhā 'l-wʿadu in kuntum ṣādiqīn</td><td></td><td>وَيَقُولُونَ مَتَى هَذَا الْوَعْدُ إِن كُنتُمْ صَادِقِينَ</td></tr>
<tr><td colspan="3">And they say: When will this promise be fulfilled, if ye are truthful?</td></tr>
<tr><td>49. Ma yanẓurūna illa ṣayḥatan waḥidatan ta'khudhuhum wa hum yakhiṣṣimūn</td><td></td><td>مَا يَنظُرُونَ إِلا صَيْحَةً وَاحِدَةً تَأْخُذُهُمْ وَهُمْ يَخِصِّمُونَ</td></tr>
<tr><td colspan="3">They await but one Shout, which will surprise them while they are disputing.</td></tr>
<tr><td>50. Fa-lā yastaṭīʿūna tawṣiyatan wa lā ila āhlihim yarjiʿūn</td><td></td><td>فَلا يَسْتَطِيعُونَ تَوْصِيَةً وَلا إِلَى أَهْلِهِمْ يَرْجِعُونَ</td></tr>
<tr><td colspan="3">Then they cannot make bequest, nor can they return to their own folk.</td></tr>
</table>

<table>
<tr><td>51. Wa nufikha fī ‘ṣ-ṣūri fa idhā hum mina ’l-ajdāthi ila rabbihim yansilūn</td><td></td><td>وَنُفِخَ فِي الصُّورِ فَإِذَا هُم مِّنَ الأَجْدَاثِ إِلَى رَبِّهِمْ يَنسِلُونَ</td></tr>
<tr><td colspan="3">And the trumpet is blown and lo! from the graves they hie unto their Lord,</td></tr>
<tr><td>52. Qālū yā waylanā man ba‘athanā min marqadinā hadhā mā wa‘ada ’r-Raḥmānu wa ṣadaqa ’l-mursalūn</td><td></td><td>قَالُوا يَا وَيْلَنَا مَن بَعَثَنَا مِن مَّرْقَدِنَا هَذَا مَا وَعَدَ الرَّحْمَنُ وَصَدَقَ الْمُرْسَلُونَ</td></tr>
<tr><td colspan="3">Crying: Woe upon us! Who hath raised us from our place of sleep? This is that which the Beneficent did promise, and the messengers spoke truth,</td></tr>
<tr><td>53. In kānat illa ṣayḥatan waḥidatan fa idhā hum jamī‘un ladaynā muḥḍarūn</td><td></td><td>إِن كَانَتْ إِلا صَيْحَةً وَاحِدَةً فَإِذَا هُمْ جَمِيعٌ لَّدَيْنَا مُحْضَرُونَ</td></tr>
<tr><td colspan="3">It is but one Shout, and behold them brought together before Us!</td></tr>
</table>

<table>
<tr><td>54. Fa 'l-yawma lā tuẓlamu nafsun shay'an wa lā tujzawna illa mā kuntum tʿamalūn</td><td></td><td>فَالْيَوْمَ لا تُظْلَمُ نَفْسٌ شَيْئًا وَلا تُجْزَوْنَ إِلا مَا كُنتُمْ تَعْمَلُونَ</td></tr>
<tr><td colspan="3">This day no soul is wronged in aught; nor are ye requited aught save what ye used to do.</td></tr>
<tr><td>55. Inna aṣḥāba 'l-jannati 'l-yawma fī shughulin fākihūn</td><td></td><td>إِنَّ أَصْحَابَ الْجَنَّةِ الْيَوْمَ فِي شُغُلٍ فَاكِهُونَ</td></tr>
<tr><td colspan="3">Lo! those who merit paradise this day are happily employed,</td></tr>
<tr><td>56. Hum wa azwājuhum fī ẓilālin ʿala 'l-arā'iki muttaki'ūn</td><td></td><td>هُمْ وَأَزْوَاجُهُمْ فِي ظِلَالٍ عَلَى الأَرَائِكِ مُتَّكِؤُونَ</td></tr>
<tr><td colspan="3">They and their wives, in pleasant shade, on thrones reclining;</td></tr>
<tr><td>57. La-hum fī-hā fākihatun wa lahum mā yaddaʿūna</td><td></td><td>لَهُمْ فِيهَا فَاكِهَةٌ وَلَهُم مَّا يَدَّعُونَ</td></tr>
</table>

Theirs the fruit (of their good deeds) and theirs (all) that they ask;		
58. Salāmun qawlan min rabbin raḥīm		سَلامٌ قَوْلًا مِن رَّبٍّ رَّحِيمٍ
The word from a Merciful Lord (for them) is: Peace!		
59. W 'amtāzū 'l-yawma ayyuhā 'l-mujrimūn		وَامْتَازُوا الْيَوْمَ أَيُّهَا الْمُجْرِمُونَ
But away for ye, O ye guilty, this day!		
60. Alam aʿahad ilaykum yā banī ādama an lā tʿabudū 'sh-shayṭāna innahu lakum ʿadūwwun mubīn		أَلَمْ أَعْهَدْ إِلَيْكُمْ يَا بَنِي آدَمَ أَن لا تَعْبُدُوا الشَّيْطَانَ إِنَّهُ لَكُمْ عَدُوٌّ مُّبِينٌ
Did I not charge you, O ye sons of Adam, that ye worship not the devil Lo! he is your open foe!		
61. Wa aniʿbudūnī hadhā ṣirāṭun mustaqīm		وَأَنْ اعْبُدُونِي هَذَا صِرَاطٌ مُّسْتَقِيمٌ
But that ye worship Me? That was the right path.		

62. Wa laqad aḍalla minkum jibillan kathīran afalam takūnū tʿaqilūn		وَلَقَدْ أَضَلَّ مِنكُمْ جِبِلًّا كَثِيراً أَفَلَمْ تَكُونُوا تَعْقِلُونَ
Yet he hath led astray of you a great multitude. Had ye then no sense?		
63. Hadhihi jahannamu 'l-latī kuntum tūaʿdūn		هَذِهِ جَهَنَّمُ الَّتِي كُنتُمْ تُوعَدُونَ
This is hell which ye were promised (if ye followed him).		
64. Iṣlawhā 'l-yawma bi-mā kuntum takfurūn		اصْلَوْهَا الْيَوْمَ بِمَا كُنتُمْ تَكْفُرُونَ
Burn therein this day for that ye disbelieved.		
65. Al-yawma nakhtimu ʿalā afwāhihim wa tukallimuna aydīhim wa tashhadu arjuluhum bi-mā kānū yaksibūn		الْيَوْمَ نَخْتِمُ عَلَى أَفْوَاهِهِمْ وَتُكَلِّمُنَا أَيْدِيهِمْ وَتَشْهَدُ أَرْجُلُهُمْ بِمَا كَانُوا يَكْسِبُونَ

<table>
<tr><td colspan="3">This day We seal up mouths, and hands speak out and feet bear witness as to what they used to earn.</td></tr>
<tr><td>66. Wa law nashā'u la-ṭamasnā ʻala āʻayunihim fa-stabaqū ʻṣ-ṣirāṭa fa-anna yubṣirūn</td><td></td><td>وَلَوْ نَشَاء لَطَمَسْنَا عَلَى
أَعْيُنِهِمْ فَاسْتَبَقُوا الصِّرَاطَ
فَأَنَّى يُبْصِرُونَ</td></tr>
<tr><td colspan="3">And had We willed, We verily could have quenched their eyesight so that they should struggle for the way. Then how could they have seen?</td></tr>
<tr><td>67. Wa law nasha'u la-masakhnāhum ʻala makānatihim fa-mā istaṭāʻū muḍīyyan wa lā yarjiʻūn</td><td></td><td>وَلَوْ نَشَاء لَمَسَخْنَاهُمْ عَلَى
مَكَانَتِهِمْ فَمَا اسْتَطَاعُوا
مُضِيًّا وَلَا يَرْجِعُونَ</td></tr>
<tr><td colspan="3">And had We willed, We verily could have fixed them in their place, making them powerless to go forward or turn back.</td></tr>
<tr><td>68. Wa man nuʻammirhu nunakkis-hu fī 'l-khalqi afalā yʻaqilūn</td><td></td><td>وَمَنْ نُعَمِّرْهُ نُنَكِّسْهُ فِي
الْخَلْقِ أَفَلَا يَعْقِلُونَ</td></tr>
</table>

He whom We bring unto old age, We reverse him in creation (making him go back to weakness after strength). Have ye then no sense?		
69. Wa mā ʿallamnāhu ʾsh-shʿira wa mā yanbaghī lahu in Huwa illa dhikrun wa qurʾānun mubīn		وَمَا عَلَّمْنَاهُ الشِّعْرَ وَمَا يَنبَغِي لَهُ إِنْ هُوَ إِلا ذِكْرٌ وَقُرْآنٌ مُّبِينٌ
And we have not taught him (Muhammad) poetry, nor is it meet for him. This is naught else than a Reminder and a Lecture making plain,		
70. Li-yundhira man kāna ḥayyan wa yaḥiqqa ʾl-qawlu ʿala ʾl-kāfirīn		لِيُنذِرَ مَن كَانَ حَيًّا وَيَحِقَّ الْقَوْلُ عَلَى الْكَافِرِينَ
To warn whosoever liveth, and that the word may be fulfilled against the disbelievers.		
71. Awa lam yaraw annā khalaqnā la-hum mimmā ʿamilat aydīna anaʿāman fa-hum lahā mālikūn		أَوَلَمْ يَرَوْا أَنَّا خَلَقْنَا لَهُم مِّمَّا عَمِلَتْ أَيْدِينَا أَنْعَامًا فَهُمْ لَهَا مَالِكُونَ

<table>
<tr><td colspan="3">Have they not seen how We have created for them of Our handiwork the cattle, so that they are their owners,</td></tr>
<tr><td>72. Wa dhallalnāhā la-hum fa-minhā rakūbuhum wa minhā yā'kulūn</td><td></td><td>وَذَلَّلْنَاهَا لَهُمْ فَمِنْهَا رَكُوبُهُمْ
وَمِنْهَا يَأْكُلُونَ</td></tr>
<tr><td colspan="3">And have subdued them unto them, so that some of them they have for riding, some for food?</td></tr>
<tr><td>73. Wa la-hum fīhā manāfiʿu wa mashāribu afalā yashkurūn</td><td></td><td>وَلَهُمْ فِيهَا مَنَافِعُ وَمَشَارِبُ
أَفَلَا يَشْكُرُونَ</td></tr>
<tr><td colspan="3">Benefits and (divers) drinks have they from them. Will they not then give thanks?</td></tr>
<tr><td>74. Wat-takhadhū min dūni 'l-lāhi alihatan laʿallahum yunṣarūn</td><td></td><td>وَاتَّخَذُوا مِن دُونِ اللَّهِ آلِهَةً
لَعَلَّهُمْ يُنصَرُونَ</td></tr>
<tr><td colspan="3">And they have taken (other) gods beside Allah, in order that they may be helped.</td></tr>
<tr><td>75. Lā yastaṭīʿūna naṣrahum wa hum lahum jundun muḥḍarūn</td><td></td><td>لَا يَسْتَطِيعُونَ نَصْرَهُمْ
وَهُمْ لَهُمْ جُندٌ مُّحْضَرُونَ</td></tr>
</table>

It is not in their power to help them; but they (the worshippers) are unto them a host in arms.		
76. Falā yaḥzunka qawluhum innā n‘alamu mā yusirrūna wa mā y‘ulinūn		فَلا يَحْزُنكَ قَوْلُهُمْ إِنَّا نَعْلَمُ مَا يُسِرُّونَ وَمَا يُعْلِنُونَ
So let not their speech grieve thee (O Muhammad). Lo! We know what they conceal and what proclaim.		
77. Awa lam yara 'l-insānu annā khalaqnāhu min nuṭfatin fa-idhā Huwa khaṣīmun mubīn		أَوَلَمْ يَرَ الإِنسَانُ أَنَّا خَلَقْنَاهُ مِن نُّطْفَةٍ فَإِذَا هُوَ خَصِيمٌ مُّبِينٌ
Hath not man seen that We have created him from a drop of seed? Yet lo! he is an open opponent.		
78. Wa ḍaraba lanā mathalan wa nasīya khalqahu qāla man yuḥyī 'l-‘iẓāma wa hīya ramīm		وَضَرَبَ لَنَا مَثَلًا وَنَسِيَ خَلْقَهُ قَالَ مَنْ يُحْيِي الْعِظَامَ وَهِيَ رَمِيمٌ

<table>
<tr><td colspan="3">And he hath coined for Us a similitude, and hath forgotten the fact of his creation, saying: Who will revive these bones when they have rotted away?</td></tr>
<tr><td>79. Qul yuḥyīhā 'l-ladhī anshā'ahā āwwala marratin wa Huwa bi kulli khalqin ʿalīm</td><td></td><td>قُلْ يُحْيِيهَا الَّذِي أَنشَأَهَا أَوَّلَ مَرَّةٍ وَهُوَ بِكُلِّ خَلْقٍ عَلِيمٌ</td></tr>
<tr><td colspan="3">Say: He will revive them Who produced them at the first, for He is Knower of every creation,</td></tr>
<tr><td>80. Al-ladhī jaʿala lakum mina 'sh-shajari 'l-akhḍari nāran fa idhā antum minhu tūqidūn</td><td></td><td>الَّذِي جَعَلَ لَكُم مِّنَ الشَّجَرِ الأَخْضَرِ نَارًا فَإِذَا أَنتُم مِّنْهُ تُوقِدُونَ</td></tr>
<tr><td colspan="3">Who hath appointed for you fire from the green tree, and behold! ye kindle from it.</td></tr>
<tr><td>81. Awa laysa 'l-ladhī khalaqa 's-samawāti wa 'l-arḍa bi-qādirin ʿalā an yakhluqa mithlahum balā</td><td></td><td>أَوَلَيْسَ الَّذِي خَلَقَ السَّمَاوَاتِ وَالأَرْضَ بِقَادِرٍ</td></tr>
</table>

wa Huwa 'l-Khallāqu 'l-'Alīm		عَلَى أَنْ يَخْلُقَ مِثْلَهُم بَلَى وَهُوَ الْخَلَّاقُ الْعَلِيمُ
Is not He Who created the heavens and the earth Able to create the like of them? Aye, that He is! for He is the All Wise Creator,		
82. Innamā amruhu idhā arada shay'an an yaqūla lahu kun fa-yakūn		إِنَّمَا أَمْرُهُ إِذَا أَرَادَ شَيْئًا أَنْ يَقُولَ لَهُ كُنْ فَيَكُونُ
But His command, when He intendeth a thing, is only that he saith unto it: Be! and it is.		
83. Fa subḥāna 'l-ladhī bi-yadihi malakūtu kulli shay'in wa ilayhi turja'ūn		فَسُبْحَانَ الَّذِي بِيَدِهِ مَلَكُوتُ كُلِّ شَيْءٍ وَإِلَيْهِ تُرْجَعُونَ
Therefore glory be to Him in Whose hand is the dominion over all things! Unto Him ye will be brought back.		

<table>
<tr><td>Sūrat al-Mulk: Kingship (67)</td><td></td><td>سورة الملك</td></tr>
<tr><td colspan="3">To be read after Ṣalāt aẓ-Ẓuhr and after Ṣalāt al-ʿIshā</td></tr>
<tr><td>Bismillāhi ’r-Raḥmāni ’r-Rahīm</td><td></td><td>بِسْمِ اللهِ الرَّحْمٰنِ الرَّحِيمِ</td></tr>
<tr><td colspan="3">In the Name of Allah, the Most Beneficent, the Most Merciful.</td></tr>
<tr><td>1. Tabāraka ’l-ladhī bi-yadihi ’l-Mulku wa Hūwa ʿalā kulli shay’in qadīr</td><td></td><td>تَبَارَكَ الَّذِي بِيَدِهِ الْمُلْكُ
وَهُوَ عَلَى كُلِّ شَيْءٍ قَدِيرٌ</td></tr>
<tr><td colspan="3">Blessed is He in Whose hand is the Sovereignty, and He is Able to do all things.</td></tr>
<tr><td>2. Alladhī khalaqa ’l-mawta wa ’l-ḥayāta li-yablūwakum ayyukum aḥsanu ʿamala wa Hūwa ’l-ʿAzīzu ’l-Ghafūr.</td><td></td><td>الَّذِي خَلَقَ الْمَوْتَ وَالْحَيَاةَ
لِيَبْلُوَكُمْ أَيُّكُمْ أَحْسَنُ
عَمَلًا وَهُوَ الْعَزِيزُ الْغَفُورُ</td></tr>
<tr><td colspan="3">Who hath created life and death that He may try you, which of you is best in conduct; and He is the Mighty, Forgiving,</td></tr>
</table>

<table>
<tr><td>3. Alladhī khalaqa sabaʿa samāwātin ṭibāqan mā tarā fī khalqi ’r-Raḥmāni min tafāwutin farjiʿi ’l-baṣara hal tarā min fuṭūr</td><td></td><td>الَّذِي خَلَقَ سَبْعَ سَمَاوَاتٍ طِبَاقًا مَّا تَرَى فِي خَلْقِ الرَّحْمَنِ مِن تَفَاوُتٍ فَارْجِعِ الْبَصَرَ هَلْ تَرَى مِن فُطُورٍ</td></tr>
<tr><td colspan="3">Who hath created seven heavens in harmony. Thou (Muhammad) canst see no fault in the Beneficent One’s creation; then look again: Canst thou see any rifts?</td></tr>
<tr><td>4. Thumma ’rjiʿi ’l-baṣara karratayni yanqalib ilayka ’l-baṣaru khāsi’an wa Huwa ḥasīr</td><td></td><td>ثُمَّ ارْجِعِ الْبَصَرَ كَرَّتَيْنِ يَنقَلِبْ إِلَيْكَ الْبَصَرُ خَاسِأً وَهُوَ حَسِيرٌ</td></tr>
<tr><td colspan="3">Then look again and yet again, thy sight will return unto thee weakened and made dim.</td></tr>
<tr><td>5. Wa-laqad zayyanna ’s-samā ad-dunyā bi maṣābīḥa wa jaʿalnāha rujūman li ’sh-shayāṭīni wa āʿatadnā la-hum ʿaḍāba ’s-saʿīr</td><td></td><td>وَلَقَدْ زَيَّنَّا السَّمَاءَ الدُّنْيَا بِمَصَابِيحَ وَجَعَلْنَاهَا رُجُومًا لِّلشَّيَاطِينِ وَأَعْتَدْنَا لَهُمْ عَذَابَ السَّعِيرِ</td></tr>
</table>

<table>
<tr><td colspan="3">And verily We have beatified the world's heaven with lamps, and We have made them missiles for the devils, and for them We have prepared the doom of flame.</td></tr>
<tr><td>6. Wa lil-ladhīna kafarū bi-rabbihim ʿadhābu jahannama wa bi'sa 'l-maṣīr</td><td></td><td>وَلِلَّذِينَ كَفَرُوا بِرَبِّهِمْ عَذَابُ جَهَنَّمَ وَبِئْسَ الْمَصِيرُ</td></tr>
<tr><td colspan="3">And for those who disbelieve in their Lord there is the doom of hell, a hapless journey's end!</td></tr>
<tr><td>7. Idhā ulqū fīhā samiʿū lahā shahīqan wa hīya tafūr</td><td></td><td>إِذَا أُلْقُوا فِيهَا سَمِعُوا لَهَا شَهِيقًا وَهِيَ تَفُورُ</td></tr>
<tr><td colspan="3">When they are flung therein they hear its roaring as it boileth up,</td></tr>
<tr><td>8. Takādu tamayyazu mina 'l-ghayẓi kullamā ulqīya fīhā fawjun sa'alahum khazanatuhā alam yā'tikum nadhīr</td><td></td><td>تَكَادُ تَمَيَّزُ مِنَ الْغَيْظِ كُلَّمَا أُلْقِيَ فِيهَا فَوْجٌ سَأَلَهُمْ خَزَنَتُهَا أَلَمْ يَأْتِكُمْ نَذِيرٌ</td></tr>
</table>

As it would burst with rage. Whenever a (fresh) host flung therein the wardens thereof ask them: Came there unto you no warner?		
9. Qālū balā qad jā'anā nadhīrun fa-kadhdhabnā wa qulnā mā nazzala-Allāhu min shay'in in antum illa fī ḍalālin kabīr		قَالُوا بَلَى قَدْ جَاءَنَا نَذِيرٌ فَكَذَّبْنَا وَقُلْنَا مَا نَزَّلَ اللَّهُ مِن شَيْءٍ إِنْ أَنتُمْ إِلا فِي ضَلالٍ كَبِيرٍ
They say: Yea, verily, a warner came unto us; but we denied and said: Allah hath naught revealed; ye are in nought but a great error.		
10. Wa qālū law kunnā nasmaʿu aw nʿaqilu mā kunnā fī aṣḥābi 's-saʿīr		وَقَالُوا لَوْ كُنَّا نَسْمَعُ أَوْ نَعْقِلُ مَا كُنَّا فِي أَصْحَابِ السَّعِيرِ
And they say: Had we been wont to listen or have sense, we had not been among the dwellers in the flames.		
11. Fʿatarafū bi-dhanbihim fasuḥqan li aṣḥabi 's-saʿīr		فَاعْتَرَفُوا بِذَنبِهِمْ فَسُحْقًا لِّأَصْحَابِ السَّعِيرِ

<table>
<tr><td colspan="3">So they acknowledge their sins; but far removed (from mercy) are the dwellers in the flames.</td></tr>
<tr><td>12. Inna 'l-ladhīna yakhshawna rabbahum bi 'l-ghaybi la-hum maghfiratun wa ajrun kabīr</td><td></td><td>إِنَّ الَّذِينَ يَخْشَوْنَ رَبَّهُم بِالْغَيْبِ لَهُم مَّغْفِرَةٌ وَأَجْرٌ كَبِيرٌ</td></tr>
<tr><td colspan="3">Lo! those who fear their Lord in secret, theirs will be forgiveness and a great reward.</td></tr>
<tr><td>13. Wa asirrū qawlakum awi 'jharū bihi innahu ʿalīmun bi-dhāti 'ṣ-ṣudūr</td><td></td><td>وَأَسِرُّوا قَوْلَكُمْ أَوِ اجْهَرُوا بِهِ إِنَّهُ عَلِيمٌ بِذَاتِ الصُّدُورِ</td></tr>
<tr><td colspan="3">And keep your opinion secret or proclaim it, lo! He is Knower of all that is in the breasts (of men)</td></tr>
<tr><td>14. Alā yʿalamu man khalaqa wa Huwa 'l-Latīfu 'l-Khabīr</td><td></td><td>أَلَا يَعْلَمُ مَنْ خَلَقَ وَهُوَ اللَّطِيفُ الْخَبِيرُ</td></tr>
<tr><td colspan="3">Should He not know what He created? And He is the Subtile, the Aware.</td></tr>
<tr><td>15. Huwa 'l-ladhī jaʿala lakumu 'l-arḍa dhalūlan fa-mshū fī manākibihā wa kulū</td><td></td><td>هُوَ الَّذِي جَعَلَ لَكُمُ الْأَرْضَ ذَلُولًا فَامْشُوا فِي</td></tr>
</table>

min rizqihi wa ilayhi ʼn-nushūr		مَنَاكِبِهَا وَكُلُوا مِن رِّزْقِهِ وَإِلَيْهِ النُّشُورُ
He it is Who hath made the earth subservient unto you, so walk in the paths thereof and eat of His providence. And unto Him will be the resurrection (of the dead)		
16. A-amintum man fī ʼs-samāʼi an yakhsifa bikumu ʼl-arḍa fa-idhā hīya tamūr		أَأَمِنتُم مَّن فِي السَّمَاءِ أَن يَخْسِفَ بِكُمُ الأَرْضَ فَإِذَا هِيَ تَمُورُ
Have ye taken security from Him Who is in the heaven that He will not cause the earth to swallow you when lo! it is convulsed?		
17. Am amintum man fī ʼs-samāʼi an yursila ʻalaykum ḥāṣiban fa-sa-tʻalamūna kayfa nadhīr		أَمْ أَمِنتُم مَّن فِي السَّمَاءِ أَن يُرْسِلَ عَلَيْكُمْ حَاصِبًا فَسَتَعْلَمُونَ كَيْفَ نَذِيرِ
Or have ye taken security from Him Who is in the heaven that He will not let loose on you a hurricane? But ye shall know the manner of My warning.		

18. Wa-laqad kadhdhaba 'l-ladhīna min qablihim fa-kayfa kāna nakīr		وَلَقَدْ كَذَّبَ الَّذِينَ مِن قَبْلِهِمْ فَكَيْفَ كَانَ نَكِيرِ
And verily those before them denied, then (see) the manner of My wrath (with them!)		
19. Awa lam yaraw ila aṭ-ṭayri fawqahum ṣāffātin wa yaqbidna mā yumsikuhunna illa ar-raḥmānu innahu bi-kulli shay'in basīr.		أَوَلَمْ يَرَوْا إِلَى الطَّيْرِ فَوْقَهُمْ صَافَّاتٍ وَيَقْبِضْنَ مَا يُمْسِكُهُنَّ إِلا الرَّحْمَنُ إِنَّهُ بِكُلِّ شَيْءٍ بَصِيرٌ
Have they not seen the birds above them spreading out their wings and closing them? Naught upholdeth them save the Beneficent. Lo! He is Seer of all things.		
20. Amman hadha 'l-ladhī Huwa jundun lakum yanṣurukum min dūni 'r-Raḥmān ini 'l-kāfirūna illa fī ghurūr		أَمَّنْ هَذَا الَّذِي هُوَ جُندٌ لَّكُمْ يَنصُرُكُم مِّن دُونِ الرَّحْمَنِ إِنِ الْكَافِرُونَ إِلا فِي غُرُورٍ

Or who is he that will be an army unto you to help you instead of the Beneficent? The disbelievers are in naught but illusion.		
21. Amman hadha 'l-ladhī yarzuqukum in amsaka rizqahu bal lajjū fī 'utuwwin wa nufūr		أَمَّنْ هَذَا الَّذِي يَرْزُقُكُمْ إِنْ أَمْسَكَ رِزْقَهُ بَل لَّجُّوا فِي عُتُوٍّ وَنُفُورٍ
Or who is he that will provide for you if He should withhold His providence? Nay, but they are set in pride and frowardness.		
22. Afa-man yamshī mukibban 'alā wajhihi ahdā amman yamshī sawiyyan 'alā ṣirāṭin mustaqīm		أَفَمَن يَمْشِي مُكِبًّا عَلَى وَجْهِهِ أَهْدَى أَمَّن يَمْشِي سَوِيًّا عَلَى صِرَاطٍ مُّسْتَقِيمٍ
Is he who goeth groping on his face more rightly guided, or he who walketh upright on a beaten road?		
23. Qul Huwa 'lladhī anshā'akum wa ja'ala lakumu 's-sam'a wa 'l-abṣāra		قُلْ هُوَ الَّذِي أَنشَأَكُمْ وَجَعَلَ لَكُمُ السَّمْعَ

<table>
<tr><td>wa 'l-af'idata qalīlan mā tashkurūn</td><td></td><td>وَالأَبْصَارَ وَالأَفْئِدَةَ قَلِيلًا مَّا تَشْكُرُونَ</td></tr>
<tr><td colspan="3">Say (unto them, O Muhammad): He it is Who gave you being, and hath assigned unto you ears and eyes and hearts. Small thanks give ye!</td></tr>
<tr><td>24. Qul huwa 'l-ladhī dharā'kum fī 'l-arḍi wa ilayhi tuḥsharūn</td><td></td><td>قُلْ هُوَ الَّذِي ذَرَأَكُمْ فِي الأَرْضِ وَإِلَيْهِ تُحْشَرُونَ</td></tr>
<tr><td colspan="3">Say, He it is Who multiplieth you in the earth, and unto Whom ye will be gathered.</td></tr>
<tr><td>25. Wa yaqūlūna matā hadha 'l-waʿadu in kuntum ṣādiqīn</td><td></td><td>وَيَقُولُونَ مَتَى هَذَا الْوَعْدُ إِن كُنتُمْ صَادِقِينَ</td></tr>
<tr><td colspan="3">And they say: When (will) this promise (be fulfilled), if ye are truthful?</td></tr>
<tr><td>26. Qul innamā 'l-ʿilmu ʿinda -llāhi wa innamā anā nadhīrun mubīn</td><td></td><td>قُلْ إِنَّمَا الْعِلْمُ عِندَ اللهِ وَإِنَّمَا أَنَا نَذِيرٌ مُّبِينٌ</td></tr>
<tr><td colspan="3">Say: The knowledge is with Allah only, and I am but a plain warner;</td></tr>
</table>

<table>
<tr><td>27. Fa-lammā ra'awhu zulfatan sī'at wujūhu 'l-ladhīna kafarū wa qīla hadha 'l-ladhī kuntum bihi taddaʿūn</td><td></td><td>فَلَمَّا رَأَوْهُ زُلْفَةً سِيئَتْ وُجُوهُ الَّذِينَ كَفَرُوا وَقِيلَ هَٰذَا الَّذِي كُنتُم بِهِ تَدَّعُونَ</td></tr>
<tr><td colspan="3">But when they see it nigh, the faces of those who disbelieve will be awry, and it will be said (unto them): This is that for which ye used to call</td></tr>
<tr><td>28. Qul arā'aytum in ahlakanīy-allāhu wa man maʿīya aw raḥimanā fa-man yujīru 'l-kāfirīna min ʿadhābin alīm</td><td></td><td>قُلْ أَرَأَيْتُمْ إِنْ أَهْلَكَنِيَ اللَّهُ وَمَن مَّعِيَ أَوْ رَحِمَنَا فَمَن يُجِيرُ الْكَافِرِينَ مِنْ عَذَابٍ أَلِيمٍ</td></tr>
<tr><td colspan="3">Say (O Muhammad): Have ye thought: Whether Allah causeth me (Muhammad) and those with me to perish or hath mercy on us, still, who will protect the disbelievers from a painful doom?</td></tr>
</table>

29. Qul Huwa 'r-Raḥmānu āmannā bihi wa ʿalayhi tawakkalnā fa-satʿalamūna man Huwa fī ḍalālin mubīn		قُلْ هُوَ الرَّحْمَنُ آمَنَّا بِهِ وَعَلَيْهِ تَوَكَّلْنَا فَسَتَعْلَمُونَ مَنْ هُوَ فِي ضَلَالٍ مُّبِينٍ
Say: He is the Beneficent. In Him we believe and in Him we put our trust. And ye will soon know who it is that is in error manifest.		

30. Qul arā'ytum in aṣbaḥa mā'ūkum ghawran fa-man yā'tīkum bi mā'in maʿīn		قُلْ أَرَأَيْتُمْ إِنْ أَصْبَحَ مَاؤُكُمْ غَوْرًا فَمَن يَأْتِيكُم بِمَاءٍ مَّعِينٍ
Say: Have ye thought: If (all) your water were to disappear into the earth, who then could bring you gushing water?		

Sūrat **an-Nabā: The Event (78)**		سورة النبأ
To be read after Ṣalāt al-ʿAṣr		
Bismillāhi ’r-Raḥmāni ’r-Rahīm		بِسْمِ اللَّهِ الرَّحْمَٰنِ الرَّحِيمِ
In the Name of Allah, the Most Beneficent, the Most Merciful.		
1. ʿAmma yatasā’alūna		عَمَّ يَتَسَاءلُونَ
Whereof do they question one another?		
2. ʿani ’n-nabā’i ’l-ʿaẓīm		عَنِ النَّبَإِ الْعَظِيمِ
(It is) of the awful tidings,		
3. Alladhī hum fīhi mukhtalifūn		الَّذِي هُمْ فِيهِ مُخْتَلِفُونَ
Concerning which they are in disagreement.		
4. Kallā sa-yʿalamūna		كَلا سَيَعْلَمُونَ
Nay, but they will come to know!		
5. Thumma kalla sayʿalamūn.		ثُمَّ كَلا سَيَعْلَمُونَ

Nay, again, but they will come to know!		
6. Alam najʿali 'l-arḍa mihādan		أَلَمْ نَجْعَلِ الأَرْضَ مِهَادًا
Have We not made the earth an expanse,		
7. Wa 'l-jibāla awtādan		وَالْجِبَالَ أَوْتَادًا
And the high hills bulwarks?		
8. Wa khalaqnākum azwāja		وَخَلَقْنَاكُمْ أَزْوَاجًا
And We have created you in pairs,		
9. Wa jaʿalnā nawmakum subātan		وَجَعَلْنَا نَوْمَكُمْ سُبَاتًا
And have appointed your sleep for repose,		
10. Wa jaʿalnā 'l-layla libāsan		وَجَعَلْنَا اللَّيْلَ لِبَاسًا
And have appointed the night as a cloak,		
11. Wa jaʿalnā 'n-nahāra maʿāsha		وَجَعَلْنَا النَّهَارَ مَعَاشًا
And have appointed the day for livelihood.		
12. Wa banaynā fawqakum sabʿan shidādan		وَبَنَيْنَا فَوْقَكُمْ سَبْعًا شِدَادًا

And We have built above you seven strong (heavens),		
13. Wa jaʿalnā sirājan wa h-hāja		وَجَعَلْنَا سِرَاجًا وَهَّاجًا
And have appointed a dazzling lamp,		
14. Wa anzalnā mina 'l-mʿuṣirāti mā'an thajjājan		وَأَنزَلْنَا مِنَ الْمُعْصِرَاتِ مَاء ثَجَّاجًا
And have sent down from the rainy clouds abundant Water,		
15. Li nukhrija bihi ḥabban wa nabātan		لِنُخْرِجَ بِهِ حَبًّا وَنَبَاتًا
Thereby to produce grain and plant,		
16. Wa jannātin alfāfa.		وَجَنَّاتٍ أَلْفَافًا
And gardens of thick foliage.		
17. Inna yawma 'l-faṣli kāna mīqāta;		إِنَّ يَوْمَ الْفَصْلِ كَانَ مِيقَاتًا
Lo! the Day of Decision is a fixed time,		

18. Yawma yunfakhu fī 'ṣ-ṣūri fatā'tūna afwājan		يَوْمَ يُنفَخُ فِي الصُّورِ فَتَأْتُونَ أَفْوَاجًا
A day when the trumpet is blown, and ye come in multitudes		
19. Wa futiḥati 's-samā'u fa-kānat abwāban		وَفُتِحَتِ السَّمَاءُ فَكَانَتْ أَبْوَابًا
And the heaven is opened and becometh as gates		
20. Wa suyyirati 'l-jibālu fakānat sarāba.		وَسُيِّرَتِ الْجِبَالُ فَكَانَتْ سَرَابًا
And the hills are set in motion and become as a mirage.		
21. Inna jahannama kānat mirṣādan		إِنَّ جَهَنَّمَ كَانَتْ مِرْصَادًا
Lo! Hell lurketh in ambush,		
22. Li 'ṭ-ṭāghīna ma-āba		لِلْطَّاغِينَ مَآبًا
A home for the rebellious		
23. Lābithīna fīhā aḥqāban		لَابِثِينَ فِيهَا أَحْقَابًا
They will abide therein for ages.		

24. Lā yadhūqūna fīhā bardan wa lā sharāban		لا يَذُوقُونَ فِيهَا بَرْدًا وَلا شَرَابًا
Therein taste they neither coolness nor (any) drink		
25. Illā ḥamīman wa ghassāqan		إِلا حَمِيمًا وَغَسَّاقًا
Save boiling water and a paralyzing cold:		
26. Jazā'an wifāqa		جَزَاء وِفَاقًا
Reward proportioned (to their evil deeds).		
27. Innahum kānū la yarjūna ḥisāba		إِنَّهُمْ كَانُوا لا يَرْجُونَ حِسَابًا
For lo! They looked not for a reckoning;		
28. Wa kadhdhabū bi āyātinā kidhdhāba		وَكَذَّبُوا بِآيَاتِنَا كِذَّابًا
They called Our revelations false with strong denial.		
29. Wa kulla shay'in aḥṣaynāhu kitāba		وَكُلَّ شَيْءٍ أَحْصَيْنَاهُ كِتَابًا
Everything have We recorded in a Book.		

30. Fa-dhūqū fa-lan nazīdakum illā ʿadhāba.		فَذُوقُوا فَلَن نَّزِيدَكُمْ إِلا عَذَابًا
So taste (of that which ye have earned). No increase do We give you save of torment.		
31. Inna li 'l-muttaqīna mafāzan		إِنَّ لِلْمُتَّقِينَ مَفَازًا
Lo! for the duteous is achievement		
32. ḥadā'iqa wa aʿanāban		حَدَائِقَ وَأَعْنَابًا
Gardens enclosed and vineyards,		
33. Wa kawāʿiba atrāban		وَكَوَاعِبَ أَتْرَابًا
And maidens for companions,		
34. Wa kā'san dihāqa		وَكَأْسًا دِهَاقًا
And a full cup.		
35. Lā yasmaʿūna fīhā laghwan wa lā kidhdhāba		لا يَسْمَعُونَ فِيهَا لَغْوًا وَلا كِذَّابًا
There hear they never vain discourse, nor lying		

36. Jazā'an min rabbika 'atā'an ḥisāba	جَزَاءً مِّن رَّبِّكَ عَطَاءً حِسَابًا
Requital from thy Lord a gift in payment	
37. Rabbi 's-samāwāti wa 'l-arḍi wa mā baynahuma 'r-Raḥmāni lā yamlikūna minhu khiṭāba	رَبِّ السَّمَاوَاتِ وَالْأَرْضِ وَمَا بَيْنَهُمَا الرَّحْمَٰنِ لَا يَمْلِكُونَ مِنْهُ خِطَابًا
Lord of the heavens and the earth, and (all) that is between them, the Beneficent; with Whom none can converse.	
38. Yawma yaqūmu 'r-rūḥu wa 'l-malā'ikatu ṣaffan lā yatakallamūna illa man adhina lahu 'r-Raḥmānu wa qāla ṣawāba	يَوْمَ يَقُومُ الرُّوحُ وَالْمَلَائِكَةُ صَفًّا لَا يَتَكَلَّمُونَ إِلَّا مَنْ أَذِنَ لَهُ الرَّحْمَٰنُ وَقَالَ صَوَابًا
On the day when the angels and the Spirit stand arrayed, they speak not, saving him whom the Beneficent alloweth and who speaketh right.	

39. Dhalika 'l-yawmu 'l-ḥaqqu fa-man shā'a 'ttakhadha ilā rabbihi ma'āba		ذَلِكَ الْيَوْمُ الْحَقُّ فَمَن شَاء اتَّخَذَ إِلَى رَبِّهِ مَآبًا
That is the True Day. So whoso will should seek recourse unto his Lord.		
40. Innā andharnākum 'adhāban qarīban yawma yanẓuru 'l-mar'u mā qaddamat yadāhu wa yaqūlu 'l-kāfiru yā laytanī kuntu turābā.		إِنَّا أَنذَرْنَاكُمْ عَذَاباً قَرِيباً يَوْمَ يَنظُرُ الْمَرْءُ مَا قَدَّمَتْ يَدَاهُ وَيَقُولُ الْكَافِرُ يَا لَيْتَنِي كُنتُ تُرَاباً
Lo! We warn you of a doom at hand, a day whereon a man will look on that which his own hands have sent before, and the disbeliever will cry: "Would that I were dust!"		

Sūrat as-Sajdah: The Prostration (32)		سورة السجدة
To be read after Ṣalāt al-Maghrib		
Bismillāhi 'r-Raḥmāni 'r-Rahīm		بِسْمِ اللهِ الرَّحْمٰنِ الرَّحِيمِ
In the Name of Allah, the Most Beneficent, the Most Merciful.		
1. Alif lām mīm		الم
Alif. Lām. Mīm.		
2. Tanzīlu 'l-kitābi lā rayba fīhi min rabbi 'l-ʿālamīn		تَنزِيلُ الْكِتَابِ لَا رَيْبَ فِيهِ مِن رَّبِّ الْعَالَمِينَ
The revelation of the Scripture whereof there is no doubt is from the Lord of the Worlds.		
3. Am yaqūlūna 'ftarāhu bal huwa 'l-ḥaqqu min Rabbika li-tundhira qawman mā atāhum min nadhīrin min		أَمْ يَقُولُونَ افْتَرَاهُ بَلْ هُوَ الْحَقُّ مِن رَّبِّكَ لِتُنذِرَ قَوْمًا

qablika la'allahum yahtadūn		مَّا أَتَاهُم مِّن نَّذِيرٍ مِّن قَبْلِكَ لَعَلَّهُمْ يَهْتَدُونَ
Or say they: He hath invented it? Nay, but it is the Truth from thy Lord, that thou mayst warn a folk to whom no warner came before thee, that haply they may walk aright.		
4. Allāhu 'l-ladhī khalaqa 's-samāwāti wa 'l-arḍa wa mā baynahumā fī sittati ayyāmin thumma 'stawa 'ala 'l-'arsh. mā lakum min dūnihi min walīyyin wa lā shafī'in afalā tatadhakkarūn		اللَّهُ الَّذِي خَلَقَ السَّمَاوَاتِ وَالْأَرْضَ وَمَا بَيْنَهُمَا فِي سِتَّةِ أَيَّامٍ ثُمَّ اسْتَوَى عَلَى الْعَرْشِ مَا لَكُم مِّن دُونِهِ مِن وَلِيٍّ وَلَا شَفِيعٍ أَفَلَا تَتَذَكَّرُونَ
Allah it is Who created the heavens and the earth, and that which is between them, in six Days. Then He mounted the throne. Ye have not, beside Him, a protecting friend or mediator. Will ye not then remember?		

<table>
<tr><td>5. Yudabbiru ’l-amra mina ’s-sama’i ila ’l-arḍi thumma y‘aruju ilayhi fī yawmin kāna miqdāruhu alfa sanatin mimmā ta‘uddūn</td><td></td><td>يُدَبِّرُ الْأَمْرَ مِنَ السَّمَاءِ إِلَى الْأَرْضِ ثُمَّ يَعْرُجُ إِلَيْهِ فِي يَوْمٍ كَانَ مِقْدَارُهُ أَلْفَ سَنَةٍ مِّمَّا تَعُدُّونَ</td></tr>
<tr><td colspan="3">He directeth the ordinance from the heaven unto the earth; then it ascendeth unto Him in a Day, whereof the measure is a thousand years of that ye reckon.</td></tr>
<tr><td>6. dhalika ‘ālimu ’l-ghaybi wa ’sh-shahādati ’l-‘Azīzu ’r-Raḥīm</td><td></td><td>ذَٰلِكَ عَالِمُ الْغَيْبِ وَالشَّهَادَةِ الْعَزِيزُ الرَّحِيمُ</td></tr>
<tr><td colspan="3">Such is the Knower of the invisible and the visible, the Mighty, the Merciful,</td></tr>
<tr><td>7. Alladhī aḥsana kulla shay’in khalaqah, wa bada’a khalqa ’l-insān min ṭīn</td><td></td><td>الَّذِي أَحْسَنَ كُلَّ شَيْءٍ خَلَقَهُ وَبَدَأَ خَلْقَ الْإِنسَانِ مِن طِينٍ</td></tr>
<tr><td colspan="3">Who made all things good which He created, and He began the creation of man from clay;</td></tr>
</table>

<table>
<tr><td>8. Thumma ja‘ala naslahu min sulālatin min mā’in mahīn</td><td></td><td>ثُمَّ جَعَلَ نَسْلَهُ مِن سُلَالَةٍ مِّن مَّاءٍ مَّهِينٍ</td></tr>
<tr><td colspan="3">Then He made his seed from a draught of despised fluid;</td></tr>
<tr><td>9. Thumma sawwāhu wa nafakha fīhi min rūḥihi wa ja‘ala lakumu ’s-sam‘a wa ’l-abṣāra wa ’l-af’idata qalīlan mā tashkurūna</td><td></td><td>ثُمَّ سَوَّاهُ وَنَفَخَ فِيهِ مِن رُّوحِهِ وَجَعَلَ لَكُمُ السَّمْعَ وَالْأَبْصَارَ وَالْأَفْئِدَةَ قَلِيلًا مَّا تَشْكُرُونَ</td></tr>
<tr><td colspan="3">Then He fashioned him and breathed into him of His spirit; and appointed for you hearing and sight and hearts. Small thanks give ye!</td></tr>
<tr><td>10. Wa qālū a’idhā ḍalalnā fī ’l-arḍi a-inna lafī khalqin jadīd bal hum bi liqā’i rabbihim kāfirūn</td><td></td><td>وَقَالُوا أَئِذَا ضَلَلْنَا فِي الْأَرْضِ أَئِنَّا لَفِي خَلْقٍ جَدِيدٍ بَلْ هُم بِلِقَاءِ رَبِّهِمْ كَافِرُونَ</td></tr>
</table>

And they say: When we are lost in the earth, how can we then be recreated? Nay but they are disbelievers in the meeting with their Lord.		
11. Qul yatawaffākum malaku 'l-mawti 'l-ladhī wukkila bikum thumma ila rabbikum turja'ūn		قُلْ يَتَوَفَّاكُم مَّلَكُ الْمَوْتِ الَّذِي وُكِّلَ بِكُمْ ثُمَّ إِلَى رَبِّكُمْ تُرْجَعُونَ
Say: The angel of death, who hath charge concerning you, will gather you, and afterward unto your Lord ye will be returned.		
12. Wa law tarā idhi 'l-mujrimūna nākisū ru'ūsihim 'inda rabbihim rabbanā abṣarnā wasam'inā farj'inā n'amal ṣāliḥan innā mūqinūn.		وَلَوْ تَرَى إِذِ الْمُجْرِمُونَ نَاكِسُو رُؤُوسِهِمْ عِندَ رَبِّهِمْ رَبَّنَا أَبْصَرْنَا وَسَمِعْنَا فَارْجِعْنَا نَعْمَلْ صَالِحًا إِنَّا مُوقِنُونَ
Couldst thou but see when the guilty hang their heads before their Lord, (and say): Our Lord! We have now		

<table>
<tr><td colspan="3">seen and heard, so send us back; we will do right, now we are sure.</td></tr>
<tr><td>13. Wa-law sh'inā la ataynā kulla nafsin hudāha wa lākin ḥaqqa 'l-qawlu minnī la-amla-anna jahannama mina 'l-jinnati wa 'n-nāsi ajmaʿīn</td><td></td><td>وَلَوْ شِئْنَا لَآتَيْنَا كُلَّ نَفْسٍ
هُدَاهَا وَلَكِنْ حَقَّ الْقَوْلُ
مِنِّي لَأَمْلَأَنَّ جَهَنَّمَ مِنَ
الْجِنَّةِ وَالنَّاسِ أَجْمَعِينَ</td></tr>
<tr><td colspan="3">And if We had so willed, We could have given every soul its guidance, but the word from Me concerning evil doers took effect: that I will fill hell with the jinn and mankind together.</td></tr>
<tr><td>14. Fa-dhūqū bimā nasīytum liqā'a yawmikum hadhā innā nasīnākum wa dhūqū ʿadhāba 'l-khuldi bimā kuntum taʿamalūn</td><td></td><td>فَذُوقُوا بِمَا نَسِيتُمْ لِقَاءَ
يَوْمِكُمْ هَذَا إِنَّا نَسِينَاكُمْ
وَذُوقُوا عَذَابَ الْخُلْدِ بِمَا
كُنتُمْ تَعْمَلُونَ</td></tr>
<tr><td colspan="3">So taste (the evil of your deeds). Forasmuch as ye forgot the meeting of this your day, lo! We forget you. Taste the doom immortality because of what ye used to do.</td></tr>
</table>

15. Innamā y'uminu bi āyātinā 'l-ladhīna idhā dhukkirū bihā kharrū sujjadan wa sabbaḥū bi-ḥamdi rabbihim wa hum lā yastakbirūn		إِنَّمَا يُؤْمِنُ بِآيَاتِنَا الَّذِينَ إِذَا ذُكِّرُوا بِهَا خَرُّوا سُجَّدًا وَسَبَّحُوا بِحَمْدِ رَبِّهِمْ وَهُمْ لَا يَسْتَكْبِرُونَ
Only those believe in Our revelations who, when they are reminded of them, fall down prostrate and hymn the praise of their Lord, and they are not scornful,		
16. Tatajāfā junūbuhum 'ani 'l-maḍāji'i yad'ūna rabbahum khawfan wa ṭama'an wa mimmā razaqnāhum yunfiqūn		تَتَجَافَى جُنُوبُهُمْ عَنِ الْمَضَاجِعِ يَدْعُونَ رَبَّهُمْ خَوْفًا وَطَمَعًا وَمِمَّا رَزَقْنَاهُمْ يُنفِقُونَ
Who forsake their beds to cry unto their Lord in fear and hope, and spend of what we have bestowed on them.		

<table>
<tr><td>17. Falā t'alamu nafsun mā ukhfiya lahum min qurrati 'ayunin jazā'an bi-mā kānū y'amalūn</td><td></td><td>فَلَا تَعْلَمُ نَفْسٌ مَّا أُخْفِيَ لَهُم مِّن قُرَّةِ أَعْيُنٍ جَزَاءً بِمَا كَانُوا يَعْمَلُونَ</td></tr>
<tr><td colspan="3">No soul knoweth what is kept hid for them of joy, as a reward for what they used to do.</td></tr>
<tr><td>18. Afa-man kāna m'uminan kaman kāna fāsiqan lā yastawūn</td><td></td><td>أَفَمَن كَانَ مُؤْمِنًا كَمَن كَانَ فَاسِقًا لَّا يَسْتَوُونَ</td></tr>
<tr><td colspan="3">Is he who is a believer like unto him who is an evil liver? They are not alike.</td></tr>
<tr><td>19. Ammā 'l-ladhīna āmanū wa 'amilū 'ṣ-ṣālihāti fa-lahum jannatu 'l-mā'wā nuzulan bimā kānū y'amalūn</td><td></td><td>أَمَّا الَّذِينَ آمَنُوا وَعَمِلُوا الصَّالِحَاتِ فَلَهُمْ جَنَّاتُ الْمَأْوَىٰ نُزُلًا بِمَا كَانُوا يَعْمَلُونَ</td></tr>
<tr><td colspan="3">But as for those who believe and do good works, for them are the Gardens of Retreat, a welcome (in reward) for what they used to do.</td></tr>
</table>

<table>
<tr><td>20. Wa ammā ’l-ladhīna fasaqū fa-mā’wāhumu ’n-nāru kullamā arādū an yakhrujū minhā uʿīdū fīhā wa qīla lahum dhūqū ʿadhāba ’n-nāri ’l-ladhī kuntum bihi tukadhdhibūn</td><td></td><td>وَأَمَّا الَّذِينَ فَسَقُوا فَمَأْوَاهُمُ
النَّارُ كُلَّمَا أَرَادُوا أَن يَخْرُجُوا
مِنْهَا أُعِيدُوا فِيهَا وَقِيلَ لَهُمْ
ذُوقُوا عَذَابَ النَّارِ الَّذِي
كُنتُم بِهِ تُكَذِّبُونَ</td></tr>
<tr><td colspan="3">And as for those who do evil, their retreat is the Fire. Whenever they desire to issue forth from thence, they are brought hack thither. Unto them it is said: Taste the torment of the Fire which ye used to deny.</td></tr>
<tr><td>21. Wa la-nudhīqannahum mina ’l-ʿadhābi ’l-adna dūna ’l-ʿadhabi ’l-akbari laʿallahum yarjiʿūn</td><td></td><td>وَلَنُذِيقَنَّهُم مِّنَ الْعَذَابِ
الْأَدْنَىٰ دُونَ الْعَذَابِ الْأَكْبَرِ
لَعَلَّهُمْ يَرْجِعُونَ</td></tr>
<tr><td colspan="3">And verily We make them taste the lower punishment before the greater, that haply they may return.</td></tr>
</table>

<table>
<tr><td>22. Wa man aẓlamu mimman dhukkira bi āyāti rabbihi thumma āʿarada ʿanha innā mina ’l-mujrimīna muntaqimūn</td><td></td><td>وَمَنْ أَظْلَمُ مِمَّن ذُكِّرَ بِآيَاتِ
رَبِّهِ ثُمَّ أَعْرَضَ عَنْهَا إِنَّا مِنَ
الْمُجْرِمِينَ مُنتَقِمُونَ</td></tr>
<tr><td colspan="3">And who doth greater wrong than he who is reminded of the revelations of his Lord, then turneth from them. Lo! We shall requite the guilty.</td></tr>
<tr><td>23. Wa laqad ataynā mūsā ’l-kitāba falā takun fī miryatin min liqā’ihi wa jaʿalnāhu hudan libanī isrā’īl</td><td></td><td>وَلَقَدْ آتَيْنَا مُوسَى الْكِتَابَ
فَلَا تَكُن فِي مِرْيَةٍ مِّن لِّقَائِهِ
وَجَعَلْنَاهُ هُدًى لِّبَنِي
إِسْرَائِيلَ</td></tr>
<tr><td colspan="3">We verily gave Moses the Scripture; so be not ye in doubt of his receiving it; and We appointed it a guidance for the Children of Israel.</td></tr>
<tr><td>24. Wa jaʿalnā minhum a’immatan yahdūna bi amrinā lammā ṣabarū wa kānū bi āyātinā yūqinūn</td><td></td><td>وَجَعَلْنَا مِنْهُمْ أَئِمَّةً يَهْدُونَ
بِأَمْرِنَا لَمَّا صَبَرُوا وَكَانُوا
بِآيَاتِنَا يُوقِنُونَ</td></tr>
</table>

And when they became steadfast and believed firmly in Our revelations, We appointed from among them leaders who guided by Our command.		
25. Inna rabbaka huwa yafṣilu baynahum yawma 'l-qiyāmati fīmā kānū fīhī yakhtalifūn		إِنَّ رَبَّكَ هُوَ يَفْصِلُ بَيْنَهُمْ يَوْمَ الْقِيَامَةِ فِيمَا كَانُوا فِيهِ يَخْتَلِفُونَ
Lo! thy Lord will judge between them on the Day of Resurrection concerning that wherein they used to differ.		
26. Awa lam yahdi lahum kam ahlaknā min qablihim mina 'l-qurūni yamshūna fī masākinihim inna fī dhalika la-āyātin afalā yasma'ūn		أَوَلَمْ يَهْدِ لَهُمْ كَمْ أَهْلَكْنَا مِن قَبْلِهِم مِّنَ الْقُرُونِ يَمْشُونَ فِي مَسَاكِنِهِمْ إِنَّ فِي ذَٰلِكَ لَآيَاتٍ أَفَلَا يَسْمَعُونَ
Is it not a guidance for them (to observe) how many generations He destroyed before them, amid whose dwelling places they do walk? Lo, therein verily are portents! Will they not then heed?		

29. Awa lam yaraw annā nasūqu 'l-mā'a ila 'l-arḍi 'l-juruzi fanukhriju bihi zar'an t'akulu minhu an'āmuhum wa anfusuhum afalā yubṣirūn		أَوَلَمْ يَرَوْا أَنَّا نَسُوقُ الْمَاءَ إِلَى الْأَرْضِ الْجُرُزِ فَنُخْرِجُ بِهِ زَرْعًا تَأْكُلُ مِنْهُ أَنْعَامُهُمْ وَأَنفُسُهُمْ أَفَلَا يُبْصِرُونَ
Have they not seen how We lead the water to the barren land and therewith bring forth crops whereof their cattle eat, and they themselves? Will they not then see?		
30. Wa yaqūlūn matā hadha 'l-fatḥu in kuntum ṣādiqīn		وَيَقُولُونَ مَتَى هَذَا الْفَتْحُ إِن كُنتُمْ صَادِقِينَ
And they say: When cometh this victory (of yours) if ye are truthful?		
31. Qul yawma 'l-fatḥi lā yanfa'u 'l-ladhīna kafarū īmānuhum walā hum yunẓarūn		قُلْ يَوْمَ الْفَتْحِ لَا يَنفَعُ الَّذِينَ كَفَرُوا إِيمَانُهُمْ وَلَا هُمْ يُنظَرُونَ
Say (unto them): On the day of the victory the faith of those who disbelieve (and who then will believe) will not avail them, neither will they be reprieved.		

32. Fā'arid 'anhum w 'antaẓir innahum muntaẓirūn		فَأَعْرِضْ عَنْهُمْ وَانتَظِرْ إِنَّهُم مُّنتَظِرُونَ
So withdraw from them (O Muhammad), and await (the event). Lo! they also are awaiting (it).		

Sūrat al-Ikhlāṣ: Sincerity (112)		سُورَةُ الإِخْلاص
Bismillāhi 'r-Raḥmāni 'r-Rahīm		بِسْمِ اللهِ الرَّحْمَنِ الرَّحِيمِ
In the Name of Allah, the Most Beneficent, the Most Merciful.		
1. Qul hūwa 'Llāhu Aḥad		قُلْ هُوَ اللهُ أَحَدٌ
Say: He is Allāh, The One.		
2. Allāhu 'ṣ-Ṣamad		اللهُ الصَّمَدُ
Allāh the eternally besought of all!		
3. lam yalid wa lam yūlad		لَمْ يَلِدْ وَلَمْ يُولَدْ
He begets not nor was He begotten		
4. wa lam yakūn lahū kufūwan āḥad		وَلَمْ يَكُنْ لَّهُ كُفُوًا أَحَدٌ
and there is none comparable unto Him.		

Surat al-Falaq: The Daybreak (113)		سُورَةُ الفَلق
Bismillāhi 'r-Raḥmāni 'r-Rahīm		بِسْمِ اللَّهِ الرَّحْمَنِ الرَّحِيمِ
In the Name of Allah, the Most Beneficent, Most Merciful.		
1. Qul āʿūdhu bi-rabbi 'l-falaqi		قُلْ أَعُوذُ بِرَبِّ الْفَلَقِ
Say: I seek refuge in the Lord of daybreak		
2. min shārri mā khalaq		مِنْ شَرِّ مَا خَلَقَ
from the evil of what He created		
3. wa min sharri ghāsiqin idhā waqab		وَمِنْ شَرِّ غَاسِقٍ إِذَا وَقَبَ
and from the evil of darkness when it prevails		
4. wa min sharri 'n-naffāthāti fī 'l-ʿuqad		وَمِنْ شَرِّ النَّفَّاثَاتِ فِي الْعُقَدِ
and from the evil of women who blow into the knots [witchcraft]		

5. wa min sharri ḥāsidin idhā ḥasad		وَمِنْ شَرِّ حَاسِدٍ إِذَا حَسَدَ
and from the evil of the envier when he envies.		
Surat an-Nas: Mankind (114)		سُورَةُ النَاس
Bismillāhi 'r-Raḥmāni 'r-Rahīm		بِسْمِ اللهِ الرَّحْمٰنِ الرَّحِيمِ
In the Name of Allah, the Most Beneficent, the Most Merciful.		
1. Qul ā'ūdhu bi-Rabbī 'n-nās		قُلْ أَعُوذُ بِرَبِّ النَّاسِ
Say: "I seek refuge in the Lord of mankind		
2. Maliki 'n-nās		مَلِكِ النَّاسِ
King of mankind,		
3. ilāhi 'n-nās		إِلَهِ النَّاسِ
God of mankind,		
4. min sharri 'l-waswāsi 'l-khannāsi		مِنْ شَرِّ الْوَسْوَاسِ الْخَنَّاسِ

from the evil of the sneeking whisperer		
5. ʿ Lladhī yuwaswisu fī ṣudūri ʾn-nāsi		الَّذِي يُوَسْوِسُ فِي صُدُورِ النَّاسِ
who whispers in the hearts of mankind,		
6. mina ʾl-jinnati wa ʾn-nās		مِنَ الْجِنَّةِ وَ النَّاسِ
from the Jinn and mankind.		

Other titles from the Institute for Spiritual & Cultural Advancement

Muhammad: The Messenger of Islam
His Life and Prophecy
By Hajjah Amina Adil
ISBN 1-930409-11-7, Paperback. 608 pp.

Since the 7th century, the sacred biography of Islam's Prophet Muhammad has shaped the perception of the religion and its place in world history. English biographies of Prophet Muhammad – founder of the faith that currently claims 1.5 billion followers – have characteristically presented him in the light of verifiable historical authenticity. This book skillfully etches the personal portrait of a man of incomparable moral and spiritual stature, as seen through the eyes of Muslims around the world. Compiled from classical Ottoman Turkish sources and translated into English, this comprehensive biography is deeply rooted in the life example of its prophet.

In the Mystic Footsteps of Saints
By Shaykh Muhammad Nazim Adil al-Haqqani
Volume 1 - ISBN 1-930409-05-2
Volume 2 – ISBN 1-930409-09-5
Volume 3 – ISBN 1-930409-13-3,
Paperback. Average length 200 pp.
Narrated in a charming, old-world storytelling style, this highly spiritual series offers several volumes of practical guidance on how to establish serenity and peace in daily life, heal emotional and spiritual scars, and discover the role we are each destined to play in the universal scheme. Written by Shaykh Nazim Adil al-Haqqani, worldwide leader of the Naqshbandi-Haqqani Sufi Order and a descendant of best-selling poet and Sufi mystic Jalaluddin Rumi.

Liberating the Soul: A Guide for Spiritual Growth
By Shaykh Muhammad Nazim Adil al-Haqqani
Volume 1 - ISBN 1-930409-14-1
Volume 2 – ISBN 1-930409-15-X
Volume 3 – ISBN 1-930409-16-8
Volume 4 – ISBN 1-930409-17-6, Paperback.
Average length 300 pp.

This series focuses on classical Sufi teachings, which open the heart to receive life-altering spiritual powers. Liberating the Soul is based on coveted lectures of Shaykh Muhammad Nazim Adil al-Haqqani, the worldwide leader of the Naqshbandi Sufi Order and descendant of best-selling poet Jalaluddin Rumi.

Classical Islam and the Naqshbandi Sufi Tradition
By Shaykh Muhammad Hisham Kabbani

ISBN 1-930409-23-0, Hardback. 950 pp. & 2-volume paperback
ISBN 1-930409-10-9, Paperback. 744 pp. with
ISBN 1-930409-22-2, Paperback. 352 pp. (see below)

This esteemed work includes an unprecedented historical narrative of the forty saints of the renowned Naqshbandi Golden Chain, dating back to Prophet Muhammad in the early seventh century. With close personal ties to the most recent saints, the author has painstakingly compiled rare accounts of their miracles, disciplines, and how they have lent spiritual support throughout the world for fifteen centuries. In simple terms, the book outlines practical steps to develop stress, anger and time management, and to identify and prioritize what is truly important in life, all of which "awakens" the inner self to a higher dimension of spiritual consciousness. Traditional Islam and the Naqshbandi Sufi

Tradition is a shining tribute to developing human relations at the highest level, and the power of spirituality to uplift humanity from its lower nature to that of spiritual triumph.

The Naqshbandi Sufi Tradition Guidebook of Daily Practices and Devotions
By Shaykh Muhammad Hisham Kabbani
ISBN 1-930409-22-2, Paperback. 352 pp.
This books presents the doctrinal underpinnings of the Sufi Tradition according to the sourcetexts of Islam, the Quran and Sunnah as well as evidences for the practices on which Sufi spiritual disciplines are based. The book then presents in detail, in both English, Arabic and transliteration, the daily, weekly and date-specific devotional rites of Naqshbandi practitioners.

The Practice of Sufi Meditation and the Healing Power of Cosmic Energy
By Shaykh Muhammad Hisham Kabbani
ISBN: 1-930409-26-5, Paperback. 100 pp.

For those who have reached a level of understanding of the illusory nature of the world around us and seek to discern the reality that lies behind it, Sufi meditation - *muraqabah* - is the doorway through which we can pass from this realm of delusion into the realm of realities.

Through meditation the seeker has a means to return to his or her perfected original self. Muraqabah is the fastest and most direct method for advancing in spiritual degrees. It is in fact a migration from one's self to God. Through meditation higher states of consciousness are attained, and the connection to the seeker's true inner self is established, built-up and maintained, providing the practitioner with a lifeline to the Divine Presence. This book presents the spiritual background behind the practice of meditation, then takes the reader step-by-step, through the basics of spiritual connection based on the ancient teachings of the Naqshbandi Sufi masters of Central Asia.

The Honor of Women in Islam
By Professor Yusuf da Costa
ISBN 1-930409-06-0, Paperback. 104 pp.
Relying on Islamic source texts, this concise, scholarly work elucidates the true respect and love for women inherent in the Islamic faith. It examines the pre-Islamic state of women, highlights the unprecedented rights they received under Islamic Law, and addresses the prominent beliefs and prevailing cultures throughout the Muslim world regarding the roles of women in familial, social service and community development, business, academic, religious, and even judicial circles. In addition, brief case studies of historical figures such as Mary, mother of Jesus, are presented within the Islamic tradition.

Available online from www.isn1.net

www.ingramcontent.com/pod-product-compliance
Lightning Source LLC
Chambersburg PA
CBHW071258110526
44591CB00010B/711
* 9 7 8 1 9 3 8 0 5 8 5 6 1 *